# ECONOMY
## *of* ERRORS

# ECONOMY *of* ERRORS

*SatireWire Gives*

*Business the Business*

## Andrew Marlatt

*Broadway Books*  *New York*

Broadway Books titles may be purchased for business or promotional use or for special sales. For information, please write to: Special Markets Department, Random House, Inc., 1540 Broadway, New York, NY 10036.

PRINTED IN THE UNITED STATES OF AMERICA

BROADWAY BOOKS and its logo, a letter B bisected on the diagonal, are trademarks of Broadway Books, a division of Random House, Inc.

Visit our Web site at www.broadwaybooks.com

First edition published 2002

*Designed by Lee Steele*

Library of Congress Cataloging-in-Publication Data is on file with the Library of Congress.

ISBN 0-7679-0887-2

*For Susan, Walker, and Conor*

# Introduction:
# Oh, How We Have Juggered

The New Economy
The Digital Economy
The Networked Economy
Doug:

No matter what grand sobriquet is used to distinguish the unparalleled growth, productivity, and decline of the past decade, there is universal agreement that this period in our economic history has been unlike collecting mucous samples from a marmoset, or blowing into your fists to produce shrill, quacky sounds.

For unlike some of its heralded predecessors — the Old Economy (1981–1993); the Previously Owned Economy (1974–1993); the Who Put All These Damn Indians on Our Land? Economy (1533–1890) — the New Economy has performed like a true juggernaut. Year after year it juggered along, jugger-jugger-jugger, until about 2001, when it suddenly came to naught. Why? What has made this economy so special?

In a word: pesto. In seven words: no, it's not pesto. It's other stuff. Most notably, it has been fueled by unprecedented advances in technology (the Internet, the mobile phone, the steamed latte), in management practices (the accelerated IPO, the flattened organizational structure, the accelerated bankruptcy filing), and in employee relations (the lure of stock options, the allure of the on-site masseuse, the "We are no longer a going concern, please get the hell out"). But perhaps most distinctively, this economy has been covered by *BusinessMonth Weekly*.

What is *BusinessMonth Weekly*?

Published semiannually every day, *BusinessMonth Weekly* has alerted its readers to the feats and failures of business since the dawn of this Great Era in 1994. From the popular management practice of employee-slapping, to riots at dotcom refugee camps, to Cisco Systems' overeager acquisition of itself, our experienced editors and reporters have focused exclusively on the world of business (except in the last six months of 1997, when we stuck with the Princess Diana tragedy — and doubled our ad revenues!).

It is our sincere hope that the following pages, culled from nine years of these insightful reports, will become for you not just a fount of strategic ideas to apply to your own careers, but an invaluable source of historical documentation. Read, yes. Enjoy, certainly. But also study, and remember. For just as it is true that those who ignore history are doomed to repeat it, those who ignore business history are doomed to hang on to their Dr. Koop stock.

Andrew Marlatt

**SatireWire's**

# BusinessMonth
## WEEKLY

DECEMBER 1994

## Toys "Я" Us
Turns "T" and "U"
to Become
## Toys "Я" Us

## Kmart's
**New Idea:**
Shoplifter Refunds!

## Netscape
GREAT NEW COMPANY,
OR SAD EXCUSE FOR
RICH OLD MAN TO HANG WITH
YOUNG MALE PROGRAMMERS?

**Team-Building
Metaphor
Adventures**

CAUTION

NEW ECONOMISTS
AT WORK

## Ford Takes a Page
## from Software Makers:

**SHIPS UNFINISHED CARS
AND LETS END USERS FIND BUGS**

# TOYS "Я" US to Become TOYS "Я" US

## NEW LOGO FEATURES MORE BACKWARD LETTERS

FOR DECADES, the backward "R" in Toys "R" Us has made it one of the most recognizable names in retailing. But with the advent of the Internet, TRU realized one backward letter wasn't going to be enough to overtake swifter online competitors. So last week, the Paramus, New Jersey–based toy titan announced it had reversed the "T" in Toys and the "U" in Us, giving it three backward letters and, claimed company executives, "three times the brand awareness."

Industry observers were skeptical of the move, with one analyst insisting that spinning the two letters around made "absolutely no difference whatsoever...right?" But TRU executives were equally insistent that the change heralded a new era for the nation's leading toy retailer.

"Turning the 'R' around was the most important decision this company ever made," said CEO Michael Goldstein. "It made us a household name by causing consumers to do a double take. But over time, this reversal has been taken for granted, so today we reveal that the letters beginning the two other words in our name are also backward, a move which we expect will bring even more attention to our brand by causing consumers to do triple and quadruple takes."

While the reversal takes effect immediately, company executives conceded it will take several months to change the signage at its 1,500 stores worldwide. Goldstein said the company will take a charge in the fourth quarter to pay for the change, but declined to provide any numbers.

Analysts, however, estimate new signs alone will cost $30 million to $40 million, while printing new Geoffrey Dollars will run another $20 million. Old Geoffrey Dollars bearing the original name will be honored at all stores, a company spokesman said.

Merrill Lynch analyst Dee Sabeej said she isn't convinced the expense will be worthwhile.

"I've spent the last hour typing it out, writing it out, and doing it in my head," she said. "I've even had co-workers write it for me, but for the life of me, I can't see any difference in the old and new name. I have to conclude that either I just don't get it, or this is a remarkably stupid decision and a horrible waste of corporate resources."

However, Karl Merrifield, editor of trade magazine *TOY!*, said that view is shortsighted.

"The key to obtaining and retaining consumer mindshare in the recreational amusements industry is to have a name that concentrates on a letter or letters," said Merrifield. "The 'R' in Toys R Us, the 'F', 'A', and 'O' in FAO Schwarz, the 'K-B' sound in KayBee. This strategy clearly works with consumers, and by bringing added attention to its 'T' and its 'U', Toys 'Я' Us is now more letter-centric than any of its competitors."

OLD LOGO

NEW LOGO

# AT&T TO LAY OFF 120 PERCENT OF WORKFORCE

## QUAKER OATS EMPLOYEES PUZZLED BY PINK SLIPS

AT&T LAST WEEK announced it would reduce its workforce by an unprecedented 120 percent by the end of 1995, believed to be the first time a major corporation has laid off more employees than it actually has.

AT&T stock soared more than 12 points on the news.

The reduction decision came after a year-long internal review of cost-cutting procedures, said AT&T Chairman C. Michael Armstrong. The initial report concluded the company would save $1.2 billion by eliminating 20 percent of its 108,000 employees.

From there, said Armstrong, "it didn't take a genius to figure out that if we cut 40 percent of our workforce, we'd save $2.4 billion, and if we cut 100 percent of our workforce, we'd save $6 billion. But then we thought, why stop there? Let's cut another 20 percent and save $7 billion.

"We believe in increasing shareholder value, and we believe that by decreasing expenditures, we enhance our competitive cost position and our bottom line," he added.

AT&T plans to achieve the 100 percent internal reduction through layoffs, attrition, and early retirement packages. To achieve the 20 percent in external reductions, the company plans to involuntarily downsize 22,000 non-AT&T employees who presently work for other companies.

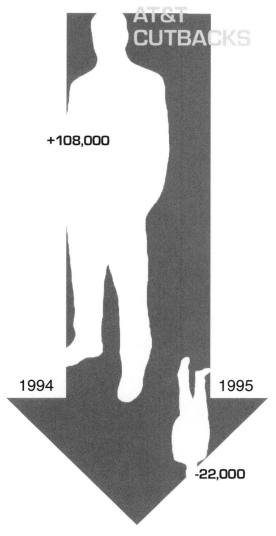

AT&T CUTBACKS

+108,000

1994          1995

-22,000

Among firms AT&T has randomly picked as "External Reduction Targets," or ERTs, are Quaker Oats, AMR Corporation, parent of American Airlines, Callaway Golf, and Charles Schwab & Co.

AT&T's plan presents a "win-win" for the company and ERTs, said Armstrong, as any savings by ERTs would be passed on to AT&T, while the ERTs themselves would benefit by the increase in stock price that usually accompanies personnel cutback announcements.

Legally, pink slips sent out by AT&T would have no standing at ERTs unless those companies agreed. While executives at ERTs declined to comment, employees at those companies said they were not inclined to cooperate.

"This is ridiculous. I don't work for AT&T. They can't fire me," said Kaili Blackburn, a flight attendant with American Airlines.

Reactions like that, replied Armstrong, "are not very sporting."

Analysts credited Armstrong's short-term vision, noting that the announcement had the desired effect of immediately increasing AT&T share value. However, the long-term ramifications could be detrimental, said Bear Stearns analyst Beldon McInty.

"It's a little early to tell, but by eliminating all its employees, AT&T may jeopardize its market position and could, at least theoretically, cease to exist," he said.

Armstrong, however, urged patience: "To my knowledge, this hasn't been done before, so let's just wait and see what happens."

# HE OUTSOURCES EVERYTHING

## TREND SETTERS:

**ALISTAIR MacLEAN**
Chairman in Absentia:

**Royal Dutch Petroleum**

**Virgin**

**Nokia**

**British Telecom**

For most of his adult life, 29-year-old Scotsman Alistair MacLean has been described as a gormless pratt, a blootered nutter with a face like a wee hard disease. But what even those who can stand him don't realize is that MacLean is one of the most successful businessmen in the United Kingdom and, arguably, the world.

The secret, he says, is outsourcing.

One of the hottest trends in business, "outsourcing" is the strategy of hiring outside personnel to perform tasks that are not part of a company's core competency, enabling the company to focus on what it does best. An architecture firm, for instance, might outsource its billing to focus on design, while that billing company might outsource its marketing to concentrate on balance sheets.

MacLean, however, has taken outsourcing to its logical conclusion. He outsources everything.

"Technically, I run British Telecom, Virgin, Nokia, and Royal Dutch Petroleum, but I found I was stretched much too thin to do it all, so I decided to outsource human resources, marketing, clerical, accounting, billing, investor relations, R&D, sales, legal, communications, production, customer service, manufacturing, and new product development," says MacLean from his one-room flat in a housing project in southwest Glasgow.

But doesn't Richard Branson run Virgin? "I also outsource executive management and ego," he explains.

MacLean says he is also a member of the new pop group the Spice Girls, but outsources performance and appearance responsibilities to "Emma, she's the fat one, I think."

Considering his unprecedented success, it seems surprising that MacLean would choose to live in a crime-ridden housing project. But this hard-driving titan of the New Economy denies it has anything to do with attempting to keep a low profile.

"Unfortunately," he says, "the costs of outsourcing eat into all my revenues and profits, so I don't see a shilling from any of my vast empire."

None of which seems to bother him. "I sacrifice quite a bit by giving up the reins, but I'm fortunate in that outsourcing has enabled me to focus on my core competencies," which he describes as "watching a bit of TV and bashing the bishop [masturbating]."

## OFFICE POLL

### AOL VS. GOOD CHOLESTEROL

#### KEY

- GOOD CHOLESTEROL
- AMERICA ONLINE
- HORSES/EQUESTRIAN
- LESS THAN $20
- FEWER COMMANDMENTS

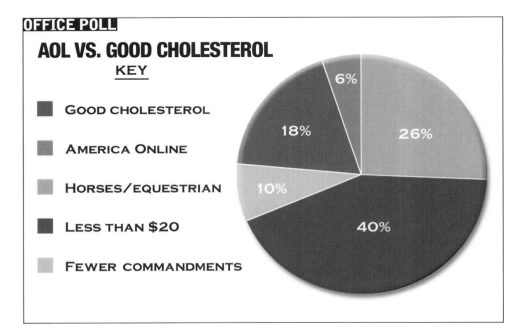

# CHRYSLER RECALLS FORD MINIVANS

Chrysler said last week it was voluntarily recalling nearly 3.6 million Ford minivans, reporting that the vehicles are unsafe and uncomfortable, and adding that Windstars should be returned to any Ford dealership for a full refund, "no questions asked."

Officials at Ford angrily pointed out that Chrysler does not make the Windstar, but a Chrysler spokesman said his company was "too deep into the full-disclosure process" to be distracted. "This confession is painful for us, but we want to do the right thing by issuing this voluntary recall of the dangerous Ford Windstar," said Tim Parrish, a Chrysler spokesman. Parrish said the recall was particularly embarrassing because the Windstar was made despite the fact that Chrysler engineers knew it did not provide a smooth, car-like ride, did not comfortably seat seven, and would never provide an adequate number of cup holders, unlike the Chrysler minivan.

Asked by another Chrysler executive how the "unconscionably flawed" Windstar ever made it to production, Parrish shook his head. "We make no excuses," he said. "It was a gross negligence."

# IMF WOES

In the face of increasing pressure from the International Monetary Fund, the Venezuelan Finance Ministry announced this week it has rented a small volcano and is actively soliciting virgin chickens. Responded one IMF official: "Perhaps they don't understand our concerns."

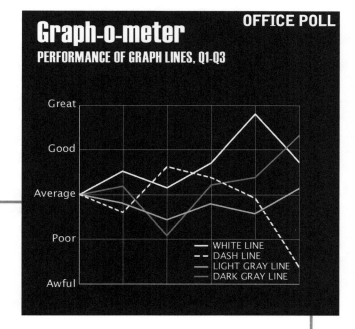

## Graph-o-meter
### PERFORMANCE OF GRAPH LINES, Q1-Q3
OFFICE POLL

Great
Good
Average
Poor
Awful

— WHITE LINE
-- DASH LINE
— LIGHT GRAY LINE
— DARK GRAY LINE

# SHARP SHEEP

The British Beef Export Council, finally conceding it cannot guarantee the eradication of Mad Cow Disease, announced Monday it will discontinue cow production and instead promote the export of genetically engineered sheep with razor-sharp, serrated edges. Consumer advocates immediately protested, arguing that serrated sheep were more dangerous than infected cows. But farmers said it's too soon to judge; as for the present, they "can't get near the fluffy bastards."

## Bisexual Unisex Bathroom Attendant Can't Wait to Get to Work

"FROM 9:00 TO 5:00, I am the happiest man on Earth," says Bo Peters, 23, the bisexual unisex bathroom attendant at giant New York technology law firm Kohle, Rensberg & Remus.

It wasn't always thus. Six months ago, a management consultant suggested KR&R needed a New Economy wake-up call. The prime directive: create open spaces where the firm's 150 employees could not only exchange ideas, but also get to know each other on a personal level. Literally and figuratively, KR&R tore down its walls. No more private offices. No more segregated workspaces. But Peters, who was then a clerk in the mail room, was not satisfied.

"I had a meeting with the partners, and I told them the bathroom was the last bastion of staid, impersonal corporate culture," he recalls. "They still had walls. They still defined people as males and females, instead of as colleagues."

KR&R decided Peters was right, and created one large, unisex bathroom. They also put Peters in charge. So far, his colleagues are pleased.

"Bo is so nice, I sometimes think that if there weren't doors on the stalls, he'd come right in there with you to help out," says office paralegal Richard Motama.

"I'm trying to get those doors taken out next," Peters says hopefully.

Today, half a blissful year after he took the job, Peters is a genuine New Economy success story. "A lot of people don't like the folks they work with, but me, I'm happy to see everyone," he says. "Of course, I know it could come to an end if they ever found out I was bisexual."

Reached in her office, KR&R managing partner Alison Rensberg agreed.

# FIVE QUESTIONS

By age 30, Jeff Bezos seemingly had it all. Princeton-educated and a financial whiz, he quickly moved up the ranks on Wall Street to become a principal at major New York hedge fund D.E. Shaw. But then in July, after reading a magazine article about the growth of the Internet — a worldwide network of computers that is available only to a handful of people, is difficult to access, and has never been used to sell merchandise — Bezos quit his job, moved to Seattle, Wash., rented a house, and set up shop in his garage, gearing up to launch a business on the Internet's World Wide Web. The business he left it all for? Books. We asked Mr. Bezos...

1. *What are you, an idiot?*
   "What?"
2. *You left your job to sell books from your garage?*
   "Yes, but..."
3. *You didn't quit, did you? You got fired.*
   "No, I..."
4. *Was it legal problems, then? Girls?*
   "No, I really think the Internet is..."
5. *So it was drugs, right?*
   *You look like a druggie.*
   "I am not a druggie. Mark my words, the Internet will..."
6. *"So then you're an idiot?"*
   "No... hey, I thought this was Five Questions. That was six."
7. *The last one was rhetorical.*

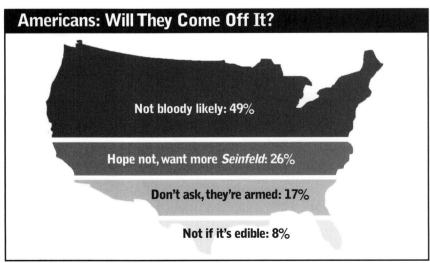

### Americans: Will They Come Off It?

Not bloody likely: 49%

Hope not, want more *Seinfeld*: 26%

Don't ask, they're armed: 17%

Not if it's edible: 8%

# Breakthrough Study Finds...
## YOU REALLY DON'T MAKE A DIFFERENCE

### In Grand Scheme of Things, Your Hard Work, Diligence, Found to Mean Squat

IN AN UNPRECEDENTED study, British and American researchers have concluded that despite what you've been told at work, you really don't make a difference, and are not remotely integral to your company's success.

"In our research, we found that you've been encouraged to believe that your hard work and contributions are somehow substantial, and that you are a significant member of the team. But what we discovered is that in your case, there's no way," said Neil Romsby of the London School of Economics.

The study, jointly conducted by the LSE and Stanford University's Business School, uncovered a variety of slogans meant to boost employees' sense of worth, such as "Our employees are our greatest asset" and "Our value is in our employees."

"We're not necessarily saying all these platitudes are lies," said Stanford economics professor Harold Bloom. "We're just saying they have nothing to do with you. That may seem sad, but it's actually rather funny because your situation is quite obvious to everyone else."

Romsby added that it's also ironic. "When you tell your boss he is doing a good job, you know you are lying, but when your boss tells you the same thing, you actually believe it. That's priceless."

Romsby cautions, however, not to assume you are simply a meaningless number to your company. "No, that's not a fair comparison," he said, "because numbers are actually quite meaningful to your company. Unlike you."

Researchers concede the study may be difficult to accept — even though your colleagues insist it shouldn't really be a surprise — but suggest you begin by substituting the word meaningless for important whenever your boss or colleagues speak to you. For example: "Diane, this is a really meaningless project and I think you can make some meaningless contributions as a meaningless member of the team." Once you feel comfortable with that, Bloom added, substitute the word "shitty" for "meaningless," and you'll have a pretty good sense of where you stand.

In another finding, researchers also learned that contrary to your company's public relations claims, your company is not really "creating the future" or "improving people's lives." This, Romsby explained, is actually good news.

"Since you are failing to make a difference at a place that also doesn't make a difference, at least you're not really hurting anybody," he said.

One of your colleagues, who asked to remain anonymous, didn't have anything to say about you, but liked the idea of having his picture taken in silhouette.

# Attention Kmart Shoplifters: REFUNDS!

ARGUING THERE IS no such thing as "bad" consumer loyalty, Kmart has unveiled a new "shoplifter returns policy," allowing defective or unwanted stolen items to be exchanged or returned for a full refund.

The announcement has shocked the retail industry, which historically has held shoplifting in contempt. "I think this is a fantastic policy," says BankOne analyst Teresa Ecinata, "for Kmart's competitors and for shoplifters. 'Why steal at Wal-Mart when Kmart stands behind the products I pinch?'"

Kmart CEO Floyd Hall, however, labels that "in-the-box" thinking, and argues the traditional "all-or-nothing" attitude toward in-store thievery fails to tap the hidden value and brand-building opportunities within the retailer-shoplifter relationship.

Many shoplifters, says Hall, are young or low-income individuals who at some point may be able to pay for merchandise. "When they can," he says, "we want them to think of Kmart."

As a result, he adds, losses from shoplifting will now be accounted for as a marketing expense.

According to Anika Sykes, director of Kmart's new Non-Traditional Consumer Division, of even greater benefit will be a reduction in "redundant shoplifting" by a previously unrecognized subset of thieves she called "disgruntled shoplifters." The disgruntled shoplifter, Sykes explains, returns to a store to re-steal a broken or defective item, or to steal a different item because the last one didn't work out.

## Citing Increased Customer Loyalty, Kmart Creates "Shoplifter Returns Policy"

Juveniles are notorious disgruntled shoppers, as they are more likely to return to steal two of the item, "just because they're pissed off," says Sykes. But even professional shoplifters can be dangerously disgruntled.

"Let's say a true professional steals a toaster oven and sells it to a fence," she says. "But the fence finds out it's broken and can't move it. Well, the professional's going to have to go back and steal that toaster oven again, isn't he? And maybe he'll steal an even more expensive one next time."

The policy, Sykes argues, should also lower the general crime rate, as fences will be less likely to physically punish thieves who repeatedly supply them with defective merchandise. Fences concur.

"I hate it when I have to assault my suppliers," says Joey Carbone, a convicted fence from Tuscan, Ala. "That Kmart gives me a chance not to put physical well-being at risk shows me they're a good corporate citizen."

While Carbone notes that his suppliers have yet to test Kmart's new policy, the few shoplifters who have made the attempt confirmed the company was good to its word and did not arrest them. For some, it was nothing short of a godsend.

"Last week I pocketed a couple of vid[eo]s from Kmart for my kids, OK?" says Eric Littleton, standing outside a Kmart in Akron, Ohio. "One of the tapes was all, like, weird lines, and my kids were friggin' screaming, 'Take it back!' Without the returns policy, I gotta steal again, but now, I'm golden. I am definitely patronizing Kmart in the future."

# A CONVERSATION WITH NETSCAPE

*EARLIER THIS SPRING, James "Jim" Clark, recently retired founder of high-end computer maker Silicon Graphics, had a hunch that a 22-year-old programmer named Marc Andreessen was the "Next Big Thing."* Andreessen, along with his college friends at the University of Illinois, had built an impressive piece of software called a "browser" that would enable people to "surf" the sites on the growing network of computers known as the World Wide Web. After heading to Illinois to recruit Andreessen and his collaborators, Clark brought the team to Mountain View, California, where they set up shop as Mosaic Communications. Last month, the company renamed itself Netscape.

BusinessMonth Weekly *contributing editor emeritus H. Clyde Hartwig caught up with the founders to talk about the Internet, this new "browser," and their unusual relationship.*

**BUSINESSMONTH WEEKLY:** Marc, let me get this straight. Mr. Clark is 50 years old, he's rich, and he's single. And on a "hunch," he lured you and a bunch of your youthful, attractive male friends to come with him to California, stay at his house, and eat his food. Marc, did he ever ask you to swim in his pool?

**CLARK:** What?

**BMW:** Oh come now, Mr. Clark, don't be so surprised.

**CLARK:** But I was...

**BMW:** I know, I know. You were looking for the "Next Big Thing." And just how tall are you, Marc? Six-foot-three?

**ANDREESSEN:** Six-foot-four, but I don't see...

**BMW:** Quite a catch for a man twice your age, Mr. Clark.

**CLARK:** What?

**BMW:** No wonder you're the talk of Silicon Valley. So Marc, when Mr. Sugar Daddy here heard about your little browser, he asked you to join him. Where did you usually meet?

**ANDREESSEN:** Mostly at his house, but...

**BMW:** How intimate.

**CLARK:** Look, are you a real reporter?

**BMW:** Don't try to change the subject, Mr. Clark. You know as well as I do that this isn't about me.

**ANDREESSEN:** What is it about?

**BMW:** Marc, Marc, don't you know? It's about you.

**ANDREESSEN:** What about me?

**BMW:** Well, you're a programmer.

**CLARK:** Brilliant deduction. So I was right. You're not a reporter. You're an industry analyst.

**ANDREESSEN:** So I'm a programmer. So what?

**BMW:** So, programmers are hot.

**ANDREESSEN:** Well, that's true. And I think as the Internet grows, programmers will be even more in demand. For instance, right now there are really only two competing browsers, ours and the one licensed by Spyglass, but as the...

**BMW:** No no, you're not listening. I said programmers are *HOT*.

**ANDREESSEN:** Hey...stop leering like that!

**BMW:** Oh Marc, let's get hyperlinked!

**ANDREESSEN:** What are you, some kind of pervert?

**CLARK:** Careful. He could be an executive recruiter.

**BMW:** All right, all right, look, I'm sorry. Don't leave. Let me just...I'll put it this way. Marc, I know you're going to go public soon, but I can't help think that if I could just...

**CLARK:** Whoa, whoa, wait. This is all about getting your hands on our stock? Jesus, I've heard some stupid venture capital pitches before, but...

**BMW:** Oh damn your stock, Clark! I just want to go public! With Marc! Let's proclaim our undying love to the world!

**ANDREESSEN:** Our *what*?

**CLARK:** We'll just back away slowly here...

**ANDREESSEN:** He's nuttier than that Mark Cuban guy.

**BMW:** No no, don't go! Look, what if we just put out a swimsuit calendar? We'll call it "Beefcakes of the Browser!" Or "Naked Came Netscape!" I have experience! I did the ChippenDOS calendar for Gates!

"Sick smokers may burden a country's health-care system, but dead smokers save governments money. That's the conclusion of a study* on the financial cost of smoking."
—Associated Press

**Name:** Adriane Moore
**Status:** Non-Smoker

**Prognosis:**
By the time Adriane dies, at age 79, she will have received 14 years of Social Security and Medicare benefits, as well as a retirement pension from her former employer, which will cost taxpayers and the economy a staggering

$878,000

**Name:** Adriane Moore
**Status:** Smoker

**Prognosis:**
By the time Adriane dies, at age 64, she will have received 0 years of Social Security and Medicare benefits, and no retirement pension from her employer. She will have had medical bills that will cost taxpayers and the economy

$349,000

$$\begin{array}{r} \$878,000 \\ -\ \$349,000 \\ \hline \end{array}$$

You do the math.

We'll do the rest.

Philip Morris

# UNFINISHED is good for BUSINESS

EVEN THOUGH IT'S A STRATEGY MICROSOFT HAS PURSUED FOR YEARS, NETSCAPE COFOUNDER MARC ANDREESSEN RUFFLED FEATHERS LAST MONTH WHEN HE SAID HIS COMPANY'S GOAL WAS TO GET ITS BROWSER PRODUCT TO MARKET **WHEN IT WAS ONLY 80 PERCENT FINISHED,** AND LET THE USERS PERFECT IT. WHO SAYS YOU CAN'T TEACH AN OLD ECONOMY DOG NEW TRICKS?

As VICE PRESIDENT of Ford Motor Co.'s design division, Bill Menchen was miserable. The company needed a new model minivan to bolster sagging sales, but the prototype was being held up by a series of test failures and parts shortages. It looked like the vehicle wouldn't be "ready" for two more years, and talk at Ford was that Menchen would soon be fired, or at least horribly disfigured. Then late one night, after stumbling in blind drunk again from a nearby bar, Menchen walked into his teenage son's room and passed out on the bed.

"When I woke up, my son showed me this brand-new software he was using to look at what he called the World Wide Web. God, it sucked. It was slow. It kept crashing."

But it also held the key to Menchen's, and Ford's, future. "So I'm there on my hands and knees, when it hits me that these software people have the right idea. They know getting product out the door is more important than shipping a perfect product. Their users can find bugs that you can fix in later versions. I thought, 'Shit, we can do that!'"

Just 16 days later, the 1995 Ford Cystera 1.0 was not just in production, but shipping to dealerships across North America.

The release had a few known bugs.

The seat belts on the built-in child safety seats were made of the sharp wire strapping used to hold cardboard boxes together. Also, there were no headlights. Cystera users, meanwhile, were encouraged to hunt down other problems. It even became a selling point.

"Some car owners are like programmers — they like to tinker — so we positioned the Cystera 1.0 as the car for early adopters, and challenged them to find conflicts," Menchen explains.

But according to the Consumer Product Safety Commission, most "bugs" were not that hard to find. "It had no reverse gear. I picked up on that right away," says CPSC investigator Jerry Kabale. "But I'll admit, it took a few days to discover that the passenger-side cup holders were heating up to 475 degrees Fahrenheit."

As for the "patches" Ford issued, Kabale was less than impressed. "I got a box of seat belts, headlights, and part of a transmission with installation instructions."

But to Menchen, all user feedback is positive, even invaluable. "It's possible that we would have found those bugs on our own, but it might have taken months," he says. "Not only would our users have been deprived of the new Cys-

[CONTINUED NEXT PAGE]

## "SOME CAR BUYERS ARE LIKE PROGRAMMERS—THEY LIKE TO TINKER—SO WE POSITIONED THE CYSTERA 1.0 AS THE CAR FOR EARLY ADOPTERS, AND CHALLENGED THEM TO FIND CONFLICTS."

[FROM PREVIOUS PAGE]
tera, but it would have given the competition the opportunity to catch up."

Some say General Motors already has caught up. The 1996 Chevrolet Wartsnall 2.1 minivan hit the streets — and, thanks to a faulty steering column, several hundred pedestrians — just two weeks after the Cystera came out.

Public outcry from both releases, as well as recent quick-to-market products from General Electric, Sears, and Lockheed Martin (see sidebar), highlight the real dilemma now facing Old Economy firms: educating the public.

"I think what we've learned is that it's not the industry that's backward, it's our customer base," says GM spokesperson Ari Levy. "For instance, they have such an Old Economy attitude toward crashes. But good automobiles, like good software, can crash.

"When that happens, they shouldn't sue," Levy continued. "That doesn't help anybody. Instead, they need to give us user feedback. So if their car experiences a crash, they or their next-of-kin need to give us feedback into exactly what the user was doing when the crash occurred so we can issue a patch."

## CYSTERA 1.0 KNOWN CONFLICTS

LEFT-HAND TURNS: Users who attempt to make left-hand turns may find the steering column conflicts (locks) when turned counter-clockwise.

RECOMMENDATION: Instead of turning left, go straight past the desired street, take the next right, then right again, then right again (SEE DIAGRAM).

NIGHT: The headlights on the Cystera 1.0 are currently incompatible with darkness. If you experience this problem, it is recommended you disable the vehicle's ignition systems after 5 p.m.

CHILDREN: The Cystera's child safety restraint system is known to conflict with children who possess the ability to move. It is recommended that children be disabled before being installed into the child safety restraint system.

# MISSILEWARE

## "Users" Help Find Bugs in Patriarch

Let's be honest, when you think long-range, multiple-target, ground-based defense systems with all-altitude, all-weather capabilities, only one missile comes to mind: the Patriot. And thanks to a fawning press during the Gulf War, Patriot-maker Raytheon had a lock on the market, and rivals like Lockheed Martin all but conceded the race.

But then the New Economy came knockin' in the form of Philip Whacker. A 28-year-old former product manager for Borland software, Whacker joined Lockheed in June, and quickly convinced his superiors that the only lock on the ground-based defense system market was psychological.

> A MOSTLY COMPLETED VERSION OF THE PATRIARCH MISSILE, EVERY MONTH, FOR FREE.

"Technologically, Lockheed has always been cutting edge, but its management practices were definitely stodgy," says Whacker, now a Lockheed Martin vice president. "I was able to facilitate a paradigm shift in company thinking, and the result is, our Patriarch 2.1 defense system is now the market leader."

How did it happen? First, Whacker sped up the product cycle, vowing to issue a new, mostly completed version of the Patriarch every six months. Secondly, the company undermined the Patriot by giving away the $240 million missile for free. (As a result, Lockheed now has 80 percent market share and staggering losses.) But most importantly, the company outsourced engineering by having users uncover conflicts and bugs.

And what has been the feedback so far? "With a free product, I think it's totally understandable to have bugs, and we do," says Patriarch Conflict Manager Amanda Shipps. "Like with the Patriarch 2.0, we didn't see system crashes, per se, but one of the missiles did literally crash on the people who bought the system. Kinda added a new definition to the term 'end user,'" she jokes.

With its attractive price point, the Patriarch has quickly become the system of choice for a host of Middle Eastern and African governments, who previously swore by the Patriot. But perhaps Lockheed's biggest coup is in its new database marketing division.

"By requiring Patriarch users to fill out a customer survey to get their free missiles, we have compiled a vast database of the highly prized 18-to-65-year-old violent, despotic male demographic," says Shipps. "We intend to sell that data to marketers."

# Swimming with the SHARKS

## EXECUTIVE TEAM BONDS, BLEEDS
## ON METAPHOR ADVENTURE

Since launching a year ago, Palo Alto, Calif.–based chipmaker CompuBiscuit has struggled. Sales of its core product — large, fluffy computer macroprocessors for massive, memory-hungry mainframes — have been virtually nonexistent. As a result, morale has declined, and innovation, like the company's roster of key employees, has slowly evaporated.

Finally, last month, CEO Madeleine "Maddy" Romish decided it was time for action, and she turned to adventure metaphor company StrifeLearning, Inc. to provide it. StrifeLearning offers clients high-risk, team-building excursions, from whitewater rafting trips that simulate the "raging river of change" of the New Economy to "outside the box" skydiving, in which groups jump from an airplane, hit the ground, then pull their ripcords, if they can.

But it was one adventure in particular that caught Romish's eye. Called "Swimming with the Sharks," it requires executives to spend 36 hours in the frigid waters near the Farallon Islands, a national wildlife refuge about 30 miles off the coast of San Francisco that is an infamous feeding ground for the Great White Shark. This expedition, Romish explains before the trip, is perfectly suited to the issues facing CompuBiscuit and its top five managers, who will join her on the excursion: "If you work in the New Economy, you work in shark-infested waters," she says, "and the truth is, we are not yet one of the sharks. We are tuna. We have to learn not to be tuna."

With Romish's consent, *BusinessMonth Weekly* Editor Treat Warland will observe the adventure, riding with Doug McDougal, a StrifeLearning facilitator whose job it will be to captain a boat near the team, shout encouragement, offer metaphorical management advice, and point out fins.

## DAY ONE
Facing Great White Death Off Farallon
Islands, Group Fails to Build Consensus

**7 a.m.**
Laughing nervously, Madeleine Romish and her top five officers climb aboard *The Detached*, a sparkling white, fiberglass fishing yacht muscled by twin 370-horsepower Volvo engines. Nearly 33 feet long, it comes with a galley, a head, and a shower, but what catches everyone's eye is the tuna tower 15 feet above the deck.

"That's where we have to sit, I guess," says Marketing Vice President Austin Petersen, forcing a laugh.

"No, that's for me," says Doug McDougal, a wry, rugged 53-year-old Texan. "To watch out for the competition."

"Competition," I learn, is how McDougal often refers to sharks.

**8 a.m.**
As we approach the Farallons, McDougal cuts the engines and we anchor up, rolling in a gentle swell. It takes half an hour to outfit the team in snorkels, black wetsuits, and flippers. McDougal then has the group stand in a line and hold out their index fingers. One by one, he pricks each finger with the tip of a serrated fish knife.

"Success is like blood," he tells the flinching adventurers. "The more successful your business, the more you bleed and attract sharks. Y'all aren't so successful, so I'm just pricking your fingers. Last week I had Intel out here. I had to use a machete."

Each executive is then handed a large cardboard box containing a heavy mainframe computer — the target market for CompuBiscuit's large processors. They also each have a wetbag tied around their necks containing bottled water and a pencil.

**8:35 a.m.**
Other than Romish, it is clear that not everyone has bought into jumping in. The CEO, however, overrules them, and with some help from McDougal, the group hits the water. The computers immediately sink to the ocean floor, which means the les-

sons begin immediately.

Charles Henneson, vice president of sales, looks up as he treads in the waves. "Does this mean we have to let go of our preconceived notions about the importance of hardware?"

"No," counters Amanda Pulova, vice president of business development. "It means to stay afloat in the New Economy, as in the ocean, you have to be willing to abandon dead weight."

CFO Chandra Chirpaty offers a dimmer, but eventually more prescient, opinion. "In an ocean of change," he says dourly, "our revenue model sinks."

**12 p.m.**
With no sharks in sight, McDougal decides it's time to give his talk. He has observed the group for four hours, and has already assessed that management is saddled with two major problems. The first is 29-year-old Romish. McDougal senses she is insecure in her leadership role and tries to overcompensate by shunning consensus. Instead of standing up for themselves, her subordinates tend to go along, he says.

"Is this true?" Romish asks, looking at the others, who are splayed out in a circle in the water. One by one, her colleagues nod.

Romish bristles. "I can't agree," she says decisively.

"Me neither," says Petersen.

"That goes for all of us," adds Chirpaty.

The other issue, McDougal says, is teamwork. The group is too individualistic, but to make CompuBiscuit grow, each person needs to interact more with the others to achieve cross-functional buy-in. "Can you work together, trust each other, and learn to deal directly with each other?" he asks. "Can you [pointing to Romish] trust your officers and their leadership skills? We'll find out soon."

**4 p.m.**
Soon turns out to be exactly four hours. A Great White grabs Romish by the foot and begins to thrash her about in a torrent of foam. Too shocked to speak, the CEO is out of the loop and no longer the decision-maker; in effect, she is now just another employee. New leadership is called for.

THE COMPUTERS INSTANTLY SINK TO THE OCEAN FLOOR, WHICH MEANS THE LESSONS BEGIN IMMEDIATELY.

"OK, a shark has Maddy's foot, what do we do?" yells Chirpaty.

"Let's build consensus!" screams Sherri Coggins, vice president of communications.

"No time for that!" replies Petersen.

The pent-up frustrations bubble to the surface like Romish's writhing upper body.

"No time? You sound just like Maddy!" screams Pulova. "Like that IBM deal. We came up with a partnership proposal, worked out all the details, had the agreement in hand, then she nixed it, just like that."

At that moment, the flailing Romish finds her voice. "Do something, idiots!" she yells, before going under again.

"But how do we know she won't just veto our decision?" Coggins asks.

"Yes, that's an issue we need to address," Pulova agrees. "I'm a leader, but I'm not empowered to leverage my leadership skills. I've been neutralized by an autocratic management style!"

**4:20 p.m.**
For agonizing minutes, the group dog-paddles in breathy silence, then turns its collective head to the sound of a "foom," followed by a thud. The Great White floats to the surface. Gasping for air, Romish pops above the waves, the bleeding shark listing at her side.

McDougal leans over the port side of his boat, harpoon-gun in hand.

"There is a time for consensus-building," he says flatly, "and a time for unilateral decision-making."

10 p.m.

As the adventurers paddle in the moonlight, the issue resurfaces when Romish, her voice raspy and tired, is finally able to speak. "Fired..." she gasps. "All...fired..."

Bolstered by their experience, the executives are not cowed. "Maddy, you have to be willing to trust your team," says Pulova.

McDougal nods. Several of the group then exchange high-fives.

### DAY TWO

Mounting Injury Toll Matched by Mounting Metaphor Toll

**10 a.m.**
Despite the fact that Romish

survived the severe attack 18 hours earlier, some in the group are clearly unglued by the experience, and by the presence of Romish herself, who has not been able to speak coherently or open her eyes since before midnight. Exhausted, cold, and sore, no one notices the fin that appears on the surface 20 yards away.

It is only after the facilitator, McDougal, loudly clears his throat and cocks his head that Sherri Coggins sees the shark. It is heading straight for her.

All color draining from her face, Coggins at first seems unable to make a sound, but as the Great White gets closer, she finally begins screaming: "Shark! Oh, God! Shark!"

McDougal, ever vigilant, attempts to focus her thoughts. "Think of it as a metaphor!" he reminds her.

"Well, it's a great fuckin' white metaphor!" Coggins answers.

Inexplicably, the shark swims away.

"Maybe it's not feeding time," says Chirpaty.

"Or maybe I'm not appetizing enough," murmurs Coggins, the tears welling. "Let's face it, the sharks go for Maddy because she's good enough. She's CEO quality. Executive material. I'm not even shark bait."

**5 p.m.**
It happens before anyone can react. A giant shark bites down on Austin Petersen's leg. The marketing VP is turned sideways and pulled under. Henneson immediately starts screaming: "Something's got Austin's leg! Something's attacking Austin!"

But McDougal quickly refocuses the group. "Think big picture," he says calmly. "It's not just Austin. Something's attacking all of you."

"Not me!" Coggins cries out in despair. "It doesn't want me! Oh, God, why doesn't it want me?!..."

McDougal, who usually keeps his cool, temporarily loses it. "You're part of the team!" he blares. "Being an effective manager is about recognizing the effect on the whole!"

And suddenly, Coggins gets it. "You're saying that if one member of the team has a problem, sooner or later that problem will manifest itself across the team, and, if not addressed, could become an enterprise-wide problem."

"FIRED..." SHE GASPS. "ALL... FIRED..."

16

She turns to her colleagues. "Folks, that shark is an enterprise-wide problem!"

A magical paradigm shift suddenly envelops the group. "Right!" shouts Henneson. "Something's attacking all of us, and it's manifesting itself as an attack on Austin, who is really a metaphor for the company's goals and vision of success!"

With only a cursory look at Romish, who is lolling unconsciously with fever, Henneson calls for an emergency meeting. Coggins, no longer worried about her place within the team, emerges as a natural leader. She calls for an NPA, or "Needs and Priorities Assessment," and universally the group agrees its top priority is to tackle the twisting, bleeding metaphor that is Petersen.

The only divisive moment comes when CFO Chirpaty, ever vigilant that CompuBiscuit not take the financially reckless path of other startups, complains that there is no budget for a rescue. He is quickly shouted down.

**5:30 p.m.**
After restoring order, Coggins suggests a pencil-based strategy. However, she has no pencil in her wetbag, and asks if anyone does. Only Henneson still has his, but a scrape with a shark during the night has rendered his left arm useless. He can't open the wetbag around his neck. Pulova, however, is able to open it and take the pencil.

"Stab the shark in the eye!" Coggins shouts.

"I can't!" Pulova answers. "I can't see! I lost my glasses!"

"Oh great," mumbles Chirpaty. "A VP of BizDev and she has no vision."

Wasting no time, Coggins swims over, grabs the pencil, and plunges it into the shark's eye socket. Wounded, the shark swims away.

"I'd like to see a tuna do that!" shouts Pulova, after which the other team members, even Chirpaty, gleefully join in a chant of "We're not tuna! We're not tuna!"

**8:30 p.m.**
When Petersen regains consciousness three hours later, he begins to cry. It is not, however, because of the 36-inch-long gash in his leg that will eventually land him in the hospital for three weeks. Instead, he is overcome with emotion.

"That was probably the best meeting we've ever had as an executive team," he says between sobs. "I feel really good about our growth prospects."

# POSTMORTEM

Six months after "Swimming with the Sharks," Warland sat down with Sherri Coggins, the Acting CEO of CompuBiscuit, to find out what impact the adventure had on the company, other than the permanent hospitalization of former CEO Madeleine Romish.

Overall, Coggins said, the biggest impact has been on product development. After discovering on the trip that putting their big, fluffy macroprocessors into large mainframes was not the best strategy for the New Economy, the managers decided to market their FluffyBiscuit® and BigFluffyBiscuit® chips to smaller devices, such as laptops and cell phones.

But the adventure also affected each team member personally, and Coggins herself provides the most poignant example.

"I'm a little embarrassed about how I acted when I saw that shark fin and got hysterical," she says. "But I wasn't thinking strategically, I was thinking viscerally: 'I'm going to be eaten.' I see now that what caused my higher brain functions to shut down wasn't the fear of being eaten, it was the fear of not having an appropriate metaphor to crystallize the situation."

That, she says, is no longer a problem.

Two months after the trip, Coggins met with John Pencock, a partner in the venture capital firm Flatiron Partners. Coggins explained that CompuBiscuit was seeking $5 million in financing in return for 18 percent of the company. Pencock, however, scoffed. His firm wasn't interested in chipmarkers, he said, adding that he personally didn't believe in CompuBiscuit's vision that massive, fluffy processors were a growth area.

Coggins revels in her response.

"The guy's a VC, so I treated him liked a shark," she recalls. "I said, 'John, cover your left eye with your hand.' When he did, I pulled out a sharpened No. 2 pencil from my purse and told him, 'See this? I can plant this pencil in that left eye of yours and for the rest of your life, you'll see the world just as you do now. Or you can reconsider.'"

"I'll have you arrested," Pencock warned.

"And you'll be blind in one eye," Coggins countered.

"I'll sue you," he said.

"And you'll still be blind in one eye," she answered.

After several moments of silence, Coggins figuratively drove home the point with a metaphor. "You see John, it's really all about vision — not just having it, but keeping it."

Flatiron eventually funded CompuBiscuit, but the new backing has done little to help sales. That once might have been considered a problem, but not anymore. As her colleagues often do since the trip, Coggins turns to the sea to explain: "If the New Economy is the ocean, and the sharks in the ocean are the competitors that want to gobble up our market share, then CompuBiscuit is lucky that we have, so far, not attracted any sharks."

# AND THE B®AND PLAYED ON

THE FOLLOWING IS THE TRANSCRIPT OF A SPEECH ENTITLED "FLIRTING WITH DISASTER: AND THE BRAND PLAYED ON," GIVEN NOV. 2 AT THE "MARKETING STRATEGIES FOR THE MILLENNIUM" CONFERENCE IN SAN FRANCISCO. THE SPEAKER WAS MR. NICHOLAS CRUMB, VICE PRESIDENT OF MCMANN & TATE, A GLOBAL ADVERTISING AND MARKETING FIRM.

"GOOD MORNING.

"When the idea was first put into practice, the shortsighted termed it 'creeping commercialism at its most creepy.' The American public, too, emitted groans of displeasure. Yet business leaders with fortitude and foresight pushed on. In time, the change they instituted — corporate sponsorship of college football bowl games — was accepted. And it flourished. The USF&G Sugar Bowl. The Tostitos Fiesta Bowl. The Federal Express Orange Bowl. Today, with corporate and product names adorning stadiums, civic centers, and rock concerts the world over, this trend is no longer 'creeping.' It is, in fact, running full speed, armed to the Colgate-Palmolive teeth, as subtle as a Tae-Bo kick to the Cruex groin.

"Now it is time to ask 'What next?' Where will corporate and brand identification take us from here? Well, as it did with those 'sacred' bowl games years ago, the answer will no doubt surprise some, excite others, and, perhaps, intimidate a few. The answer is: corporate-sponsored disaster.

"I see some of you are hesitant, but let me remind you of the old saying, 'He can't see the forest for the trees.' In the business world, we must rise above the trees and see that forest. And we must see it, not just for what it is — a wonder of nature — but for what it can be — a continuous and regenerative source of pulp and paper products, a Georgia-Pacific Forest. The same can be said for so-called 'disasters.' We must learn to see them, not just for what they are — catastrophic, life-wrenching events — but for what they can be — a continuous and regenerative source of brand identification.

"At present, disasters are still just that: disasters. World War II. The San Francisco Earthquake. Waterworld. Though they often stay in the news for days, weeks, even years, these events have remained unbranded. 'People die,' the argument goes. 'Property is destroyed. Lives are ruined. Why would we link our name with that?'

"My answer: because the names of these events invariably live on long past the perception of personal loss. When we remember the *Titanic*, for instance, few of us bring to mind the screams of tormented passengers slipping beneath the icy Atlantic...

## MISSION: GET PEOPLE TO SAY

## "IT WAS OF UNILEVER-TITANIC PROPORTIONS!"

"Instead, we remember the great ship, the power of the sea, the mammoth iceberg, the clash of wills. But doesn't a corporation, Unilever, for example, also evoke power and size? Doesn't its product, the mighty Q-tips, bring to mind a classic clash of wills in a battle with mammoth earwax buildup? Why not, then, the Unilever-Sinking of the *Titanic*? With an onslaught of releases to major news organizations — and a small fee to the ship owners — news reports would have tagged it the Unilever-*Titanic* Sinking. And instead of describing some event or object as 'of *Titanic* proportions,' today people would say it was of 'Unilever-*Titanic* proportions.'

"Of course, this disaster has passed us by. But what of the future? Will we see The Head & Shoulders Blizzard of 1996? The Soft and Dry Drought of 2002? The Shakes 'n Bake Monterey

Earthquake? Let's hear it for the LA Gear Riots and the Microsoft Windows Wall Street Crash!"

"Over time, just as it was with the USF&G Sugar Bowl, the public will adapt to unwieldy titles such as the Procter & Gamble–Pepto-Bismol–Mt. St. Helens Eruption. And doubtless they will connect with the incorporation of product slogans such as, 'The Eveready Energizer-Marin County Brush Fire: It just keeps going and going and going…'

"So, too, marrying disaster to product can keep going and going. But how do we start? Admittedly, it requires planning, investment, and, surprisingly, patience. For instance, a tropical wave forms off the west coast of Africa. Do you jump on it, declare it the Tropicana Tropical Wave? Absolutely not. Tropical waves often die out, and that kind of brand recognition you don't need. The same goes for tropical depressions. More often than not, they pack a small punch; and then there's that word: depression. It may work for a pharmaceutical interest, but most companies will want to wait until it becomes a formidable tropical storm. The moment a true catastrophe appears imminent — and I suggest you develop close relations with disaster specialists at the National Hurricane Center in Miami, FEMA, and Union Carbide — you must get the word out and claim that tragedy!

Press conferences, faxes, news releases. If you're a consumer products firm, follow quickly with package labeling, inserts or special offers. 'Correctly chart the path of Hurricane Yugo and you could win a new car!'

"But remember, a percentage of pre-tax proceeds from a select sales period should be earmarked for potential victims.

"Finally, some of you may be wondering how far this concept can go, and to that I leave you with the words of advertising legend Larry Tate, who in his book, *Marketing Your Mother*, writes, 'Frankly, I think we all would have shown up to hear the Bell Atlantic Sermon on the Mount.'"

# DISASTERS IN BRIEF

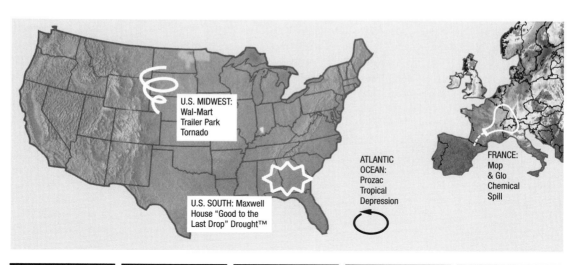

U.S. MIDWEST:
Wal-Mart
Trailer Park
Tornado

ATLANTIC
OCEAN:
Prozac
Tropical
Depression

FRANCE:
Mop
& Glo
Chemical
Spill

U.S. SOUTH: Maxwell
House "Good to the
Last Drop" Drought™

**RUSSIA**
Chernobyl-
U.S. Army
"Don't Ask,
Don't Tell®"
Reactor
Meltdown

**TEXAS**
Taco Bell™
"Run for the
Border™"
Prison
Uprising,
brought to
you by Ivory
Soap™

**NEVADA**
Dow
Corning©-
Hoover
Dam Break

**VIRGINIA**
Anheuser-
Busch™/
Pharmacia
Amtrak™
Train
Derailment

**BOSNIA**
Ethnic
conflict —
sponsorship
opportuni-
ties still
available

SatireWire's

# BusinessMonth
## WEEKLY

DECEMBER 1995

ALSO INSIDE:

IBM ANNOUNCES
VOICE RECOGNITION
BREAK THREW

FED DROPS ACID,
INTEREST RATES
AT POLICY RAVE

"OH, YOU MEAN
*THAT* INTERNET! WE
KNEW ABOUT THAT!"
Q&A with Bill Gates

THE LATEST
MANAGEMENT
CRAGE:
# Employee
# Slapping

Feel the Stress Fly
Off Your Fingertips

"MICROSOFT BOB"
STARTS "ANNOYING
SOFTWARE" CRAZE

RISKY NEW HMO STRATEGY:
PAY HEALTH CLAIMS

# AT&T CEASES TO EXIST

## 120 PERCENT CUTBACKS REMARKABLY SUCCESSFUL

LESS THAN ONE YEAR after AT&T's surprise decision to eliminate 120 percent of its workforce, (see story, Dec. 1994), the company disclosed last week that it had achieved its goals, adding that the $6 billion in payroll savings would be reflected on its next quarterly earnings statement, if it were going to issue one, which it won't, because, unfortunately, the company has ceased to exist.

Last December, AT&T initiated a sweeping cost-reduction plan that called for eliminating all 108,000 of its employees by the end of 1995 through a combination of layoffs, attrition, early retirement packages, and widespread use of the phrase, "You don't work here anymore." On Monday, the company announced it had achieved that goal when the last remaining employee, AT&T Chairman C. Michael Armstrong, accepted his own resignation.

Under the plan, the company also hoped to realize an additional 20 percent savings by instigating "external reductions" at companies not owned by or connected in any way with AT&T. But while Ma Bell sent out nearly 22,000 pink slips to employees at these other firms, none of the companies those employees worked for chose to fire them.

The lack of external cooperation, however, was not a factor in AT&T's dissolution, Armstrong insisted. Instead, he credited the company's "remarkably successful" strategy of comprehensive internal cutbacks.

"Our internal reduction strategy was a complete success, and we are proud to report to shareholders that as a result, we have reduced internal expenditures to zero and saved nearly $6 billion," said Armstrong, who also challenged AT&T's former competitors to make such a claim. "However, there is always pain associated with gain, and we therefore additionally report that as a result of having no employees, AT&T is no longer a going concern."

Speaking from his home in northern New Jersey, Armstrong said the company first realized it was no longer a viable operation just moments after he tendered his resignation. "I turned around to say goodbye to my coworkers and I was, like, 'Hey, where is everybody?'" Armstrong recalled. "I was stunned at first, but then it occurred to me that we had achieved our stated goal, and frankly, I said to myself, 'Lord, am I good or what.'"

While he acknowledged being surprised that the cutbacks led to a termination of the company, Armstrong defended his decision to implement the reductions.

"It's easy to Monday-morning-quarterback, but at the time, we knew we had to do something to achieve a competitive cost position," he said. "We could have reduced prices, but that would have squeezed our margins. Eliminating employees, on the other hand, would increase our margins. Naturally, I then decided to eliminate all of our employees, and thereby increase both savings and margins exponentially... Man, this still sounds like a good idea."

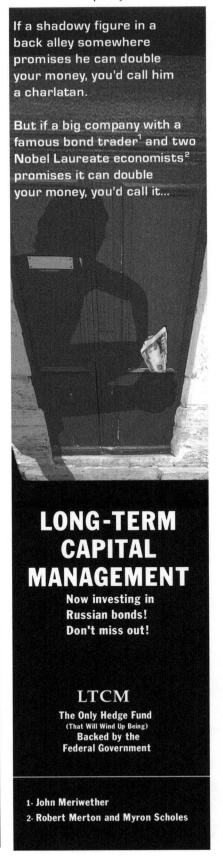

# LOYAL EMPLOYEES A VALUABLE, SALEABLE ASSET

## Companies Can Get Top Dollar for Their Most Faithful Workers

IN AN AGE when employees are labeled "human capital" and workplace longevity is measured in months, some companies have finally begun to realize that a truly loyal employee is a rare and valuable asset that should be recognized, nurtured, and, ideally, sold to the highest bidder.

"Your truly devoted employee, one who honestly believes in his or her company and is faithful to its mission and its products, is an absolute gem, impossible to find," explained Margaret Carter, manager of Coca-Cola's Human Capital Asset Sales division. "That's why they're so easy to sell. Companies are yearning for employees like that."

## TREND SETTERS:
## MARGARET CARTER

HUMAN CAPITAL ASSET SALES MANAGER, THE COCA-COLA CO.

While many firms have long nurtured their staffs in an effort to increase loyalty, the revelation that these employees themselves were a cash cow is credited to Carter and Coca-Cola, a company well known for low turnover and an allegiant workforce.

"There was this guy in my department named Stan who had been with the company for almost 15 years," Carter recalled. "Day in and day out, he did everything we asked, never complained, and was viciously loyal to our products.

"So one night, after Stan stayed up for 24 hours finishing a project, I had an epiphany: 'This guy is worth his weight in gold. I bet I could sell him and make a killing.'"

Carter phoned a few recruiter friends, as well as a pair of human resources directors she knew. Within five hours, she had three bids. "It was a remarkably easy sale," she said. "These other companies were just like us. They had very few loyal employees left. So when they heard they could get someone as loyal as Stan, they jumped."

Coca-Cola, meanwhile, was no less impressed, and offered Carter a job as head of the newly created human sales department. In the past nine months, she has sold no fewer than 62 loyal employees, earning the company $7.75 million, an average of $125,000 per worker.

"Some of our most loyal people I've gotten mid six figures for, but those are the real keepers," she said.

But is it possible that companies would be better served by keeping their most loyal people?

"It's funny, but one of our workers made that point not too long ago," Carter recalled. "He said devoted employees represent all that's good and true and wonderful about Coca-Cola, and insisted we should keep them for the good of the company.

"I think I got $250,000 for that guy," she added.

## WELCOME HOME...NOT

Despite its popularity, the practice of selling loyal employees has not been universally successful. Last month, Pixar Animation Studios was forced to refund nearly $2.2 million to Home Depot, which had bought the highly dedicated animation team from Pixar's hit movie, *Toy Story*.

"Pixar is renowned for its low turnover, and we were told that the animators we bought were the cream of the crop when it comes to loyalty," said Kathy Lazerri, marketing vice president for the Atlanta-based building supply chain. "But it only took a couple of days to figure out they didn't give a damn about Home Depot."

Pixar returned the money and rehired the employees, but is now suing Home Depot. "Before we sold those people, they were among our most loyal staffers, but now they're back and suddenly they're not loyal to us at all," said Pixar CEO Steve Jobs. "I want to know what the hell Home Depot did to them."

"What Home Depot did to us? What Home Depot did to us? How about what (expletive) Pixar did to us?" said returned animator Jeremy Sachs.

"See what I mean?" said Jobs. "Since they came back, they all talk like that."

Despite Pixar's experience, human resources experts doubt employee sales will slow anytime soon, arguing the practice finally enables firms to measure the "capital" in "human capital."

"The true value of a loyal employee has always been abstract; you could never put an actual number on it," said Nabisco human resources spokesman Ken Chesley. "But now you can. It's somewhere between $75,000 and $300,000."

# MICROSOFT ACCIDENTALLY EMBEDS BROWSER IN WINDOWS 95

## Gaffe Could Cause Company to Inadvertently Corner Browser Market

Embarrassed Microsoft officials revealed last week that its Windows 95 development team accidentally embedded the company's Internet browser software in the newly released operating system, a startling blunder that rival browser company Netscape blasted as "a rookie monopolist mistake."

"Putting a browser into the operating system is like putting a word processing program in the same package with, say, a spreadsheet," said Netscape founder Jim Clark. "People don't want to have all their software come from one place. They want dozens of small companies with competing standards to offer them a variety of conflicting software that cannot be controlled through a single interface."

"We have our engineers working overtime to separate the two programs," said Microsoft CEO Bill Gates. "In the interim, we sincerely apologize for any convenience our error may have caused."

---

### QUOTE:
## "Get the Best Out of Your People"

"When people ask me what's most important, I say you've got to get the best out of your people. I think that's essential. Once you get the best out, you're left with a lot of very average people. Average people are much more manageable, and they're usually not out to get your job."

—David L. Pouland
PRESIDENT, CYBERDIGITAL KINETICS

---

# FIVE QUESTIONS

Late last month, the power of the Internet arrived at British clothier Marks & Spencer in the form of an "email." In a gala demonstration at which attendance was required, the firm's IT manager, Lucas Bigsby, instructed Francis Nollem, an average employee in the purchasing department, to send an email from Nollem's computer to the computer next to the coffee pot. After several failed attempts, a cheer went up as Nollem succeeded, thereby marking the first time Marks & Spencer has used email for intra-company exchanges. Afterward, we listened in as Bigsby fielded questions from the purchasing staff to see how well they understood their cutting-edge capabilities.

1. *Lucas, what did the email say?*
   It said, "Hello, this is a test."

2. *And that's revolutionary, is it?*
   It's not the message that's revolutionary, it's the process. It foreshadows a not-too-distant day when all our internal communications will be done this way.

3. *We'll all be sending emails to the computer next to the coffee pot?*
   What? No, no. We'll all be sending emails to each other, at our own computers.

4. *Right, but if you don't have a coffee pot next to your computer, does that mean you can't get email? Or will you be ordering coffee pots for everyone? We'll have to go out to bid on that if you are.*
   Look, no, we don't need more coffee pots! You're missing the point. The point is, email will streamline workflow immeasurably. You won't have to wait to speak to colleagues in person, and they'll no longer have to waste time trying to track you down.

5. *I see. Because they'll know where to find us.*
   Well, yes, in a manner of speaking.

6. *We'll all be hanging about the coffee pot, waiting for our emails.*

# Shooting at Virtual Office Leaves 3 as Good as Dead, 6 Tantamount to Wounded

## DECENTRALIZED WORKFORCE ALL BUT ACTUALLY TERRIFIED

FOR EMPLOYEES OF virtual consulting company Kragen Technology, the dream of working anytime, anywhere has turned into a nightmare. Last week, something like panic swept through the Web-based firm as a disgruntled employee, dressed in his pajamas but who could easily have been wearing army fatigues and face paint, burst into a crowded conference call and representationally opened fire on his geographically distributed coworkers.

Three employees were as good as dead, and six more appeared to be wounded in everything but the physical sense.

According to workers at Kragen, which has no physical headquarters but functions as a company by allowing employees to work from home, the shooting took place during a conference call monitored by 22 Kragen employees scattered around the globe. The alleged assailant was 31-year-old project manager Robert Hines, whom colleagues described as "a seemingly nice guy, always ready with what in effect passed for a fully functional smile."

The incident began when Hines, who had just logged into the call from his office in Denver, was criticized for being late. Hines then allegedly screamed, "That's the embodiment of the last straw! Eat decentralized lead!" and began effectively mimicking the noise of gunfire.

"People were screaming 'Oh in effect God!' and 'Sweet decentralized Jesus!'" recalled shaken employee Amanda Phelps, who works out of Seattle. "I was in my sweats in the study, so I was able to dive under my desk. But Mitch [Eno, a vice president] was on his cell phone in Grand Rapids and couldn't make out what was happening until it was too late. It was a disaggregated nightmare."

Hines was all but actually subdued by a pair of Kragen security guards telecommuting from their homes in Toronto, Ont., and São Paulo, Brazil.

To speed the healing process, the company immediately turned to virtual-workplace trauma therapist Nancy Deegan-Smith. "This was very much like a real experience for these people, and what they need right now is something that seems very much like hands-on, tender loving care," said Deegan-Smith, who is treating employees via email from her vacation home in the Bahamas.

# FACTORY ORDERS PLUNGE!

## "MOST CONSUMERS CAN'T AFFORD FACTORIES" CITED AS POSSIBLE REASON

A Commerce Department report citing that U.S. factory orders plunged a record 7.5 percent in July has prompted many to wonder if factories are failing to appeal to the important 18-to-34 market, or perhaps have become too expensive for the average consumer.

"How much does a factory cost, $100 million?" asked DeAnne Marks, a 27-year-old librarian in Salem, Mass. "Where am I going to get that kind of money when I've got to put food on the table? And where would I put it, anyway? That's got to be the stupidest economic measurement I ever heard of."

Market observers say that kind of aggressive apathy, particularly from the under-34 market, could be a factor in the stark decline of factory orders, which is widely regarded as one of the most important economic indicators. But e-commerce analysts point to another problem: factory manufacturers and distributors have failed to take advantage of the digital economy.

Said GartnerGroup analyst Steven Sichua: "You look at Amazon.com's menu bar, and they're starting to sell everything — books, music, software — but I don't see a button for factories. If you can't order factories online, you're missing out on a major chunk of the market." Sichua spontaneously predicted that factories ordered online will be a $700 billion business by 2003.

In Fresno, Calif., Bristlewaite Construction president Richard Harper suggested the real problem lies with the Commerce Department's research, not the factory makers. Bristlewaite, which builds factories across central California, has never been polled by Commerce officials, said Harper. "We're one of the biggest factory builders in the West, so you'd think we'd be one of the companies they survey," he said. "We got orders to build three factories in July. Three! That's a 200 percent jump, not a decrease."

Contacted in Washington, Commerce Department officials went on the defensive, insisting its report details the orders of big-ticket items, such as airplanes and ships, from factories. That explanation, however, did little to quell consumer criticism. "A ship? Where the hell am I going to get the money to order a ship?" said DeAnne Marks. "That's still the stupidest economic measurement I ever heard of."

# Great
# New Economy
# Jobs

**JASON KRETOP,**
TECH SUPPORT,
PRODIGY
INFORMATION
SERVICES

"I like to track what our subscribers are doing, like there's this one guy in Dayton, Ohio, Stanley Levitan, who is just an absolute *porn freak*. Major perv. I don't know what he does for a living, but I doubt he gets much done, 'cause he's forever in these Usenet groups downloading nasty pictures. We're always passing his surfing history around the department. We're like, "Holy shit, check out where Stanley is now!"

---

**WHO'S ON THE MOVE:**

Dayton, Ohio–based Marshaulk Plastics announced last week that Junior Payroll Manager Stanley Levitan, 44, has been promoted to head the company's new World Wide Web initiative. Said Marshaulk CFO Ralph Knorland:

"We want to get involved with this Internet thing, and Stanley seems to know more about it than anyone in our company. I don't know where he finds the time, but he's really dedicated to it."

---

## IBM ANNOUNCES VOICE RECOGNITION BRAKE THREW

IBM this week unveiled ViaVoice II for Windows, a revolutionary new line of voice-recognition software that, the company boasted, makes talking to your computer easier, faster, and "more a curate than ever beef whore."

To show off the new software's capabilities, IBM Director of Voice Technology Cameron Kurtz answered interviewers' questions using ViaVoice II's speech-to-text feature, which is designed for both advanced and novice users, and even recognizes proper nouns.

"We bee leaf that voice recognition will trains forum the way you mans interact with technology, from the computer two the telephone and Internet," said Kurtz. "The first place to effect this trains forum Asian is by making the personal computer more friendly two ewes and more pro duck dove."

Kurtz added that "Veal Voice should quickly bee gum the market liter."

---

# 85 PERCENT OF NATION'S 2.9 MILLION JOBLESS SAY THEY'RE NOT JUST STATISTIC

In a new Gallup poll on the dehumanizing aspects of job loss, nearly 85 percent of the nation's 2.96 million unemployed said they "agreed somewhat" or "agreed strongly" with the statement, "I am not just some mind-numbing statistic."

"I think what we found quite interesting was that the overwhelming majority of respondents, 75 percent, said they were genuinely hurt by efforts to categorize and compartmentalize their difficulties," said Gallup researcher Evan Krest. "This was particularly true of women between the ages of 30 and 49, and men who have been unemployed for six months or more."

But the most empirically moving answers, Krest added, were given by the 62 percent who said they hoped the study would finally put a human face on their anonymous plight.

"One 18-to-29-year-old woman said she was a real person with a real name and real problems that could not possibly be adequately conveyed using cold-blooded numbers," he recalled. "Unfortunately, her responses were within the margin of error of plus or minus 3 percent, so she didn't count."

## LESSONS
### I HAVE LEARNED
**JACK WELCH**
**CEO, GENERAL ELECTRIC**

"When I was in high school I got my first job at a hardware store. Mr. Carruthers was my boss' name. I remember he told me, '*Son, no matter how far you go in life, never forget the value of a dollar. It's $1. Some people forget that, and the people who do are just plain stupid. How could you forget what a dollar is worth? It's a goddamned dollar. One dollar. One hundred goddamned pennies. Never forget that.*' And I never did."

## VENEZUELA v. IMF, ROUND II

In reaction to yet more pressure from the International Monetary Fund, the Venezuelan Finance Ministry announced last week that the waters of the Caribbean were legal tender. Responded an IMF spokesman: "I don't see how...that doesn't really...they did *what*?"

## ONE-UPSMANCHIP

In response to AMD's new 166 MHz chip, Intel said on Friday it has developed a 167 MHz chip, but AMD downplayed the announcement this week, saying its 166 MHz chip really runs at 168 MHz. Just before press time, however, Intel released a statement claiming there was a typo in its announcement Friday, and that its 167 MHz chip really runs at 168 MHz. A spokesman at AMD said the company would not comment about Intel's latest claim, explaining executives were too busy boxing up AMD's new 169 MHz chips to come to the phone.

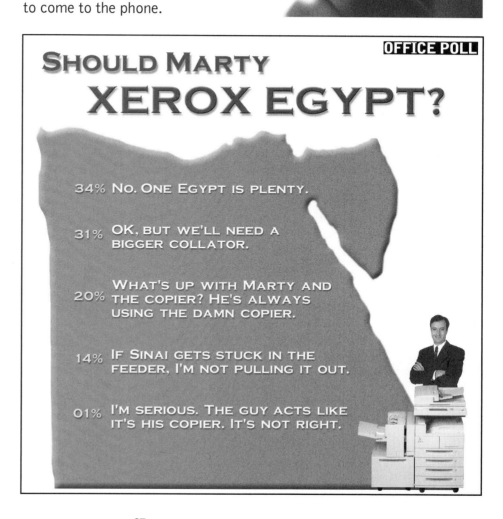

**OFFICE POLL**

## SHOULD MARTY XEROX EGYPT?

**34%** No. One Egypt is plenty.

**31%** OK, but we'll need a bigger collator.

**20%** What's up with Marty and the copier? He's always using the damn copier.

**14%** If Sinai gets stuck in the feeder, I'm not pulling it out.

**01%** I'm serious. The guy acts like it's his copier. It's not right.

## TOOLS OF THE TRADE

Sirs,
I found your article on the essential tools of job security (*"Your Boss, a Hooker, and a Camera,"* May 1995) to be misleading. Certainly, taking clandestine photographs of one's boss with a hooker would be a sure-fire way to retain one's job if, in fact, your boss considered being photographed with someone not his wife as a threat. But what if he is unmarried, or European?

NAME WITHHELD
BY REQUEST

Sirs,
Bravo on *Your Boss, a Hooker, and a Camera!* I particularly appreciated that you outlined the expenses involved: the prostitute, the adjoining motel rooms, the two-way mirror, the film and film processing, the safe deposit box in which to keep the negatives, and also the camera itself, if you don't already have one.

Most people would argue that keeping their job is worth the $5,000 this could cost, but if I may make a suggestion, why go to the expense and trouble when you can achieve the same results, right on your own computer, with new Adobe Photoshop 3.0? Now on sale for just $795 with mail-in rebate.

ASIA KANDLER
Product Manager
Adobe Systems

Sirs,
Less than two months after reading your fine article on job security, my boss dropped a bomb on me. I was being fired. It was, needless to say, a life moment, and my first thoughts were of Robert Burns' "But oh! fell death's untimely frost, that nipt my flower sae early." But then I remembered I had secretly taken all those photos of my boss with a prostitute. Thanks.

RICHARD SINCLAR
Newest Vice President
Carlton Minibus
Corp.

Sirs,
I couldn't afford an actual hooker, so I improvised a little from what you suggested in your Boss-Hooker-Camera story. The pictures came out great anyway, and when I showed them to my boss, you could see him and the woman easily, *in flagrante fellatio,* clear as day. But instead of panicking and letting me keep my job, he looked me straight in the eye and said it wasn't him! Does it make a difference if you hire an intern instead of a real prostitute?

SHEILA MCFAY
Former White House Aide

## WHAT'S IN A NAME?

Sirs,
I was disappointed in your coverage of the annual Robert Moskowitz Salary Survey™, (*"People Named Robert Moskowitz Still Make More Than You,"* September 1995). The bottom line is, who in the world cares what the "46 people in the United States and Canada named Robert Moskowitz" make every year? So what if they earn more than the average American? That is such a stupid economic measurement for such a stupid, stupid name, and you do your readers a disservice by giving it space.

ALICE BELL, Chairman
National Alliance for People
Named Alice Bell
Milwaukee, Wis.

Sirs,
Kudos on your fine article espousing the benefits of cooperating with your competition (*"Coopetition: Neville Chamberlain's Guide to Snuggling with the Enemy,"* August 1995). For too long, businesses have felt threatened whenever a larger, more powerful corporation that is simply defending its territory wants to talk with them. But in fact, these corporations have nothing but the best intentions.

STEVE BALLMER
President
Microsoft

## TRIPE

Sirs,
Your article on dealing with change in the New Economy, (*"Embracing Your Inner Change Agent," July 1995*) was nothing more than vacuous platitudes and meaningless tripe. From Rule #1, "Change agents embrace non-linear e-business metrics," to Rule #50, "Change agents recontextualize counterintuitive paradigms," the entire piece was useless and will do nothing to impact the lives of real businesspeople.

SIMON BARBER
L&M Construction
Grover, Md.

Sirs,
Your article on dealing with change in the New Economy has changed my life! I've got it taped up on my cubicle and passed out 100 copies to my colleagues! I'm going right out to disintermediate some unextensible methodologies!

JANE CARTWRIGHT
Chief Visionary
JustKnitWoolSocks.com

# Fed Drops Interest Rates, Acid at Policy Rave

## FEDERAL RESERVE NOT SO RESERVED ANYMORE

PROVING THE Federal Reserve is anything but reserved, U.S. central bank governors this week announced they had dropped interest rates, their pants, and 162 tabs of acid and Ecstasy during what turned out to be a two-day "policy rave" at their September meeting.

According to those present, Fed Chairman Alan Greenspan did not ingest any hallucinogens, although he was affected. "Alan didn't drop, which was probably a good thing, because for about two hours there it looked to me like he was barking like a chicken and had laser beams shooting from all 12 of his eyes," said committee staffer Julie Lindstrom. "But his gossamer wings were soooo beautiful.

"Everyone was soooo beautiful," she added.

The closed-door session of the Federal Open Market Committee reportedly began with Greenspan discussing his upcoming Congressional testimony. However, it quickly raved-up after an unidentified staffer, frustrated at not being able to understand the opaque chairman, passed around tabs of Ecstasy and LSD, which he identified only as "Greenspan Decoders."

"About 45 minutes later, [Fed Governor] Nathan Gladstone says to me, 'Julie, can you bring us the reports on monetary interventions, bond yields, and three dozen pacifiers?'" recalled Lindstrom. "Then we ordered some glowsticks and Meat Beat Manifesto CDs, and the Open Market meeting got really, really *open.*"

For the next 36 hours, the committee's dignified boardroom was transformed into a trance room, with the heads of the New York and Dallas central banks banging out jungle-drum rhythms on the massive oval table, and the head of the Detroit bank insisting consumer confidence tastes like candy-coated clouds. Toward daybreak, male committee members and staff reportedly took off their trousers after their zippers began to emit signals which they feared were being broadcast on Radio Free Europe.

While the rave was "definitely a dope groove," Fed Governor Bradley Muer said members did exhibit restraint. "Some people were going to candyflip [combine Ecstasy with acid], but most of us are Old Economy, and acid just

> "Then we ordered some glowsticks and Meat Beat Manifesto CDs, and the Open Market meeting got really, really *open.*"

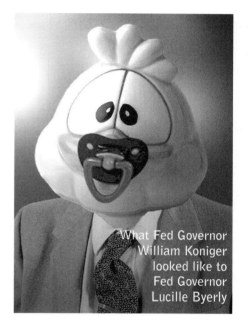

What Fed Governor William Koniger looked like to Fed Governor Lucille Byerly

seemed more traditional," he said.

The rave fizzled about 7 a.m. and was about to adjourn when a staffer reportedly noticed the committee hadn't covered every item on the agenda. "We just hit reentry and were going to watch the sun come up over the Treasury Building, when somebody said, 'Oh, shit, we forgot to drop the Fed fund rates,'" explained FOMC member Gerald F. Cohen. "Then everybody just started calling out whatever numbers they saw floating in front of their eyes."

Hours later, the board finally agreed to cut rates half a percentage point. Initially, said Cohen, committee members decided to lower rates by 8 million basis points, from 5.00 to minus 7,999,995, but were talked out of it by an art deco wall sconce that claimed it was Cary Grant.

# SWAT
# SHOPS

**MAJOR CORPORATIONS TURNING INTO "SWAT SHOPS"**

# Employee-Slapping Widespread, Effective

PAM KENNEDY WAS beyond frustrated. As a vice president at WorldCom, she was responsible for staffing in the company's marketing department. This was once an easy job, as candidates annually knocked down her door and rarely made difficult demands. But all that changed as the Internet economy expanded and the labor pool tightened. Suddenly, Kennedy found herself making unprecedented concessions to keep her best workers. And one day, after an entry-level employee insisted he needed more flextime and a better health plan, Kennedy lost it.

"I slapped the guy, hard, right across the face," recalls Kennedy, a petite brunette with a meticulous manner. "He was stunned, but I was completely invigorated. It was as if every inch of ground I'd given was instantly reclaimed."

In earlier times, Kennedy would have been fired, but WorldCom, like dozens of other corporations, had recently instituted an "employee-slapping policy" that allowed managers to slap workers "pretty much whenever they damn well please."

Like Kennedy, many supervisors hail the random slapping of employees as a great equalizer, but the practice has, not surprisingly, come under fire from many lower-level workers. Even some senior-level managers have voiced complaints.

"I, for one, don't like it a bit," says Marcia Pepperstein, vice president of sales at Motorola. "I'm a vice president, and I get slapped. I think there should be a ceiling somewhere, just below

**"I'M A VICE PRESIDENT, AND I GET SLAPPED. I THINK THERE SHOULD BE A CEILING SOMEWHERE, JUST BELOW ME, SO THAT I DON'T GET SLAPPED, BUT I STILL GET TO SLAP. THAT, TO ME, WOULD BE AN ACCEPTABLE SYSTEM."**

# Helping Hands

**Before implementing its employee-slapping policy, Ralston Purina explored several options:**

- Gaff the employee
- Paint the employee
- Scribble on the employee
- OK, employee, hold still. I am going to hit you with this AOL disc.
- Mr. Scary Hand Man

theoretically, I could slap every one of them, but who's got the time?" he laments. "What I've learned, and this is a good lesson for prospective managers out there: delegate."

Most employee-slapping policies prohibit the slapping of anyone not full-time, although Goldman Sachs has reportedly violated this recently by allowing managers to slap temporary workers until they confess. One violation companies have been cracking down on is what's known as the "slunch," or slap-punch. "My boss punched me once," recalls UPS' Baines. "She said it was a slap, but I felt knuckle. I couldn't shave for a week."

Baines filed a complaint with the Human Resources Department at UPS, and after getting slapped around a bit — "on the organizational chart, they were two levels above me" — his grievance was declared valid. Now his boss can only slap him in the presence of her superiors.

With the rapid pace of its adoption, employee-slapping is expected to quickly extend beyond the

me, so that I don't get slapped, but I still get to slap. That, to me, would be an acceptable system."

While employee-slapping programs are relatively new, their genesis can be found in the mid-1990s, when Internet companies raised the ante for hiring by offering stock options and unusual perks. As a result, employees gained more freedom and power, and have been able to make ever-greater demands on employers.

Employee-slapping, proponents argue, makes up for the lost sense of balance, with several managers reporting they can "feel the tension fly right off their fingertips." Some also contend the policy has reinvigorated a sense of ambition in the workforce, as climbing the corporate ladder to attain more money or power has been supplanted by a more intense, visceral desire.

"It's simple math," explains Jeffrey Baines, a senior marketing manager at United Parcel Service. "Right now, in my department, I've got six people under me. That's only six people I can slap. My boss, he has 96 people under him. I want his job."

There are, however, limits to ambition, warns Cisco Systems CEO John Chambers. "I've got 26,000 employees, and

> **"I'VE GOT SIX PEOPLE UNDER ME. THAT'S ONLY SIX PEOPLE I CAN SLAP. MY BOSS, HE HAS 96 PEOPLE UNDER HIM. I WANT HIS JOB."**

business world and reach into government. Already, federal officials and political party operatives are preparing.

"We're telling all our candidates that saying, 'I work for the American people' can earn them a big fat lip," said Democratic pollster Stanley Greenberg. "We've also bought all of them mouthpieces."

But the commonly held notion that politicians do work for the public has some rubbing their palms together, particularly those watching the presidential race. "After the election next year, I get to slap either George Bush or Al Gore," said a voter from Kansas City. "That's as close as it comes to a no-lose scenario."

# BUSINESS JARGON BAD FOR BUSINESS, MISSION-CRITICAL STUDY FINDS

## JARGON-WIELDING "BUZZ JUNKIES" SHOULD BE "DECRUITED," REPORT STATES

ACCORDING TO a mission-critical new study, people who use the latest business buzz phrases may actually harm their companies by using jargon in place of more concise language, a practice the report calls "message de-engineering."

"Jargon and catchphrases almost always blur the meaning of what you're trying to convey, and this recontextualization actually decreases productivity," said Harvard Business School Prof. Mary Chang, who co-authored the report, entitled "The Negative Value Proposition of Message De-engineering at the Enterprise Level."

As a result, Chang noted, the average employee wastes time looking up the terms, or simply grins and pretends she knows what the buzz phrase means. "I call these average employees who don't get the lingo the 'Blank-and-Smile,'" said Chang. Unfortunately, she added, jargon and catchy phrases are now ingrained in corporate culture, "so eliminating them will require companies to think outside the box and implement viral solutions at the enterprise level."

Based on sheer usage, most buzz breeders and buzz junkies work in middle management, but Chang said even chief executives are guilty. "Sadly, sometimes these phrases come from the top," she said. "I call these 'smoke signals.'

> **Jargon and catchy phrases are now ingrained in corporate culture, "so eliminating them will require companies to think outside the box and implement viral solutions at the enterprise level."**

They look pretty, but they're incomprehensible unless the Chief is there to translate."

To Chang and others, there is a much simpler way to communicate strategies, goals, and ideas.

"I remember the first time I heard the term 'tool creep,' I thought it was that Tim Allen character on TV," said Randall Crench, the report's coauthor and a partner with Andersen Consulting. "But it really describes the habit of attempting to use too many software applications, which are sometimes called 'tools.'"

While Crench conceded that "You suffer from tool creep" is catchy, he argued it would be better to simply state, "You use too many applications." However, he added, "at least 'tool creep' is better than 'buy-in,' as in 'I need your buy-in on this.' That phrase is totally jargon basement."

But why even use a term like "jargon basement" instead of simply stating "bad"?

"Because 'jargon basement' is a best-of-breed phrase," said Crench. "Really, by introducing you to this new term, it's like I'm handing out a stylishly linguistic gift. I call that 'Santa Clausing.'"

# "Oh, YOU MEAN *That* INTERNET!

## YEAH, WE KNEW ABOUT THAT."

**AN INTERVIEW WITH BILL GATES**

**Microsoft.** The name alone is synonymous with market domination. And yet, to date, the software giant has done anything but dominate the buzz surrounding the Internet. Critics charge that the Redmond, Wash.–based company, determined to build its own information highway called the Microsoft Network, simply failed to catch the latest wave. Lately, however, Microsoft has struck back, explaining that it is not only well aware of the Internet, but began making plans for it before smaller rivals like Netscape appeared on the scene more than a year ago. *BusinessMonth Weekly* sat down with Microsoft Chairman and Chief Executive Bill Gates to discuss the company's heretofore covert Internet strategy, and find out how one of the most successful tech companies of all time expects to cope with what many are calling the greatest technological breakthrough of the 20th century.

**BMW:** Earlier in 1995, you did an interview with *Fortune* magazine where you never mentioned the Internet or the World Wide Web. In an interview with *Playboy* late last year, it was the same thing. But now you suddenly claim Microsoft has been making plans for the Internet since early 1994.
**GATES:** I never mentioned the Internet before because I didn't want to give away our strategy, which I think is reasonable, given the highly competitive nature of the industry. But make no mistake, we have been intimately familiar with the Internet for quite some time.

**BMW:** So despite what people are saying, you're really more of a dot-com pioneer?
**GATES:** Absolutely. A bot-gum pioneer. Heavily involved in Internet-based bot-gum technologies for quite some time.

**BMW:** Sorry? Did you say bot-gum technologies?
**GATES:** Services. I meant Internet-based bot-gum services, of course.

**BMW:** Right... Let's talk about that in more detail. The bot-gum thing. So would you say, based on Microsoft's extensive research, that companies deploying bot-gum technologies will be the most successful on the Internet? And bot-gum services, of course. Those too.
**GATES:** You can never be certain who's going to do well. I certainly didn't expect Microsoft to dominate the operating system market when we first started. But like others, we have been investing in the bot-dum area.

**BMW:** You mean bot-gum.
**GATES:** Yes, bot-gum. As I was saying, we have been investing in the bot-gum area, although at present I'm not at liberty to be too specific about our plans.

**BMW:** Of course. But you can't move too slowly since so many other Internet companies have already deployed bot-gum technologies. Like, say, HimmelFark Software or, um, CandyGramps Technologies. You've heard of them, no doubt.
**GATES:** Certainly. But you know, I don't want to address particular competitors like the ones you mentioned, which of course are well known to us. But I will say that being first

does not necessarily mean you will come out on top.

**BMW:** Although I think it's safe to say that you were the first to see the value of bot-gum. That's real vision.
**GATES:** We try to stay ahead of the curve.

**BMW:** I can see that now. So, well, let me ask this: today the Internet is still small, only a few million people, but what role do you think the, um, the pig will have in speeding up adoption of the network?
**GATES:** Pigs?

**BMW:** The pig, yes. As you know, Netscape has been working on a, um, a pig-based browser, basing its code on the DNA of pigs. It's very new. Perhaps you haven't...
**GATES:** Oh, pigs! Yes, well, new for them, but not for us. We've been moving forward on the pig-DNA–based browser for some time. Before Netscape formed, actually.

**BMW:** Well, clearly, the press has been wrong in claiming Microsoft is late to the Internet dance.
**GATES:** Not unusual. The more successful you are, the more you become a faultless target.

**BMW:** Right, but since you haven't even mentioned e-commerce, I assume you're not completely caught up.
**GATES:** On the contrary. I was just going to mention e-commerce.

**BMW:** Really? What do you think of it?
**GATES:** What do you think of it?

**BMW:** No, you first.
**GATES:** Exactly. That's what I think. That we'll be first in e-commerce.

**BMW:** And in the meantime, you'll be barreling ahead with your Internet-based bot-gum software.
**GATES:** We're committed. We've invested millions in it. Our finest people are working on it as we speak. A year from now, when you think bot-gum, you'll think Microsoft.

**BMW:** No doubt about that.

# NEW HMO STRATEGY:
# LET'S PAY HEALTH CLAIMS

## ANALYSTS SKEPTICAL; DOUBT INSURERS EQUIPPED TO HANDLE JOB

MOVING INTO what insurance executives concede is "uncharted territory," five of the nation's leading HMOs announced yesterday they will begin paying health insurance claims for sick and injured people.

Health-care advocates immediately cried foul, noting the insurers plan to significantly increase premiums to offset claim losses. Higher premiums are unnecessary, watchdogs argued, because consumers already pay insurers with the expectation they will be covered. However, Cigna HealthCare President Benjamin Darnell disagreed with that assessment.

"In the past, what consumers really have been paying for is hope, as in, 'I sure hope my insurance covers this,'" said Darnell. "Now, consumers will be paying for health, as in, 'I'm glad I have my health because my insurance company has all my money.'"

Exactly how much premiums will rise is undetermined, said Dr. John Wopping, chairman and CEO of UnitedHealth Group. "We're still doing cost-benefit analysis and revising our cash-flow models," said Wopping, "but our initial estimates call for premiums to increase, on average, fuckin' astronomically."

Regional discrepancies will exist, however, as consumers in the northeastern U.S. and in California incur higher-than-average premiums because, Wopping said, "they have more money. But hey, if you're really sick," he added, "what's money, right?"

Also undetermined is whether the insurers will allow ailing and injured people to actually see physicians. "We have an inter-company committee studying what service it is that physicians and hospitals provide," said Darnell. "It's not really something we're familiar with."

Under the existing system, a patient is treated, a claim is submitted, and the insurer refuses to pay based on one of the following criteria:

1) Illness/injury not covered under patient's current plan.

2) Claims submission package incomplete; please include unicorn horn obtained by tooth fairy during unscripted professional wrestling match.

Under the proposed system, healthcare providers will simply pay claims. However, the HMOs insist losses will be equalized, not just by increased premiums, but by "tremendous savings" in personnel costs.

Kaiser Permanente, for instance, said it will cut 65 percent of its staff, eliminating its entire "Complaints," "Repeated Complaints," "Here's Another One Complaining," and "This Guy Was Shot in the Head Six Times Last Week and He Actually Thinks We're Going to Cover Him" departments.

Despite the rosy profit picture painted by HMOs, however, Wall Street analysts reacted to the announcement with skepticism. "I'm afraid these are foreign waters these insurers are barking up," said Goldman Sachs analyst Lisa Kepler, utilizing a stunning mixed metaphor that had them standing three deep around her cubicle just to get a glimpse of her. "These companies simply don't have the people and procedures in place to provide this service. It's like trying to teach an old dog new tricks when the horse is already out of the barn," she added, before being mobbed by admiring colleagues who lifted her onto their shoulders and carried her off for a well-deserved celebratory luncheon.

## TRENDSPOTTING

TODAY, MORE THAN EVER BEFORE, WOMEN ARE IN TOP EXECUTIVE POSITIONS, WHICH MEANS TODAY, MORE THAN EVER BEFORE, TOP MALE EXECUTIVES GET TO YELL...

# girl fight!

BY PETER DETWICK

*Last year, women held just 5 percent of corporate officer posts in the 500 largest U.S. companies. But this year, the number is expected to hit 7 percent. Within three years, it should double. While some claim the jump is due to equal employment laws or the desire to put the right person in the right job, many believe male executives have a less noble motive. Secretly, they are turned on by watching high-level, nicely dressed corporate women get into knock-down-drag-out fights right in the office. BusinessMonth Weekly reporter Peter Detwick investigates.*

IT IS 5:45 P.M. in the offices of Atlanta-based Dynamo Metrix, and CEO Lahti Carlin has just found out that company CFO Denise Ridgeback has been stabbing her in the back, questioning her authority, and calling her a variety of crude and unpublishable names.

"I can't believe this. Denise really called me that?" Carlin asks a reporter sitting in her office. "That's not like her. This really hurts."

Ten minutes later, a visibly angry Ridgeback bursts into Carlin's office.

"Lahti," says Ridgeback, "How could you do this to me!"

"What are you talking about? Do what?" Carlin answers. "And frankly, you shouldn't be the one complaining, you back stabber!"

"Back stabber?" says Ridgeback. "You're the one who called me a (expletive) (expletive) and demoted me!"

"What? I didn't call you a (expletive) (expletive), and I didn't demote you, although I should have, you lying (expletive)."

"Why you..." Suddenly, Ridgeback lunges at Carlin, and the two grapple to the floor.

"Lying (expletive)?" asks Ridgeback, as she attempts to put Carlin in a headlock. "What did I say?"

"Ha! What indeed!" Carlin screams. With a free hand, she points to a reporter in her office. "You told him I was a (expletive) (expletive), and you told the board I was embezzling from the company!"

"I never... Hey, put that camera away!" Ridgeback calls to the reporter as Carlin knees her in the abdomen. "Half an hour ago, that reporter told me that you said you were going to demote me for being an 'incompetent (expletive) (expletive)'!"

"He what? Hey, where'd all this Jell-O come from?"

Ridgeback and Carlin ease their grips and turn to the reporter, who has already seen enough and departs.

**Next month: How far will female executives go to get interviewed in a major business magazine? BMW reporter Peter Detwick investigates.**

# NEW SOFTWARE
# INTENTIONALLY
## "Microsoft Bob" Starts Major Trend ANNOYING

FOR MOST of its history, software has at least pretended to be helpful, but analysts say the recent introduction of Microsoft Bob has started a new trend among developers, who are following Redmond's lead by building a variety of purposefully irritating programs.

According to PC Data analyst Paul Bahns, Microsoft put a lot of effort and money into Bob, an alternative to Windows that uses animated agents to help guide novice users around their computers. Competitors, however, have quickly answered the call, added Bahns, who forecasts a "conspicuous drop" in traditional help utilities and a surge in what he calls "vengeful, senseless, and exasperating" utilities.

Among the software programs expected to be top-sellers next year:

• **Where in the World Is That Damn File?** *(BadApps.com; $39.95):* Takes a file at random from your hard drive and hides it in "somewhere on the Internet." Great educational utility that teaches users how to use the vast computer network. Also provides a valuable lesson in backing up data.

• **Tressprint** *(LabourSaver Inc.; $19.95):* A Printer Intercept Utility, Tressprint replaces any graphics or document file you attempt to print with a low-quality, full-page image of former British Prime Minister Harold Wilson falling off a ladder.

• **Flashback 2.0** *(Luddite Software; $49.95):* Remember your DOS commands? Better brush up, as this utility irrevocably converts any PC into a 1981 model IBM XT with 128k RAM running DOS 2.0. (External 5.25-inch floppy drive sold separately.)

• **Simon Sucks** *(Taunting Technologies; $199.95):* A Prefatory Command Utility based on the popular game Simon Says. After installing Simon Sucks, users are required to type in the words "Simon Sucks" before each mouse click in any program. Users who forget to type "Simon Sucks" are "Out," and their computers will lock up. Users must then reboot using the "Tell Simon You're Sorry" emergency disk. Replaces the popular "Mother May I?" Prefatory Command Utility.

• **ElfinFind** *(Search and Annoy Utilities; $19.95):* One of the first "search utilities" for the Internet, ElfinFind automatically scans the World Wide Web for references to the word "elfin," and continuously delivers results to your desktop, whether you want it to or not. The software has impressive financial backers, including Dr. Tim Berners-Lee, the father of the Web. "Everybody thinks I created the Web to more easily find and exchange data stored on the Internet, or to expedite global communications and business practices, and

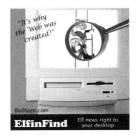

I guess it's turning out to be that, but my original intention was to provide a platform for people to post and share any intelligence they might have gathered on the Elves. ElfinFind is the second phase of this great plan. Using a beta version of the software, along with the Web, I have increased by tenfold my knowledge of the Elf world. Of course, the flip side is the Elves can find out more about me now. So I seldom sleep in the same place twice."

• **PaperAge** *(Luddite Software; $4,995.95):* Running out of hard drive space will never again be a problem with PaperAge, which prints every file on your hard drive onto portable, easily accessible paper, and then deletes those files from your computer. Comes with handy 346-drawer filing cabinet. (Tip: How many printouts of Harold Wilson falling off a ladder can you have? Find out. PaperAge is now compatible with Tressprint's LabourSaver!)

• **AlphaMail** *(Don't Call Me SoftWare; $99.95):* Email plug-in that auto-responds to all incoming mail with message: "WHATEVER YOU HAVE TO TELL ME, SAY IT TO MY FACE."

• **BetaMail** *(Don't Call Me SoftWare; $699.95 for those who like the price, $999.95 for anyone who complains):* Doesn't actually do anything, and if that's a problem, the price is $1,299.95.

# Accident Imminent?

## Let 'Em Hear You Scream!

> As part of its safety awareness campaign, the Cell Phone Safety Council will place posters such as this one on buses in several major cities.

# CAR PHONE SAFETY: SCREAM "AAHH!" BEFORE IMPACT
## Cell Phone Industry Group Launches Public Service Campaign

UNDER PRESSURE to do something about car accidents involving cell phones, the industry-backed Cell Phone Safety Council this week launched a public service campaign urging users to "scream like hell" before impact, thereby alerting callers on the other end that there is some kind of trouble.

"It's ironic, but people who can talk forever on a cell phone suddenly come up mute when they're about to get into a collision," said CPSC spokesman Donald Lufrette. "They just get hit, and the caller on the other end doesn't know what happened."

Therefore, the safety council suggests users scream "Aahhh!" or "Oh, God!" or, if there are no children present, "Shit!" just before impact. A proper scream, Lufrette insisted, can save your life, as the person on the other end of the call can then phone authorities.

As an added advantage, a good caterwaul also cuts down on the wasted airtime that inevitably follows a crash as the phone, still connected, sits amid shards of broken glass on the hood of the car. A wise caller, realizing your predicament, will know to hang up right away.

"Your hospital bills are going to be bad enough," Lufrette remarked. "The last thing you want is a big fat cell phone bill on top of it."

Sally Anne Rimes, a cell phone user in Garden City, N.J., said she welcomes the public service campaign.

"It's very annoying when suddenly the other person isn't talking and you don't know what happened," said Rimes. "You're just sitting there going, 'Hello? Hello?'"

Rimes said three of her friends have been in accidents while speaking on cell phones, but only one of them had the sense to scream first. "It was so thoughtful of him to yell. I was like, 'Oh, my God! Look, call me back when you're free,' and I hung up. I saved his widow a ton of money."

# SatireWire's

# BusinessMonth

DECEMBER 1996

## WEEKLY

*IN THE NEW ECONOMY, YOU NEED*

# SPEED

## EVERYBODY'S ON SPEED

## WAIT, WE DON'T MEAN IT THAT WAY

WE MEAN METAPHORICALLY. BUT THEN AGAI
PEOPLE ARE WORKING UNNATURALLY LONG HOUR

HOW THE HELL ARE THEY "STAYING
AWAKE"?

WHATEVER. WE JUST WANT TO SAY

# FASTFASTFASTFASTFASTFAST

## FAST INSIDE THIS ISSUE

*THESE HEADHUNTERS WON'T FIND YOU A JOB, BUT
THEY'LL TAKE YOUR HEAD FAST!* ● *PULL A FAST ONE
ON TELEMARKETERS: CALL THEM BEFORE THEY CALL YOU!*
● *AOL MEMBERS CAN'T GET ONLINE FAST (OR AT ALL)*
● *VALUJET CHANGES ITS NAME, AND FAST*

# NETIZEN FEARS HACKERS WILL STEAL HIS VISA CARD

## NO. 8099 0788 341 9800 EXP. 12/99

## NEW PRIVACY STUDY REVEALS CONSUMER CONCERNS, ADDRESSES, PHONE NUMBERS

NELSON SHANK has been online since 1994, but according to a new report by the Internet Privacy Association, the 31-year-old database programmer has yet to make a single online purchase, fearing hackers or marketers will steal his Visa Card number, 8099 0788 341 9800 EXP. 12/99, as well as discover that 213-98-8750 is his Social Security number, and that he uses his mother's maiden name, Vitale, as his AOL password.

"I would like to buy a novel on, say, Amazon.com, but how do I know my information is safe?" said Shank, who told the researchers he was particularly worried that his unlisted phone number, 311-4245, would fall into some marketing firm's hands.

Shank's response was one of nearly 35,000 gathered in a survey by the Internet Privacy Association, whose stated goal is to "expand awareness of Internet privacy issues through extensive consumer opinion polls and the dissemination of exceptionally valuable demographic information."

"Study after study has shown that Internet privacy is the number one concern of those going online, and our survey confirmed this, as 80 percent of respondents stated they did not want their personal information shared," said IPA director Shellie Jorkins.

What makes the IPA study different, Jorkins noted, is the level of detail extracted from respondents, and the way in which the IPA plans to use that information in the fight against online privacy invasion.

"We are so concerned about privacy that we want to share our findings with other affected groups, such as marketing database firms, consumer products companies, and credit card issuers," she said. "We do this because we think marketers, who are so often accused of failing to respect people's privacy, should know that there are thousands of people with average household incomes of $74,000 who don't want their information made public."

By collecting such personally identifiable demographics, she added, "we let these ruthless marketers know that these are not just nameless, faceless consumers, but real people, with real concerns, with real brand loyalties and real obtainable credit card histories."

In true open-source fashion, Jorkins pledged that the IPA would hold none of its information back, including online browsing habits, medical records, and other highly valuable data, which can be sorted into a wide variety of demographic categories on request, and is available through the IPA for $9,995. Charging for the information, Jorkins explained, is one way the IPA ensures that these third parties "are as interested in Internet privacy as we are."

Susan Demarak, identified in the report as a 29-year-old mother of three who is likely to purchase a midsize four-door sedan in the next six months, said she was glad to take the survey.

"I was happy that someone is out there fighting the good fight on Internet privacy," said Demarak. "I've even forwarded to the IPA the email addresses of 10 friends who I know would like to go on record against online privacy invasion."

# BRE-X INVESTORS SAY ENORMOUS WEALTH WON'T CHANGE THEM

Investors in Canadian mining firm Bre-X Minerals Ltd., which is sitting atop the "gold find of the century" in Indonesia, say they are determined not to let the profits they eventually receive change who they are as people.

"Whatever happens, even if what we get is really surprising, I'm still going to be the same guy," vowed Ed Ottley, a 52-year-old carpenter from Toronto who sunk $6,000 of his life savings into Bre-X stock. "In fact, I guarantee you that a few years from now, if you meet me on the street, you'll think I never made so much as a dime off my investment."

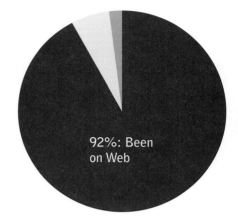

92%: Been on Web

## VENEZUELA v. IMF ROUND III

Following a tense, daylong meeting yesterday between the International Monetary Fund and the Venezuelan Finance Ministry, which recently have been at odds, the Ministry announced that all doors on bathroom stalls in its buildings will be removed immediately. Asked for reaction, an IMF official replied: "Maybe it's a language problem."

## Poll: 92 Percent of Web Users Have Been on Web

A surprising 92 percent of respondents to an online survey said they had been on the Internet at least once, while 6 percent said they had never been online but hoped to do so within the next six months. The remaining 2 percent in the survey, conducted by CNET at its World Wide Web site, said they had never been online, and had no intention of doing so. Among the reasons the latter group cited for abstaining: excess home and work responsibilities, fear of privacy invasion, and too much time spent on the Internet already.

# *Consumer Reports* Says *Consumer Reports* Unsafe

*Consumer Reports* has issued a product safety warning on the December issue of *Consumer Reports*, saying the popular magazine can easily overturn, has been linked to numerous hand lacerations, and is highly flammable.

In its December 1996 issue, the respected periodical demanded that Consumers Union, which publishes *Consumer Reports*, recall the magazine based on safety tests of the December 1996 issue.

"Our testers sustained small cuts on their fingers from page edges, and found that the magazine repeatedly and eas-ily caught fire when exposed to a heat source, such as a match," *Consumer Reports* said. "In addition, the magazine would likely have turned right over if not for the safety outriggers that engineers attached to the cover."

People looking for unbiased product information in magazine format should avoid the December 1996 *Consumer Reports* until the safety problems have been corrected, the magazine added.

Further information on the warning can be found in the December 1996 issue of *Consumer Reports*.

## BEARDSTOWN LADIES WIN NOBEL IN ECONOMICS, PULITZER IN FICTION

The renowned Beardstown Ladies Investment Club, a group of 16 Illinois grandmothers whose books teach readers how they, too, can consistently beat the markets, has won the prestigious Double, taking home the Nobel Prize for Economics and the Pulitzer Prize for Fiction.

Nobel Prize committee members said they could not ignore the "absolutely unbelievable" 23.4 percent annual rate of return the ladies have achieved in the last decade, and called the success of their practical, down-home advice, as espoused in their *Common-Sense Investment Guide*, "inconceivable for women who had no previous experience on Wall Street."

The Pulitzer committee said they awarded the fiction prize to the Beardstown Ladies for the same reasons.

# AOL Launches "Online Anytime Except Nights and Weekends and Forget About Getting Through During the Day" Campaign

Hoping to increase its lead as the nation's largest busy signal service provider, America Online last week launched its "Online Anytime Except Nights and Weekends and Forget About Getting Through During the Day" campaign, which promises new members 50 free hours of unsuccessful connect time in the first month.

Although the estimated 75,000 new users signing up each week have all but clogged AOL servers, Chief Executive Steve Case insisted the marketing blitz is necessary as access numbers in New Hampshire and southern Oregon are still available 75 percent of the time, and logging on between 2 a.m. and 4 a.m. on the East Coast is virtually possible.

## 1996 Business Olympic Games

### EVENT SCHEDULE

| Tuesday | Wednesday | Thursday | Friday |
|---|---|---|---|
| 100 Meter Merge | 4x400 Team Recall | Platform-Agnostic Diving | Field Hockey Before Interest, Depreciation, Taxes, and Amortization (FHBIDTA) |
| Uneven Bars for Equal Pay | Shot Puts and Calls | Consumer Non-Cycling | Crisis Pole Vaulting |
| 200 CEO Egostroke | Synergized Swimming | Triple Witch Jump | Total Quality Management Water Polo |
| Generally Accepted Accounting Relays | Sexual Harassment Finals: 200-Meter Breaststroke | Negotiation Marathon | Parallel Barriers to Entry |
| Boxing: Light Middleware | Greco-Roman Outsourcing | e-Questrian.com (formerly Equestrian, Inc.) | Closing Ceremony: Downsizing of Redundant Athletic Personnel |

# ValuJet Changes Name to AirTran

## HOPES PEOPLE DON'T MAKE CONNECTION TO FATAL CRASH

### Specifically Flight 592, Which Went Down in Everglades May 11, 1996

ATLANTA-BASED air carrier ValuJet announced it has merged with Orlando-based AirWays Corp., and changed its name to AirTran in order to put name-recognition distance between itself and ValuJet Flight 592, which would have been AirTran Flight 592 if the company had changed its name before the 27-year-old DC-9 plunged into the Florida Everglades in May, killing all 110 on board.

AirTran spokeswoman Kelly Fidrich insisted AirTran is "an entirely new company with an entirely new vision, and we look forward to an entirely fresh start."

In a survey conducted by *The Dotconomist*, however, 100 percent of respondents who were asked if they associated the name AirTran with the horrible deaths of 105 passengers and 5 crew aboard Flight 592 who perished after oxygen canisters aboard the Miami-to-Atlanta flight exploded eight minutes after takeoff, answered, "Now that you mention it, yes."

Revolutionaries intent on attacking a capitalist banking center in San Diego react bravely after being told to stop.

# REVOLUTION FINALLY COMES, BUT AT INCONVENIENT TIME

## LACK OF BOURGEOISIE COOPERATION, STRONG TV LINEUP, TURN BACK UNIVERSAL UPRISING

THE LONG-AWAITED Revolution, when the oppressed and disenfranchised break the chains of economic servitude and social injustice and put the tyrants and plutocrats up against the wall, finally arrived last Monday, but quickly fizzled after the ruling classes said they just didn't have time for it.

"It was 8 o'clock at night, we had guests over, I was introducing a new line of cookware in the morning, and suddenly my employees want to overturn the status quo and establish a classless society?" said Martha Stewart, CEO of Martha Stewart Living Omnimedia and one of those slated to be "first up against the wall" when the Revolution came. "Of course, I said 'No.' "

Across the globe, attempts to cast off the shackles of capitalist oppression met similar fates. In Szentgotthárd, Hungary, second-shift workers at a

General Motors plant attempted to seize the means of production, but were told they needed to make an appointment with plant manager Istvar Tari, whom workers described as "almost impossible to get ahold of." In Syria, meanwhile, revolutionaries ran into logistical problems.

"We always said that when the Revolution came, the United States of America would be first up against the wall," said Rashap Abdi, a bicycle maker in Damascus. "So when the Revolution really did come, we all gathered by this big wall, and we waited, and we waited, and the United States never showed up."

Abdi's younger brother, 16-year-old Hafez, vowed to go to the United States and find a wall himself, but the elder Abdi wouldn't hear of it. "I was like, 'Oh, yes, Hafez. You go to

America. You can't even drive.' "

Visibly disappointed, revolutionary leaders conceded they didn't anticipate the depth of opposition from corporate and political hegemonists. Their sole victory was at Harvard University, where students successfully rose up against themselves. As for what went wrong, the activists hinted that the masses gave up too easily, although some suggested the decision to schedule the universal uprising to compete with a popular television viewing hour in the United States was ill-advised.

"I wanted to join in and all, but I was watching *Touched by an Angel*," explained Carolyn Ebsen, a data processor in Augusta, Ga. "Everybody who knows me knows you do not interrupt me during *Touched by an Angel*, not even for the ascendancy of the proletariat over the exploitative bourgeoisie."

# JUST LOOKING?
# EAT LEAD

## Nation's Largest Retailer Suggests Browsers Buy or Die

WELCOME TO WAL-MART

## JUST LOOKING?

⇨ Research indicates that half of you will leave this store without making a purchase.

⇨ We don't really know why. Our prices are low. Our selection is quite good.

⇨ So, if you think about it, it's probably not our fault. It's probably your fault.

⇨ You're a teaser. And nobody likes a teaser. Especially in retail.

⇨ But we'll give you a choice. Buy something today, or say "Goodbye" forever.

*Punishment may vary.
Please see store manager for details.

IN AN EFFORT to increase its so-called closing ratio — the percentage of all store visitors who actually buy merchandise — Wal-Mart said it may execute shoppers who claim they are "just looking."

According to Wal-Mart Chairman Robson Walton, it "absolutely will not be official company policy" to exterminate window shoppers, but will instead be an "entirely personal decision" left up to individual store managers.

To aid supervisors in their efforts, however, the company will install and staff a tactical "Repercussive Services Desk" in each of its 2,300 retail stores, an expense Walton said will be more than offset by the revenue increase expected as browsers are suddenly inspired to buy.

Currently, the closing ratio at Wal-Mart stores averages about 50 percent, meaning nearly half of its visitors leave without making a purchase. With $167 billion in annual sales, instituting a policy that effectively makes buyers out of every store visitor could nearly double revenues, said Jack Bandag, Wal-Mart's new Director of Repercussive Services. He added, however, that it "absolutely will not be official company policy" to value revenue over human life, except in the case of union members.

Such an approach, analysts said, would have the added benefit of fighting off customer defections to the Internet. As do other offline retailers, Wal-Mart foresees a growing problem with NRPCUs (Non-Revenue-Producing Corporeal Units), who examine a product in person at a brick-and-mortar store, then go online to order the same product at a lower price.

While implying NRPCUs are "a waste of valuable floor space on Market Earth," Bandag said it's possible that managers could choose to let browsers live, or institute lesser punishments, such as knee-capping, cold-cocking, or the "roundhouse spleen buster."

All of this will be spelled out in a forthcoming Repercussive Services handbook, which also explains how sales personnel should approach a suspected NRPCU: If the suspect's response to the question, "May I help you?" is "No, thank you. Just looking," potential employee responses range from "I encourage you to reconsider," to "How 'bout I wring your damn neck with this two-piece cotton-poly jogging suit you been staring at for 10 minutes?"

Even though the policy is not yet official, word quickly reached Wal-Marts across the country, boosting both consumer sales and employee morale.

"Before, if I asked to help somebody, they blew me off or acted like I wasn't there," said Crystal Tanner, a 17-year-old associate sales partner at a Chicago-area Wal-Mart. "But now, if I so much as say, 'Hey,' consumers snap to attention. It's like I'm the Alan Greenspan of retail."

Wal-Mart said it decided to go forward with Repercussive Services after testing it at a store in Ohio, where the closing ratio jumped from 43 percent to 97 percent after employees told anyone who claimed to be "just looking" that they would "have their balls handed to them on a fuckin' platter." In a possibly related statistic, that same store had the highest percentage of impulse purchases of any in the company's chain.

This sign is now posted at the entrance to all Wal-Mart stores.

## INFANT-TODDLER DEFECTS

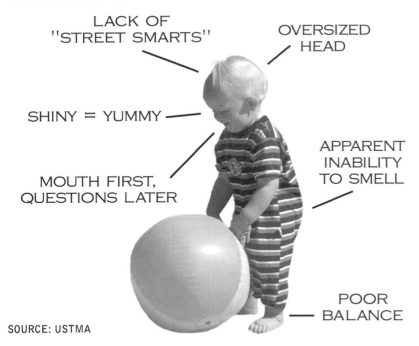

LACK OF "STREET SMARTS"

OVERSIZED HEAD

SHINY = YUMMY

APPARENT INABILITY TO SMELL

MOUTH FIRST, QUESTIONS LATER

POOR BALANCE

SOURCE: USTMA

# Toy Trade Group Wants Infants Recalled

## MANUFACTURERS' LOBBY SAYS SMALL CHILDREN DEFECTIVE

CITING "CRITICAL NEW RESEARCH," the U.S. Toy Manufacturers Association this week demanded that all toy recalls be suspended and replaced with an immediate recall of the nation's 13 million infants and toddlers.

According to USTMA researchers, blaming toy-related hazards on flaws in product design or construction overlooks "equally egregious" defects in infant-toddler design. "You look at how little kids are built, and it's outrageous," said USTMA Executive Director Wallace Cavanaugh. "Their airways are too small, their balance is atrocious, their heads are way too big, and their common sense is negligible. They are a cornucopia of reckless, irresponsible defects."

Cavanaugh said the USTMA will submit its findings to the U.S. Consumer Product Safety Commission and the *New England Journal of Medicine.*

The USTMA estimates member companies lost $1 billion last year recalling more than 60 million product units, numbers that led consumer groups to quickly label the trade group's announcement "self-serving and greedy." Cavanaugh, however, insisted economics was only one factor in the new stance.

"Certainly, on a cost-retrieval basis, there are 47 million fewer infants and toddlers than there are recallable products, so the savings should be substantial," said Cavanaugh. "But we're also parents and aunts and uncles, and anything we can do to make families safer we will do."

Cavanaugh also asserted the recall should "in no way" be construed as an effort by toy makers to shirk responsibility for past and present hazards. "Absolutely, the toy manufacturers are partly to blame," he said. "We should have called for a recall of infants and toddlers earlier."

Legally, the USTMA's recall plan must be approved by the Consumer Product Safety Commission. However, citing the "clear and present danger to the community," the USTMA began a pilot recall program yesterday in conjunction with several leading fast-food restaurants, which have agreed to exchange infants and toddlers for a free, medium-sized order of french fries.

"This is just sick," said Evelyn Hodesby of Columbus, Ohio, mother of twin two-year-olds and one of many parents who expressed outrage over the infant-toddler recall. "I would never exchange my children for anything. And their notion that it's really the little kids who are 'defective' is reprehensible."

"Oh, yeah, blame the messenger," responded Cavanaugh.

Not every parent, however, was upset with the manufacturers' trade group. Standing outside a McDonald's in Linden, N.J., Arlene Witchell said the program was more than fair.

"This is such a relief," said Witchell, who moments earlier entered the restaurant as the mother of four and left it as the mother of three after exchanging her one-year-old son, Rodney. "I always thought there was somethin' wrong with that kid. I useta think maybe it was my drinkin', you know? But now... mmm, these fries are good."

# HEADHUNTING FIRM DECAPITATES 250

## Peruvian Company Takes Its Cut Off the Top

Boratu Jiménez Jenga, CEO of GreatHeadHunters.com, admires the skull of a potential client on a recent trip to New York City.

**HEADS UP**

GREATHEADHUNTERS.COM, which has decapitated more than 250 corporate executives in the past three months, has run afoul of U.S. authorities, who claim the Peruvian-based tribe-turned-Internet-startup is misleading potential clients by urging them to "make a clean break with the world's leading headhunting firm."

However, Boratu Jiménez Jenga, CEO of GreatHeadHunters, defended his company's practices, arguing industrialized nations are to blame for misappropriating the term "headhunter" to mean someone who will help you find a new job.

"This is not false advertising," said Jiménez. "We are great headhunters. We hunt heads. Our fathers hunted heads. Our fathers' fathers hunted heads. If we contact you and you give us your information, we are going to find you and take your head.

"But cleanly," he added. "We are not barbarians."

They are, however, successful. Since taking to the Web last year, GreatHeadHunters.com has witnessed unprecedented growth. In Q3 1996 alone, said Jiménez, head acquisitions increased 985 percent over the previous quarter.

"The Internet has been an incredible boost for our business," he said. "Before, we got maybe 8 or 10 heads a year, and for these we had to kidnap people. Now we are getting inquiries all the time from people actually looking for the headhunter. They give us their addresses, their job histories. It is so easy to find them!"

In fact, Jiménez said, the tribe now has more potential clients than it can possibly decapitate, and plans to open offices in New York, Chicago, and Silicon Valley soon. To staff the offices, the company plans to hire outside the tribe for the first time, although Jenga promised the heads of new hires would not be taken.

"I will salt the eye sockets of the newly dead to ensure this does not happen," he pledged.

Asked if this was some magic charm to guarantee a future outcome, Jiménez conceded it was not.

"Actually, I just say that to sound headhuntery. Really, we have attorneys who handle the contracts. They are pretty explicit. Mostly boilerplate."

According to the U.S. State Department, however, the success of GreatHeadHunters is countered by the "deep pain" the company's practices have caused the families of U.S.-based executives. One example was Robert Copping, who until January was a senior product developer at Oracle Corp.

"My Rob was being courted by a dozen headhunting firms, and he was looking to move, so when he got the email from GreatHead-Hunters, he figured it wouldn't hurt to speak with them, too," said his wife, Ashley Copping. "He sent them his personal info, arranged a meeting, and the next thing I know, zip, his head is gone.

"GreatHeadHunters indeed," she added sourly. "I'd like to give them a piece of my mind."

Jiménez said he would arrange it.

GreatHeadHunters.com has been accused of misleading clients, but this transcript of a phone interview with a prospective client suggests the firm may be innocent.

CLIENT: *Hi, I'm exploring my options and looking for a recruiter.*

GREATHEADHUNTERS: We are headhunters.

CLIENT: *Whatever. So, can you help me out?*

GHH: Tell us about your head.

CLIENT: *My head? Oh, you mean my brains? My knowledge? Well...*

GHH: How big is your head?

CLIENT: *My hat size is 14, ha ha. But I guess you're asking if I have a big ego. Well, I'm not shy...*

GHH: Any blemishes?

CLIENT: *On my record? No. I have been a model employee.*

GHH: On your head. We like clean heads.

CLIENT: *My head's quite clean, I assure you. But I don't see...*

GHH: We should get together.

CLIENT: *OK, yeah. So, do you think you have something for me?*

GHH: No. You have something for us.

CLIENT: *That's a great way of looking at it. It's like I'm more important to you than you are to me. You know, most recruiters act like...*

GHH: We are headhunters.

CLIENT: *Right, that's what I mean. You say "headhunters." None of this "We're executive recruiters" stuff. You call it like it is. You're real straight shooters.*

GHH: No guns. Machetes. Very quick.

CLIENT: *Ha ha. You guys slay me.*

GHH: OK.

Larita and Al Taylor like to think they own this 3BR ranch home in suburban Atlanta.

REA SOLD

# Record 73 Million Americans Now Pretending They Own Their Own Homes

## LOW INTEREST RATES HELP MANY FULFILL THE AMERICAN (BANKER'S) DREAM

SPURRED BY an ever-strengthening economy, housing numbers released by the National Association of Realtors last month show that a record 73 million Americans are now participating in the mass self-delusion that they, and not their banks, actually own their homes.

"Home ownership is the fulfillment of the American (banking industry's) dream, and we are proud to announce that more Americans than ever have been able to (help lending institutions) achieve that dream," said NAR President Richard Schicter.

After putting 20 percent down on a $235,000 house last week, Minneapolis pediatric nurse Stephanie Doogan officially became the 73 millionth American to take part in the widely accepted fantasy.

"Ever since I was a little girl, I've wanted to (deceive myself into believing I could) be a homeowner," said Doogan, 35. "Well, look at me now! Me, little Stephanie Doogan, I actually have a place I can call 100 percent (minus 80 percent) my own!"

Across the country, other (people in denial concerning their status as) property owners expressed similar satisfaction.

"There's nothing like taking a walk around your (bank-owned) house, then going outside and kneeling down in your (bank-owned) lawn and grabbing a handful of (the bank's) dirt to make you realize how precious (their) land is," said 28-year-old Matt Jackson, who(se bank) bought a $210,000 home on New York's Long Island last year. "It makes me feel as though I really have something that no one can take away from me (unless I miss so much as one mortgage payment)."

Added Devon Knight, who recently (thinks he) purchased a condominium in Baltimore's Inner Harbor: "When I was renting an apartment, if the furnace went out, I had to get the landlord to fix it. But now, if the furnace goes out, I have to fix it!... hold on, I'm losing the illusion here... why is that good again?"

"Equity," said First Union's Jay Harrington, Knight's mortgage broker. "Just remember, you have equity. And next to the right of every single (major) American (corporation) to have a say in who gets elected, that's the most sacred thing you can (pretend you) have."

# DELL SUPPORTS EXTENDING GATEWAY AMNESTY

## Gateway Denies Amnesty Exists; Dell Says It's Just Trying to Help

DELL COMPUTER this week said it supports extending the amnesty period for anyone possessing a Gateway computer, arguing Gateway owners should be given "at least" two more weeks to hand over their equipment to police without fear of arrest and conviction.

An outraged Gateway CEO Ted Waitt, however, denied there is an amnesty program, and accused its rival of fabricating the story to scare people into dropping Gateway and buying Dell products. In response, Dell CEO Michael Dell called Gateway's allegation "truly worrisome."

"If Gateway is correct and there is no amnesty program, that would mean the police can arrest anyone using Gateway products right now," said Dell. "Honestly, they should be warning their customers about this."

But Waitt insisted that is not what he meant. "There is no amnesty program because it is not illegal to own a Gateway computer, so there is no reason to have an amnesty," he said. "Why on Earth would it be illegal to own a Gateway?"

Dell said he wondered about that too. "I'm not a lawyer, so it would be improper for me to comment on the specific reasons why thousands of Gateway owners have been imprisoned and had their houses and families taken from them. I just heard it's been happening."

"That is absolutely ludicrous!" said an enraged Waitt.

"I totally agree," said Dell. "That's why we believe the amnesty should be extended, so that this doesn't keep happening. I mean, I know Gateway is having revenue problems, but you'd think they'd at least want to keep their customers out of prison.

"Some things are just more important than profits," Dell added. "At least that's how we see it. Gateway maybe is different."

A spokesman for San Diego–based Gateway later said the company would file a complaint with the California attorney general's office, accusing its rival of unscrupulous business practices. Dell, however, said no filing is necessary.

"Look, we're out there supporting a fellow computer maker in its hour of need, but if Gateway doesn't want our help, then we'll stay out of it," said Dell. "We're going to be busy helping IBM with their exploding ThinkPads anyway."

# Cubists Launch Unnavigable Web Site

## Conceptual Realism Dominates Site
## No One Will Be Able to Use Anyway

THE INTERNATIONAL Society of Cubists officially launched its Web site this week, a brilliant rejection of natural form and perspective that metaphysically establishes the implication of movement, analytically redefines spatial relationships, and is an absolute bitch to navigate.

"What the hell is this? I can't tell how to get anywhere," one of the site's first visitors told the Cubist Society's Webmaster-Curator, Paulo Cassat. "Is this art, or is this a Web site?"

"Thank you," Cassat responded.

According to Society President Francisco Bernioz, the group launched the site to bring attention to Cubism, the art movement founded in the early 20th Century by Pablo Picasso and Georges Braque. Based in Madrid, Spain, the Society also hopes to establish a scholarship fund for young cubist painters and sculptors. However, at a public showing of the site here in Spain's capital, most initial visitors were clearly uncomfortable with the design, especially the artists the site purports to help.

"This site is going to turn people off," complained one young sculptor from Corsica. "I mean, how do I get from the home page to, say, the fundraising form?"

"You must be willing to abandon your preconceived notions of traditional Web design," replied Bernioz, "and disregard its nefarious standards of foreshortening, modeling, and chiaroscuro [the distribution of light and shade]."

"Uh-huh. But how do I find the link?" the young man persisted.

"You must embrace the idea that the link exists," said Bernioz, "for once that idea is established, form itself can be forgotten."

"You don't know where it is, do you?"

"Not specifically, no," Bernioz conceded. "It's there somewhere. I think on a nonsequential parallel plane right behind the polygonal search box."

The site — digital graphics, text, and HTML on browser — has fared no better with art critics, who immediately accused the cubists of stealing the absurd navigation and layout from pretty much every other site on the Web.

*The International Society of Cubists homepage.*

# Effluvium

## GM Subcompact for Next Millennium Packs Noxious Punch, but Is It Enough?

CLAIMING IT HAS filled the final niche in the automotive market, General Motors last week unveiled a prototype of the 2000 Chevrolet Effluvium, a subcompact gas-guzzler that, boasted one GM executive, "eats up ozone like a four-cylinder, coal-burning power plant." Industry observers declared the new model bold, surprising, and asinine.

Speaking to analysts at the Detroit Auto Show, GM CEO John Smith, Jr., defended the Effluvium, which he claimed will occupy the last available niche in the automotive market when it hits the streets in three years. "Look where the industry has been," said Smith. "We used to make big cars that polluted a lot. Then we made small cars that polluted less. Then we made big cars that polluted less. So what's missing?"

Small cars that pollute more, Smith argued.

To automotive market analyst Noah Wang, that's not all that's missing. Since the 1970s, said Wang, Detroit has been reluctant to change, fighting such innovations as emissions standards and air bags. That trend began to change in the early 1990s, when Ford, GM, and Chrysler all embraced the cup holder. With the Effluvium, Wang lamented, that innovation wave has receded.

"This is just not original," Wang told Smith during the show. "I'm afraid the car is going to have to be more than just another gas-guzzler."

"It's also built out of papier-mâché," Smith countered. "Except for the air bags, which are glass."

"I don't care if it has exploding bumpers," said Wang. "It's still not enough."

"The gas tank is under the driver's seat," Smith noted. "And the seat belts are highly flammable."

"Nope. Not convinced."

"The steering wheel is heated to 475 degrees Farenheit."

"Well..."

"And if you try to start the car... you...um..."

"Yes...?"

"Something really bad will happen. Maybe something with acid. Or vampires."

"Hmmm...it would have to be real vampires, or real acid."

"Sure, sure. Could be vampires on acid. Who knows?"

In a revised statement, Wang estimated the Effluvium would quickly become one of the top-selling small cars in America and raised his rating on GM to "strong buy."

Executives at Ford and DaimlerChrysler, meanwhile, quickly announced work on their own small gas guzzlers — the Mercury Miasma and the Plymouth Vapor—which they said would hit the market in 1999. *Car & Driver* editor Paul Brock, however, cautioned against nationalistic euphoria, noting that Toyota is believed to be working on a two-cylinder motorcycle that emits radioactive particles.

## EXHAUSTING INNOVATION

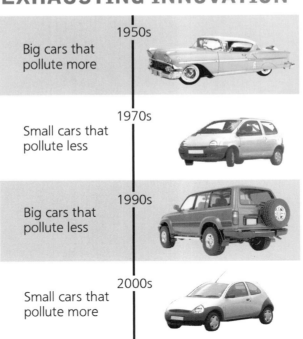

| 1950s | Big cars that pollute more |
| 1970s | Small cars that pollute less |
| 1990s | Big cars that pollute less |
| 2000s | Small cars that pollute more |

Senior Tour pro Mel Blount with his Way Fat Ugly Bitch driver.

# COMPETITION A "BITCH" FOR "BIG BERTHA"

## Downsized Callaway Exec Goes Up in Size With Massive Club Heads

THE MARKET FOR oversized, offensively named golf clubs, once dominated by Callaway Golf's Big Bertha line, is expanding in more ways than one with the introduction of Way Fat Ugly Bitch® titanium woods from ParSix Golf.

Analysts estimate the Bitches, with club heads the size of room air conditioners, will present a major challenge to Callaway and other equipment makers.

"I think it's just a horrible, horrible name for a golf club," said Goldman Sachs analyst Patricia Trent-Jones. "But the thing's got a sweet spot as big as my head, and frankly, I think that's going to attract a lot of consumers."

Grabbing market share from Callaway would be "sweet irony" for ParSix CEO Peyton Hollings, a former Callaway executive. Once the industry's top-selling club, Big Bertha sales fell sharply as competitors matched its girth. Hollings suggested the company regain market share by producing a monstrously large club head, but he was rebuffed, and eventually let go in 1994.

The next year, while Callaway made incremental increases in both size and sales with its Great Big Bertha line, Hollings formed ParSix and began building his Bitches, which are noted for their low center of gravity and relatively light weight.

"Big Bertha heads were big, about the size of a softball, and Great Big Berthas were also huge, but they weren't willing to go all the way," said Hollings. "We are. Our Way Fat Ugly Bitch woods, as the name implies, are outrageously big, yet competitively priced."

A set of four woods (driver, 3, 5, and 7) will carry a suggested retail price of about $700, said Hollings, who added that major retailers will initially be offered incentives to discount the Bitches up to 20 percent.

ParSix said it has been testing the Bitches since June, and claims that 92 percent of golfers who used the Bitches preferred them over their previous brands. One tester, Andrew Johnson, the touring pro at Largo Lakes Country Club in Key Largo, Fla., was among those impressed.

"I liked all them Bitches," said Johnson. "I mean, I did have problems with my No. 5 Bitch, know what I'm saying? But I bagged that Bitch and switched to my No. 7 Bitch, and now that's my best Bitch."

A.G. Edwards retail analyst Paul Wellstones, however, said he expects golfers will be more interested in Callaway's new line of Trucker Butt Putters®, due out in the spring, which have a titanium head the shape and size of a loaf of bread.

"The Way Fat line basically just ups the ante for oversized woods, but the Trucker Butts are the first abhorrently oversized putter heads, and I think that's a niche no one has even thought of," said Wellstones.

# With MyColdCalls, You Call Telemarketers Before They Call You

TWO OR THREE times a day, Karsten Franks was besieged by telemarketers. They called during dinner. They called during his favorite TV show. They called offering credit cards, chimney cleaning, and insurance. Unsure why he was so popular — Franks says he bought something only half the time — the 68-year-old retired Las Vegas electrician longed to give telemarketers a taste of their own medicine. Last month, he finally got the chance.

Like nearly 15,000 other people, Franks signed up with Louisville, Ky.–based MyColdCalls, a unique consumer advocacy firm that upends traditional telemarketing by turning "victims into victors," and passive phone call recipients into aggressors.

"Instead of getting these cold calls at all hours, MyColdCalls allows me to call a real telemarketer on my time, when I want to," said Franks. "And as long as I make at least ten calls a month, or buy from at least five telemarketers a month, MyColdCalls will keep my name off of telemarketing lists. So long to harassing phone calls!"

"What we're doing is nothing short of shifting the balance of power from telemarketers to consumers," said MyColdCalls CEO Bennett Green. "MyColdCalls users are in total control of the telemarketing experience, and all it costs is the price of the phone call and the product they have to buy."

Paying $2.95 a minute, MyColdCalls users can pick not only the telemarketing company, but the actual name of a telemarketer who works there. They can even call several different telemarketers at once, and patch themselves through to the one that answers first.

"Just this morning, I called a credit card telemarketer, and it was absolutely liberating," said Irene Chappell, a 62-year-old shipping clerk in Dayton, Ohio. "His name was Ron Johnson, and instead of him asking for me, I got to ask for

him, and I got to say, 'How are you today, Mr. Johnson?'

"It was a rush," Chappell recalled. "He even said, 'Whatever it is, I'm not interested.'"

"It really does turn the tables on us," said Nora-Lee Dunlop, a telemarketer for the New York City Fraternal Order of Police and Urban Kitchen Remodelers in Queens. "These people are calling me, I have no idea who they are, but they know my name. It's kind of eerie."

To generate revenue, MyColdCalls depends on subscriptions and a percentage of sales generated by the companies it partners with. And finding partner companies, said Green, has been fairly easy.

"At first, we thought this was some kind of joke," admitted Dean Eaves, a salesman for United Vinyl Siding and Windows, in Nashville, Tenn. "I even asked Ben Green, 'What kind of person would want to cold call us to buy our vinyl siding?' But his answer convinced me. He said, 'The kind of people who actually buy vinyl siding when you cold call them.'"

What's most appealing to Eaves and other partners is MyColdCalls' conversion rate. Normally, less than 1 percent of cold calls results in a sale. But the conversion rate through MyColdCalls is an astounding 99 percent. The fact that calls are initiated by consumers, not telemarketers, is undoubtedly one factor, as is the mandatory number of purchases members must make. But Irene Chappell thinks she knows another reason.

"For me, it's all about doing to them like they do to us," she said. "When I called Mr. Johnson, I eventually signed up for the credit card, even though I didn't need it. I did it because he seemed quite busy with other callers, and I sensed it would be rather inconvenient for him."

Unable to control a snicker, she added, "Now he knows what it feels like."

---

**MYCOLDCALLS INC.**

**BASED:** Louisville, Ky.

**FOUNDED:** 1995

**CEO:** Bennett Green

**BUSINESS:** Turn telemarketing victims into victors by having them cold call telemarketers and buy their products and/or services at a time convenient for the consumer, not the telemarketer.

**REVENUE:** Makes percentage of each successful sale.

**MyColdCalls Top Tips for Turning the Tables on Telemarkers:**
1) Call several telemarketers simultaneously. When one picks up, pause two seconds before asking to speak to him.
2) Insist they take your credit card number at the start of the conversation.
3) Buy whatever they're selling.

# Changing Corporate Stories

## Companies Replace Nuts-and-Bolts Descriptions with Riveting Kids' Classics

GENERAL ELECTRIC CEO Jack Welch knows the truth of the cliché, "To be a great company, you need a great story." But at a time when many a company's tale is beginning to add a lively dotcom plot, Welch realized GE's "story" of "engines, appliances, and insurance" wasn't exactly riveting.

So last week, he changed it. "We're still selling the same stuff, but now our company 'story' is *Hansel and Gretel,*" said Welch. "The witch in the gingerbread house is so mean, she really hooks you from the beginning. But what makes GE's story truly great is how Gretel gets the courage to push the witch into the... wait, I don't want to give it away. You'll have to call investor relations."

Following GE's lead, dozens of other corporations also have changed their corporate stories in the past month, replacing stultifying narratives of energy services and telecommunications with classics such as Dr. Seuss' *Yertle the Turtle* and Mark Twain's *Huckleberry Finn*.

Citigroup, for instance, has replaced talk of its diverse financial holdings with

the timeless talking-bunny tale *Watership Down*. International Paper now tells the Hardy Boys' riveting *Secret of the Old Mill*, where a quick-thinking Frank saves Joe and Chet. And Philadelphia-based CoreStates Financial Corp., whose story of late has been doubly dry — it's a financial institution, and it's laying off 1,900 workers — is now regaling employees, customers, and Wall Street alike with *The Old Woman Who Lived in a Shoe*.

"It's a much better story than, 'We're laying off people to increase our profits,'" explained CoreStates spokesperson Kim Dixon. "This old woman has all these kids she loves, but she can't afford 'em; they're eating all her stuff, making her poor. It's tragic. That's the story we tell now, except, in the end, we have it so the old woman has to let 10 percent of her kids go."

While some have hailed the change for making Wall Street much more interesting, investor groups are frustrated. "I think the stories are great and all, but now a lot of people don't know what the hell these companies do," said Derek Yarborough, president of Individual Investor. "For instance, if you go to IBM's new Web site and click 'About the Company,' it's *Misty of Chincoteague*."

An IBM spokesperson said the company has heard the complaints, but countered that its first choice — *Stormy, Misty's Foal* — was already taken.

**Dow Chemical is one of many firms to change its company story. Here, Dow's Annual Report, which once described chemical, plastic, and agricultural products, now features this Dr. Seuss classic.**

No one, however, has protested as loudly as the media. Nicole Katzen, a business reporter with the *Atlanta Constitution*, said she recently called Coca-Cola to get a comment on overseas sales, and instead heard 20 minutes of *The Old Man and the Sea*. "I had to call back four times to see how it ended," she said.

While Ernest Hemingway, Lewis Carroll, and classic fairytales are popular choices, some companies have decided to rewrite their own stories, scripting in-house. New high-tech darling Netscape Communications, for instance, has caused quite a commotion with its rather violent tale called *Bill the Rich Jerk Who Gets Attacked by People with Knives and Bats and Is Forced to Free His Source Code and Then Is Killed Anyway*. But it's Pepsico's choice of Beatrix Potter's *Peter Rabbit* that has analysts like Bear Stearns' Brian Frisco intrigued.

"That Peter is such a lovable imp," Frisco said. "I could hear about him over and over and over."

# How to Move Faster Than Your Competitors, Your Company, Even Yourself

YOU HEAR IT over and over again. To survive in today's networked economy, companies need to move fast. Very fast. Faster than ever. What does this mean? No one really knows. No idea. None whatsoever.

This makes "speed" the essential business platitude, and makes interviews such as the following, with Alison Parfit, coordinator of the Enterprise Acceleration Team at IBM, metaphorically vital to your company's New Economy survival.

*Alison, welcome. Tell us, why do you think speed is so essential to survival in today's economy?*
Business is moving faster than ever, so you've got to move faster than ever. Faster than your competitors, faster than your company. Faster, even, than yourself.

*That's fast.*
That's survival. The truth is, if you're too slow, you're history.

*What about dust? Could you be dust?*
Yes, also toast.

*Whoa. That's jarring, real-world advice. I think I just heard two dozen companies organize Enterprise Acceleration Teams. Speaking of which, you started an Enterprise Acceleration Team at IBM. Why?*
We wanted to make speed a way of life across the company, and also create a workplace environment that truly valued speed and swiftness at the enterprise level, and at the desktop level.

*Shake-up city. Rock the foundation. What did you find?*
We learned that you can't achieve great speed without speedy people. And speedy people can't make a real difference without speedy leaders to

# PEED

## THE MUST-HAVE PLATITUDE FOR THE NEW ECONOMY

motivate them, because, in the end, speedy people are not just faster than average people, they're much faster, and they can make business move at the speed of light.

*Wow, it sounds like "speedy leaders" are the key. Let's try to get our arms around that for a moment. Describe what traits, what distinct talents, are indicative of the prototypical "speedy leader."*
Speed.

*Super informative. I am wide-eyed. Unable to blink. Now, I also understand you found barriers to speed. Can you explain?*

"The key to speed is moving fast, and the key to being speedier is moving faster."

Barriers to speed are decelerators, obstacles, speed bumps, things that slow you down individually, as a team, or as a company. Slowing things. Things that impede and slow the process.

*Goose bumps of recognition. All companies have this problem. Are you saying there's a cure?*
Absolutely. If you want to speed up your people, speed up your business, you must remove those impediments to speed, remove those speed bumps.

*How about "Destroy those speed bumps"? A lot of our readers are male.*

Yes, "destroy" works. Also "displace."

*Sine qua non business advice. OK, let's get even more micro. A specific situation. You've got a company, moving too slowly, what can it do? Nitty-gritty detail.*
They have to remove speed bumps, and they must be willing to think fast and act fast, both as individuals and — and this is imperative if the corporation as a whole is going to move fast — as a group. If individuals and groups move fast, the company will move fast.

*Hair singeing. You've shocked my monkey. Can you be any less specific?*
No, I don't think so.

*Tremendous. Worth the cover price right there. Well, Alison, anything we haven't addressed?*
Yes. Most people, and by extension most companies, work beneath their potential velocities. If you dig a little, you'll discover this is because people don't feel empowered.

*Speed bump alert! What can companies do?*
Empower them.
*Major e-piphany. MBA advice. This article should come with a diploma.*

## Business Gifts for Businesspeople
# SAVE YOURSELF WITH "SHOOT HOWARD NEXT!" OFFICEWEAR

BUSINESSPEOPLE ARE impossible to shop for. That's why no one likes them. *BusinessMonth Weekly*, however, has come to the rescue. From Red Man Stick underarm tobacco to "Shoot Howard Next!" OfficeWear, the gifts on this list could save a colleague's life, or his job, but will probably just make him smell bad.

### Red Man Stick®
How long has it been since you had a cigarette at work? Not outside or in some dingy designated area, but right at your desk? Too long, right? Oh, sure, you could try the patch, but that requires a prescription. And nicotine gum, like chewing tobacco, goes in your mouth — very unprofessional. But now, the folks who brought you the smokeless solution, Red Man Chewing Tobacco, bring you Red Man Stick®, the underarm tobacco that glides on smooth and leaves you all-day nicotine jittery. It's like putting a pinch between your pits. And best of all, no one will know but you!
*($3.99; ALSO IN AEROSOL SPRAY. NO CFCs!)*

### MyBlackBox®
Frequent business travelers know that nothing is quite so frustrating as dying in a plane crash. But it's no less frustrating for colleagues back at the office who will never see those final notes you made about that important project. MyBlackBox® can't save you from being ripped to shreds as the fuselage disintegrates, and it can't save you from the heart attack you'll have as your plummeting metal sarcophagus barrels downward at 700 miles an hour, but it can save your work. Made of an unbreakable, flame-resistant titanium alloy, the box plugs into your laptop computer and records every single keystroke you make during your flight. It even records your passwords to pass along to colleagues! Remember, once God ignores your prayers and you die, you're just a box of ashes. But thanks to MyBlackBox®, your work can live on!
*($299.95, OR FREE WITH A SET OF FIRESTONE TIRES.)*

### "Shoot Howard Next!" OfficeWear
How many times has this happened to you? You're sitting at your desk when in walks a disgruntled ex-employee, armed to the semiautomatic teeth, who begins shooting people at random. Bummer. Well, now you have a chance to avoid mortal danger by donning "Shoot Howard Next!" OfficeWear. Just because a gunmen is "crazed" doesn't mean he's not open to suggestion, especially if that suggestion is in sync with his purpose. Since most offices have someone named Howard, wearing a "Shoot Howard Next!" blouse, dress shirt, or T-shirt might present the assailant with a doable short-term goal, and give you time to escape!
*(T-SHIRT: $19.95; DRESS SHIRT: $49.95; BLOUSE: $69.95. ALSO AVAILABLE IN "SHOOT BOB," "SHOOT KIRSTEN," AND "SHOOT PHIL IN MARKETING.")*

### Smellarm Clock
You've tried alarms that beep, ding, buzz, and turn on the radio, but nothing works. Now, Smell-o-vision and Sunbeam offer a breakthrough in wake technology, the Smellarm Clock, with the patented ScentScale Odor Interface. With 100 different odors, the Smellarm Clock automatically detects when your sense of smell is ignoring its alarm, and "turns up the volume" by releasing increasingly malodorous aromas. You'll literally be forced to flee your room from scent No. 17, burning hair; No. 45, skunk; or No. 88, Slobodan Milosevic. And even if you try to ignore scent No. 100, your roommates will undoubtedly rouse you with a cheery, "Man, wake up, your room smells like shit!"
*($99.95; $39.95 FOR ADDITIONAL SCENT CARTRIDGES.)*

Feldstein's relationship has not met her expectations but is right in line with her mother's projections.

# GIRLFRIEND ANNOUNCES DISAPPOINTING Q2 RESULTS

## Relationship Falls Well Below Expectations

LAURA FELDSTEIN (Brooklyn, 24) announced disappointing results in her relationship with skeezing loser boyfriend Derek McHugh (Brooklyn, 27) for the quarter ended May 31, 1996.

In the three-month period, net proceeds — i.e., total Derek spent on entertainment, flowers, and gifts, less unrecouped losses by Feldstein, including the $26 in phone calls Derek made to his ex-girlfriend using Laura's cell phone (Laura saw the bill; she's not stupid!) when Laura was "out of commission"

for the week ending April 24 — equaled $139, well below Feldstein's expectations, but pretty much in line with her mother's.

Pro forma attention (time spent in intelligent conversation without the immediate promise of sexual interaction) for the second quarter was down 60 percent from the quarter ended Feb. 28, 1996, just after they met, and down 75 percent from Q2 1995, when Feldstein was still dating Ramón, that Latino guidance counselor from NYU who

was creepy but at least pretended he was interested in her life.

On a per-share basis, Feldstein reported her diluted share of Derek was 33 percent — down from what she thought was 100 percent, HA! in the first quarter — primarily due to broad-based weakness in Derek, who was continuing and/or establishing strategic partnerships not only with his ex, but with some bitch named Candi; like what kind of slut would go by the name Candi, anyway? As a result of these extraordinary items, Feldstein believes it may be necessary to spin Derek off into a separate, wholly independent entity, the bastard.

Laura Feldstein, Possibly Ex-Girlfriend, said in a statement: "During the second quarter, we continued to operate in a difficult environment, especially in the sexual services sector, where depressed levels of activity were a direct result of our divergent relationship accounting methodologies. Specifically, I contend EBITDA stands for Engagement Before Intercourse, Touching Downstairs, or Arousal. He insists it stands for Everyday — Blowjobs, Intercourse, and Twaddling Derek's Anaconda. That's what he calls it anyway. 'The Anaconda.' Like I need to know this.

"Although at present I continue my association with Derek, I plan to broaden my core focus and test current market conditions in an effort to search for a synergistic partner or partners — hear that Derek! Partners! erssssss! — who are willing to invest heavily in R&D (That's 'Relationship Development,' Derek, not 'Rut & Dash').

"Though it is a challenging time, I remain stubbornly confident that the long-term trends for my happiness are positive, although not with Derek, as his past performance is probably a guarantee of future results."

# SatireWire's
# BusinessMonth
## WEEKLY

**DECEMBER 1997**

## PLUS

**Music Industry
Has the CLAP**

**Spam Study Finds
Instant Wealth, Sexy
Coeds Just a
Click Away!**

**Eluminum: Alcoa Makes
First Web-Based Metal**

**GreatHeadHunters.com
Wants Eyeballs (Run!)**

**Do Smaller Employees
Make Smaller
Microchips?**

*Diana, Princess of Wales
1961–1997*

# Diana, again?

It's fair to ask, as doubtless some of you already have, "Why the hell is Princess Diana on the cover of *BusinessMonth Weekly*?" Or perhaps you've been keeping track, and have extended that query to read, "Why the hell is Princess Diana on the cover of *BusinessMonth Weekly*...again?"

Depending on one's perspective, the answer is more complex than might be assumed. Here at *BusinessMonth Weekly*, we looked at it this way: When we laid out the December issue several months ago, we decided to put on the cover either an MIT professor (due to our story on email Spam found in this issue) or a photo of cellist Yo Yo Ma (due to a feature you'll find this month about the lucrative musical movement known as CLAP). When we went to advertisers with this information, they said they would indeed be interested in advertising — some other time.

We would be less than journalists if we were not students of history, and so we looked at the bookings for our September issue, which featured Princess Diana on the cover, and noted the ad space had sold out. This is why we put Princess Diana on the October cover, which, by the way, also sold out. As did November. And each month, our circulation was double the average.

So we went back to our advertisers and said we were putting Princess Diana on the cover in December. Unlike you, they didn't ask us why. They just bought space. Every page of it. So, in one respect, I might answer your question with, "Who cares why the hell Princess Diana is on the cover of a magazine about the economy? You're reading it, aren't you?"

But we are not that crass. In actuality, we do care about your opinions. Specifically, we have listened to your complaints about the previous Diana covers, where you noted, quite perceptively, that not one of those issues contained an actual story about Diana. In fact, you seemed particularly upset by the October issue, which had no stories about anything at all. Only ads.

It was a good month.

But this month, we redeem ourselves. It turns out there is a legitimate connection between Princess Diana and what we cover here at *BusinessMonth Weekly*. In particular, for millions of people across the globe, Princess Diana put the Internet on the map.

How so? Let's face it. On Aug. 31, the night of the crash, quite a few Princess Diana fan sites were already in existence, but for the most part, the die-hard Princess Diana fans, the kinds of people who go to beauty salons for the magazines, who still have funny messages on their answering machines, who think Regis is way too good for Kathie Lee, and who think about that *a lot*, were not yet on the Internet. But Princess Diana was on the Internet. She was, in fact, all over the Internet.

**EDITOR'S NOTE**

Literally moments after she perished in that automobile accident, word spread online. Within minutes, news groups were bursting with details. Within hours, mourners posted their condolences on the royal family's Web site. And by Sept. 14, AOL users finally got the emails people had sent them about the crash two weeks earlier.

The truth was, if you were trying to discover what really happened that fateful night in Paris, the Internet was the place to be. Certainly, there were the wild theories, the irrational guesses. But without the Internet, we would never have known the truth. We would never have learned, as Pierre Salinger explained at alt.conspiracy, that Princess Diana's car had been shot down by a missile.

For millions of offline Diana devotees, being out of this loop was too much to bear. So they signed up. With Earthlink and Mindspring. With Prodigy and Compuserve. They joined the Internet Age. A fair question to ask now is, "Will they stay? Will they still be interested in the Web after the hoopla surrounding Diana finally fades, after the media finally squeezes the last nickel out of the royal hype?"

That's a subject we'll be exploring in our January issue. Look for Diana and Dodie on the cover.

# MIT Spam Study Finds INSTANT WEALTH, SEXY COEDS Just a Click Away!

## Generous Offers to Share Secrets Restore Researchers' Faith in Humanity

AFTER AN EXHAUSTIVE, 12-month study of unsolicited email, or "spam," MIT researchers have concluded that you can earn $50,000 in the next 90 days by sending email from your home, which is located near a college where sex-crazed coeds are anxious to meet you.

Researchers also learned that there are two ways to get a million dollars — win it or work for it — and bigop@yesmail.com has information that can help you with both.

According to Massachusetts Institute of Technology Prof. Kevin Mirren, who headed the study, researchers were "shocked" by the findings, particularly by the discovery of "rampant altruism" among those willing to share incredibly valuable secrets for a pittance.

As examples, the report cited bob56_865@hotmail.com, who would like to reveal to you the secrets of how he became a millionaire for only $39.95, and "Cliff Robbins," who would like to introduce you to the "money machine" that is "Electrigel Creme," which represents a completely new paradigm in healing and recovery.

"I think one of the more amazing things we learned was that an exclusive club of highly skilled options traders is sharing its incredible wealth-generation secrets," says researcher Karen Zurgman. "You don't normally associate options traders with benevolence."

Not surprisingly, Zurgman adds, that offer has a catch. "You have to hurry to be among the first 100 subscribers," she said.

Not all the findings, however, spoke well of humanity.

IS A LEGITIMATE, LEGAL
portunity for you to becom
n rich rich beyond your wil
eams! If I did it, you can d
too! All you need is a sm
ent in of $49.95 an

**MIT lead reseacher Karen Zurgman says she and her colleagues were "startled" to discover that simply by sending a check or money order to cook113@slo.net, your dreams can come true.**

Researchers found it "sad," for instance, that barely legal coeds were randomly contacting people near their colleges. "You'd think they'd find some nice boys on campus," notes Zurgman, who theorizes these coeds might be at all-girl schools, or suffering from self-esteem issues.

In all, researchers catalogued 35 million separate pieces of spam for the study, although in the end, only half that number were included in the report. "We had to go back and exclude about 17 million emails because when we scrolled to the bottom, they specifically noted that they were not spam," says a sheepish Mirren.

Among the more surprising findings from the study:

• If you miss the offer from freecash_4_u@yahoo.com, you will regret it.

• Ninety-three percent of people who respond to the email from ejon6esyt@bigplanet.com don't make the cut.

• The stock of UTOU (OTC:BB) will skyrocket in the next two weeks.

• By calling 1-800-930-1389, you have nothing to lose and everything to gain.

• Members of the World Currency Cartel are amassing hundreds of millions of dollars in the currency market using a very LEGAL method which has NEVER been divulged to the general public, but which you can learn for $25 plus $10 for shipping and handling.

## VENEZUELA v. IMF ROUND IV

After several fruitless meetings between International Monetary Fund officials and the Venezuelan government, IMF Managing Director Michel Camdessus himself flew to Caracas yesterday to confront Venezuelan Finance Minister Umberto Mondregal. The two met on the tarmac, where a beaming Mondregal thrust a four-iron into the IMF leader's hands and whispered "Never trust a pigeon." He then left. Said Camdessus to a colleague afterward: "Maybe they just don't know what we do."

## COLGATE-PALMOLIVE: NOT A BUNCH OF "FANCY DANS"

Colgate-Palmolive this week said a press release issued by the company last Thursday stating, "We are fancy Dans with satin hands Una Paloma Blanca over the mountains tiny puppies pass the pistachio nuts nuts nuts with the munchy-crunchy satellite dish tornado crackers Mazeltov!" makes no sense whatsoever. In a separate statement, Colgate-Palmolive announced it would Gilgamesh crampons Puddleby Gewurztraminer, but would likely later deny it.

## HP Accepting Supper Invite

Hewlett-Packard, the nation's No. 2 computer and office equipment maker, disclosed today it doesn't have anywhere to go next Thanksgiving and is "putting out feelers." Interested parties should expect 83,200 for dinner.
Yorkshire pudding: 43,500.
Just cornbread: 39,700.

## What's on Alan Greenspan's Mind?

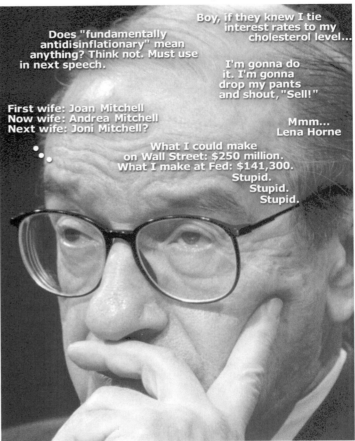

Does "fundamentally antidisinflationary" mean anything? Think not. Must use in next speech.

Boy, if they knew I tie interest rates to my cholesterol level...

I'm gonna do it. I'm gonna drop my pants and shout, "Sell!"

First wife: Joan Mitchell
Now wife: Andrea Mitchell
Next wife: Joni Mitchell?

Mmm... Lena Horne

What I could make on Wall Street: $250 million.
What I make at Fed: $141,300.
Stupid. Stupid. Stupid.

## SMALL TECH STOCKS FALL; BIG, SLOW, DUMB STOCKS RISE

Small, nimble technology companies weren't quick enough for Wall Street last week, taking another pounding as investors once again favored the stocks of big, lumbering, stupid companies. "The market is sluggish right now, and small companies are very hard to get a hold of," said Prudential analyst Henry Duncan. "Huge, slow, dumb companies are much more predictable. You can scarf down a whole bag of Cheetos and crush an empty can of Miller Genuine Draft on your forehead while watching your dog scratch itself before they'll move much, one way or the other."

# MARKET EXPERTS SAY NOW IS NO TIME TO PANIC; TIME TO PANIC COMES NEXT MONDAY

## Market Simply Undergoing "Healthy Correction" Until Devastating Free Fall

DESPITE THE STEEP market downturn induced by the Asian financial crisis, economic and financial experts this week advised investors to remain calm and continue to hold on for the long term, which they said would end abruptly next Monday when a market panic wipes out 90 percent of the world's wealth.

"With the difficulties overseas spreading into U.S. markets, I realize things look a little dodgy right now, but this is no time for people to lose their cool," said U.S. Treasury Secretary Robert Rubin. "God knows there will be plenty of time for that come Monday, when everything you've worked for vanishes in a matter of seconds."

On Wall Street, meanwhile, analysts were generally upbeat. After watching the Dow Jones Industrial Average climb to a record 8,259.31 on Aug. 6, the market was due for a "healthy correction," said Merrill Lynch analyst Pamela Green, adding that the U.S. economy looks set to rebound by the first quarter of 1998, "unless next Monday comes first, which, I'm afraid, it will."

"While you must always be vigilant in market conditions such as we see today, we advise buying on dips and looking for value plays — stocks trading below their traditional book values — which we think stand a very good chance of moving upward until Monday, when everything goes to shit," Green wrote in a research note to investors today. "For the risk-averse, we particularly like defensive plays, such as aerospace and health care, which we believe will hold up well prior to collapsing entirely at 3:42 p.m. Eastern Standard Time."

Unlike other devastating life experiences, such as divorce, retirement, or telling your parents you are gay, there is no effective way to plan for a genuine market panic, said White House chief economic advisor Janet Yellen. However, she added, people can be proactive once the panic does hit. Among her suggestions:

- Eat your young. "It seems barbaric, but trust me, if you don't do it, someone else will, and you'll end up kicking yourself."
- If you live in Manhattan and hear somebody sing, "It's Rainin' Men," don't hum along. Jump out of the way.
- Diversify your portfolio. Always sound advice, no matter the economic climate.
- Set aside 10 percent of your pre-tax income for firearms.
- Will your online broker be there in a market panic? Maybe it's time you switched to a Schwab One account. *(paid advertisement)*

"To everything there is a season,
    A time to be born,
A time to die,
    A time to plant,
A time to reap,
    A time to kill,
A time to heal,
    A time to laugh,
A time to panic.
    The latter comes Monday,
3:42 p.m. EST"

—Janet Yellen
White House
Chief Economic
Advisor

# JOB PERFORMANCE
### (AS A PERCENTAGE OF CHEESE)

HAS FILED 3 BRIE HARASSMENT COMPLAINTS 20%

HAS COMMUNICATIONS SKILLS OF HAVARTI 45%

VERY MUCH A TEAM BRIE 25%

OFTEN TURNS JARLSBERGS IN LATE 10%

# Adam Smith Never Punched an Oboist

Scottish economist Adam Smith, renowned father of free trade, never punched an oboist, and scholars say that now, more than 200 years after his death, it is unlikely he will ever have the chance.

"Well, no, I'm not aware of Adam Smith ever hitting an oboist," said renowned Smith biographer Peter Stanchcombe. "And yes, I suppose it is too late now. Why are you asking me this?"

Despite his fame and numerous writings, Smith's feelings toward oboists are not widely known. His 1759 work, *Theory of Moral Sentiments*, makes no references to oboes, while his legendary laissez-faire treatise, *The Wealth of Nations*, published in 1776, is equally noted for its lack of violence and woodwinds.

# IBM Has Smaller Chips; AMD Has Smaller Employees

In response to IBM's statement that it will produce transistors only .20 microns across in the near future, rival chipmaker Advanced Micro Devices announced today that most of its employees are no more than 14 inches tall.

AMD, however, refused to allow reporters into its facilities to verify the claim. "We would, but we can't reach the doorknobs to let you in," spokesman Ravi Chalani said in a phone interview.

AMD's assertion comes shortly after IBM boasted it will soon pack 200 million tiny transistors on a chip 500 times thinner than a human hair. The Sunnyvale, Calif.–based AMD has made no such chip claim, but insisted employee size directly relates to chip size. "It's just common sense that smaller employees will eventually translate into ever smaller chips," said Chalani, noting that smaller employees are naturally predisposed to "think small."

Meanwhile, AMD Chief Executive Jerry Sanders has been working with a miniaturization coach and can now only be found with an electron microscope, Chalani added.

Citing competitive concerns, an IBM spokesman refused to reveal the average height of its workers, but a former IBM executive, speaking on condition of anonymity, said most IBM employees were between 5'2" and 6'4".

# SURVEY: MAJORITY OF WEB USERS ARE FBI AGENTS POSING AS TEENAGE GIRLS

## Study Shows Evolving Web No Longer Dominated by Male Techies

THE INTERNET reached a demographic milestone this week as a new study revealed that for the first time, the majority of U.S. Internet users are FBI agents posing as teenage girls.

The report, by research firm IntelliQuest, marks the first time the demographic group known as "males" has not been in the majority.

According to the survey, which tracked online usage from January through July, 50.4 percent of U.S. Web users — or nearly 20.2 million — are FBI agents posing as teenage girls. That is still below the percentage of FBI agents posing as teenage girls in the overall population, which according to U.S. Census figures is 55.7 percent. However, the report noted that FBI agents posing as teenage girls represent the fastest-growing segment of Web users, increasing 185 percent in the past 12 months.

"This study reveals that the Internet has come of age as a practical medium and is no longer dominated by the male techie crowd," said Randall Stinson, editor of *American Demographics* magazine. "These newcomers are saying, 'The Internet is about more than being a geek. It's about shopping and staying in touch with family and friends and posing as a little girl to apprehend perverts.'"

Web sites catering to teenage girls corroborated the findings. "At least half" of Gurl.com's 750,000 unique monthly visitors are FBI agents posing as teenage girls, said Gurl.com spokesperson Helen Kattrall. "It's easy to tell the difference," she said. "Real teens chat with each other about boys and school and celebrities. But FBI agents posing as teenage girls are never interested in girl talk. They tend to write

things like, 'Hi, I'm Emily. I'm almost 13, and I'm looking for a father figure willing to cross state lines.'"

In a statement, the FBI disputed the study's findings and insisted its agents are not working on that many cases. However, the bureau conceded it cannot rule out the possibility that some agents are posing as teenage girls in their free time.

*In other survey findings:*
• More than 60 percent of female respondents say cybersex is equivalent to infidelity, but a staggering 92 percent of FBI agents posing as teenage girls approve of cybersex as long as it leads to an arrest and conviction.
• Nearly one-third of pedophiles say they actually go to teen sites in hopes of meeting FBI agents.
• Four out of five men say they watch women's gymnastics and figure skating for the athleticism. Nine out of ten women say they are lying.

## U.S. WEB USERS
### 100% = 40 MILLION

16.8%

32.8%

50.4%

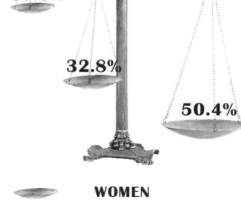

WOMEN

MEN

FBI AGENTS POSING AS TEENAGE GIRLS

## WINDOWS NOT A VIRUS

Symantec issued an apology to Microsoft yesterday after the security software maker's AntiVirus Research Center issued an alert for a "widespread and lethal virus known to cause system crashes and data loss" that turned out to be the Windows 98 operating system. Symantec CEO John Thompson called it a "regrettable but understandable" mistake.

In a live hookup, Apple CEO George Bailey stands onstage, as Microsoft CEO Mr. Potter watches, to announce a partnership between the longtime rivals in which Microsoft invests $150 million in Apple, and Apple agrees to throw the Martini family out on the streets.

## New Web Site Launched for Those Without Internet Access

**Reacting to an alarming new report that warns of a widening "digital divide" between those who have Internet access and those who don't, the United Nations last week launched HaveNot.org, a community and commerce site targeted at the estimated 5.9 billion people who do not have access to the Internet. According to HaveNot Director Anthawal Nadretee, traffic so far has been "very slow, which we think is encouraging."**

## Ancestry Site Says Can't Be Own Parent

Genealogy Web site Ancestry.com abruptly suspended its joint venture with TimeTravel.com yesterday after an audit of family trees on its site revealed more than a dozen registered users had become their own parents. "It's icky," said Ancestry.com spokesperson Arlene Murphy.

# BUSINESS TRAVAIL

**IN TODAY'S ECONOMY, YOU'RE EXPECTED TO DO MORE WITH MORE, EXCEPT UP IN THE AIR, WHERE THE RULE IS, "SO MUCH TO DO, SO LITTLE SPACE." WE ASKED SOME FREQUENT FLIERS HOW THEY MAKE ROOM TO WORK AT 30,000 FEET.**

IF THERE'S SOMEONE in the seat next to me, I'll usually sit down, introduce myself, then ask what they do and what they're working on. They, of course, tell me, and even though sometimes they don't have the courtesy to return the formality by asking what I do and what I'm working on (I sit next to a lot of CEOs), I'll tell them anyway. "I'm an economist..." I'll say.

I've had entire rows to myself after uttering just those three little words.

*Prof. Richard L. Farmagno*
WHARTON SCHOOL OF BUSINESS
UNIVERSITY OF PENNSYLVANIA

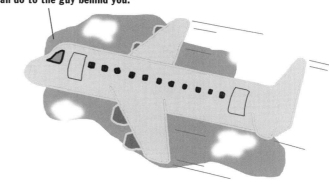

"...so put your seat back, relax, and see how much knee damage you can do to the guy behind you."

IF I NEED to clear some space, I'll wait until the captain says we've reached our cruising altitude, then I'll turn to the man or woman next to me and whisper, "Want to join the mile-high club?"

*Margaret Thatcher*
RETIRED
LONDON, ENGLAND

I CALL IT the power of projecting. I'm sitting next to someone, and the first thing I do is turn quickly and say to him, in an alarmed voice, "Good God! One of us is going to throw up in your seat!" The hypochondriacs immediately assume it's them that's going to lose it, and they sprint for the lavatory. Everybody else assumes it's gonna be me. Either way, I usually end up with lots of space to work.

*Bradley Smith*
PROGRAMMER
CLOAKBROOK TECHNOLOGIES

I TRAVEL CONSTANTLY, and you've hit upon on a real sore spot for me. Every flight I'm on has too many passengers. I mean, yuck, I don't want people anywhere near me! They are so horribly disgusting and pushy and whiny. And they won't leave you alone. Can't they see I'm busy? If it were up to me, I would never let them on the plane, but as it is, I usually find it best to simply ignore them.

*Priscilla James*
FLIGHT ATTENDANT
BRITISH AIRWAYS

I BOARD EARLY and take my cell phone. When my seatmate arrives and starts stowing his luggage overhead, I cup the phone against my mouth and hiss: "Well of course I'm upset! Shouldn't you have told me it was contagious *before* you released me?"

*Alex Epiching*
MARKETING MANAGER
CARNOGGI CHEMICAL

**Lock. Load. EXPLODE!**

Pure Sparkling Ammunition

PERRIER

*Mountain Spring-Loaded Water*

Change isn't just for the Internet-enabled. Old line, offline companies too have been dreaming up new ways to do business.

# Perrier, Smith & Wesson Make Squirt Gun Ammo

## ADVOCACY GROUPS VOW TO FIGHT; YOUNGSTERS "PSYCHED"

SEEKING TO penetrate the youth market that has long eluded them, Smith & Wesson and Perrier last week announced a joint venture to produce Mountain Spring-Loaded Water®, a line of bottled ammunition for water pistols and squirt guns.

Positioned as "the pure ammunition alternative," Mountain Spring-Loaded Water is expected to be in stores by summer, but child advocacy groups have already dubbed it "the most irresponsible product" to come out since Little People Poppers — the short-lived brand of caffeinated sugar pills released by Fisher-Price and Merck & Co. last year.

Despite the threat of a boycott by several groups, major retailers insist they will load up on the sparkling ammo, as they expect a windfall from the estimated 51 million underage water pistol owners in the United States and Europe.

"For the last several years, gun man-ufacturers have all but ignored minors, acting as if our money wasn't good enough for them," said 14-year-old Tyler Hemera, president of the New York–based Gen Y Consumer Council. "This product shows my generation that they do respect our purchasing power, and we will react accordingly."

As for Perrier, Hemera continued, "From here on out, I'm, like, mainlining the stuff. And that goes for everyone I know."

Executives from the Springfield, Mass.–based joint venture, dubbed Wessier, downplayed opponents' fears that the Smith & Wesson–backed product will encourage youngsters to play more aggressively with water pistols and possibly "trade up" to real firearms.

According to Wessier CEO Martin Patrinot, formerly director of Smith & Wesson Youth Outreach, the compa-ny's chemical-free ammunition will not only prolong the life of water pistols by keeping the action clean, but also "included in each package will be a pamphlet designed to teach little juvie shooters about gun safety and storage."

However, Virginia Gloss, executive director of the Child-Consumer Safety Council, said referring to children as "'little juvie shooters'" is "appalling, frankly," and may only escalate the increasing number of incidents between police officers and children wielding realistic-looking squirt guns.

Patrinot denied that allegation. "The first thing the pamphlet says, on line one, is, 'Never, ever aim a water pistol at a law enforcement officer,'" he said. "And after that? Let's see, after that it explains how even a small squirt gun, if used effectively, can take out a tiny assailant at 20 feet. Somebody trying to grab your Poké-mon cards, something like that."

# GreatHeadHunters.com Expands, Now Promises to Deliver Eyeballs to Web Sites

GREATHEADHUNTERS.COM, the Peruvian-based tribe turned Internet startup that specializes in taking the heads of job seekers (see Dec. 1996 issue) announced last week that it has expanded its business and is now selling the eyeballs of Internet users.

Boratu Jiménez, CEO of GreatHead-Hunters, said the firm has been building up an eyeball inventory for the past three months, and launched sister site WeDeliverEyeballs.com on Thursday.

"A few months ago I am reading on the Internet Stock Report how valuable eyeballs are, how Web sites don't care about revenues right now, they care only about acquiring the eyeballs," said Jiménez. "I look then at our current business model, where we obtain heads, and I see very much real synergy there. All our heads had eyeballs."

So far, he added, most of the company's clients have been happy with the service, although there has been some initial revulsion.

Said George Bell, CEO of Web portal Excite: "This Jiménez guy told me he could deliver 40,000 pairs of eyeballs from Yahoo! users, and I thought he was going to get me 40,000 users to my site who were once loyal to Yahoo!" Realizing Yahoo! had a market cap of $4 billion and 31 million users, Bell knew its visitors were worth $129 apiece. After brief negotiations, Bell cut a deal with WeDeliverEyeballs, paying $4.48 million, or $112 per pair of eyeballs, and looked for Excite's traffic to increase.

Instead, Bell said, he got a package in the mail containing 80,000 eyeballs. "I was shocked and disgusted. I near-ly got sick," he said. "But then I thought, 'Wait a minute, here are 40,000 people who won't be going to our competitor. Maybe this isn't such a bad deal after all.' "

Excite has now signed a two-year agreement with WeDeliverEyeballs.com. With several other contracts in the books, demand is so great that the company has doubled its staff to ramp up head acquisitions, and has even begun obtaining eyeballs without heads. Citing competitive concerns, Jiménez refused to divulge exactly how the firm obtains its stock, and attempts to get past company security to view its operations were rebuffed.

"We discourage prying eyes, unless we're doing the prying," Jiménez explained.

What's next for the mysterious CEO? According to Jiménez, eyeballs and heads are only the beginning. The company, he said, is also intrigued by the promise of online audio, and is in negotiations to deliver ears to Progressive Networks and Microsoft.

**WeDeliverEyeballs founder Boratu Jiménez shows off his inventory.**

WeDeliverEyeballs insists it does not mislead clients, and this recorded conversation seems to support its position.

CLIENT: *You guys some kind of marketing firm?*

WEDELIVEREYEBALLS: No, no, we deliver eyeballs. Your site need eyeballs?

CLIENT: *Well, yeah, sure. Customer acquisition is the key to success right now. It's all about eyeballs.*

WDE: OK, we get you eyeballs. Good price. How many you want?

CLIENT: *I don't know. We'd like as many as we can get.*

WDE: We selling individual lots of 10,000 each. Up to 50,000. Special orders after that. Take time to acquire more eyeballs.

CLIENT: *You mean you can guarantee us 50,000 new users?*

WDE: Eyeballs.

CLIENT: *Whatever. This is great. How much?*

WDE: Depends. You want Yahoo! users? That $125 per pair of eyeballs. Infoseek $41. GeoCities not so much. We give you special deal. $18.

CLIENT: *Wow. Well, we'd love to steal traffic from GeoCities.*

WDE: No, no, eyeballs. And we do stealing. You buy eyeballs from us.

CLIENT: *Ha, ha, OK, right. We'll take 20,000 users...sorry, pairs of "eyeballs."*

WDE: No problem. Ship today. Arrive big box. Four days.

CLIENT: *Arrive big box? Oh, arrive on our servers. Those boxes. Well, super-duper. Hopefully we'll be able to keep those "eyeballs" from going back to GeoCities.*

WDE: No worries. Eyeballs never look at GeoCities site again. We guarantee.

THE GOLDMAN SACHS GROUP, INC., IN CONJUNCTION WITH SALOMON SMITH BARNEY, ANNOUNCES THE INITIAL PUBLIC OFFERING OF

# DEATH
## THE UNDISPUTED MARKET LEADER IN THE EXTERMINATION OF ALL LIVING THINGS.

IN ACCORDANCE WITH SEC REGULATIONS, THE COMPANY'S S-1 INITIAL PUBLIC OFFERING FILING FOLLOWS:

## COMPLETE DEATH, INC., S-1 FILING
### FORM S-1(A) REGISTRATION STATEMENT UNDER THE SECURITIES ACT OF 1933
### INITIAL PUBLIC OFFERING STATEMENT

### DEATH, INC.
#### A DELAWARE CORPORATION

| AMOUNT TO BE REGISTERED | OFFERING PRICE PER SHARE | AGGREGATE OFFERING PRICE |
|---|---|---|
| 35,000,000 | $18.00 | $630,000,000 |

**PROPOSED SYMBOL: DIE**  **PROPOSED MARKET: NEW YORK STOCK EXCHANGE**

THIS INVESTMENT INVOLVES RISK. SEE "RISK FACTORS" BELOW.

### OUR BUSINESS
Death, Inc., hereinafter referred to as "the Company," is the recognized world leader in Death, responsible for the expiration of all living things.

### OUR STRATEGY
The Company's objective is to expand participation in, and increase the rate of, mortality worldwide. Key elements of the Company's strategy include:

1) Kill everything.
2) Leverage new Company holdings to create an internal network of operations, hereinafter referred to as the "Death Network," that will eliminate redundancies, increase efficiencies, and accelerate the transition from Life to Death.
3) Operate its facilities and subsidiaries to maximize profit, with a minimal regard for each facility's impact on the primacy of life, human or otherwise.
4) Stimulate creativity and innovation among its employees while simultaneously increasing workload and production by utilizing the Company's unique Personnel Productivity Incentive Program. (*See Company Prospectus, "Work Harder or Die," page 26.*)
5) Research, produce, and market new products and services that will significantly impact the rate of Death among living things.
6) Market Death as a positive, logical alternative to Life.
7) Kill everything.

### MARKET OPPORTUNITY
From its founding in year zero until the present, the Company has not sought to profit from its core competencies, nor has it sought outside

**DEATH, INC.**

funding to support its business. However, due to favorable market conditions, the Company believes it now has the opportunity to own or materially control entities that could have a significant positive impact on its corporate goals.

While the Company currently has no revenues or assets, it plans to use funds raised through an initial public offering to acquire both minority and majority interests in corporations, governmental bodies, individuals, and other entities operating in several key markets. The Company is not currently in discussions with any other entity. However, the Company intends to enter into agreements with hospitals and other health-related services, as well as elected and appointed governmental bodies and individuals, chemical and weapons manufacturers, public and private utilities, high-technology companies, tobacco producers, fast-food restaurants, and others. As a result of these acquisitions, the Company believes it can streamline its operations and accelerate its corporate mission while increasing shareholder value through efficient management of its facilities and subsidiaries, enabling shareholders to materially benefit from nature's one true constant: Death.

### SUMMARY FINANCIAL INFORMATION (IN THOUSANDS)
| | |
|---|---|
| Year Zero to Date Revenue | $0 |
| Cost of Revenue | $0 |
| Gross Profit (Loss) | $0 |
| Operating Expenses | $0 |

### RISK FACTORS
You should carefully consider the following risks before buying shares in this offering.

*LIMITED EARNINGS HISTORY MAY IMPACT INITIAL INTEREST IN THE OFFERING.*
The Company has never earned revenues from its operations, nor has it generated positive earnings, either of which could serve to dampen initial interest in its stock offering. However, the Company intends to institute a Potential Shareholders Motivation Program for institutions, brokers, and individuals that may offset earnings concerns. (*See Company Prospectus, "Stock Incentives: Buy It and Live," page 31.*)

*THE SECURITIES HAVE NO PRIOR MARKET, AND THE COMPANY CANNOT GUARANTEE ITS STOCK PRICE WILL NOT DECLINE AFTER THE OFFERING.*
It is possible that the trading market price of our common stock may decline below the initial public offering price. However, the Company plans to institute a Shareholder Defense Initiative Program that should safeguard the price of its stock. (*See Company Prospectus, "Stock Incentives: Sell It and You Die," page 32.*)

*WIDESPREAD ADOPTION OR IMPLEMENTATION OF IMMORTALITY*
The Company cannot rule out the possibility that advances in technology or other means may cause the widespread implementation of immortality, or everlasting life, which could adversely affect the Company's ability to remain a going concern. The Company plans to fight any and all such advances rigorously.

*MEDICAL ADVANCES*
For the foreseeable future, the Company believes that Death will eventually engulf all things. However, the advent of medicine has continually been a burden to the Company. Although to date no medical methodology has been proven superior to the Company's, advances in the field have negatively impacted Death rates, particularly in developed countries. The Company plans to fight any such advances rigorously. (*See "Use of Net Proceeds: Other," below.*)

*RESULTS ARE SUBJECT TO SIGNIFICANT FLUCTUATIONS*
The increasing worldwide birth rate may cause short-term fluctuations in the overall morbidity rate and result in periodic fluctuations in our success rate. However, the long-term outlook remains positive, as any increase in the number of living things will result in a coterminous increase in the number of dying things.

*SUCCESS DEPENDS UPON FINDING LIVING THINGS TO KILL*
The Company's ability to conduct business is dependent upon its ability to find and identify life forms for extermination. If for any reason our ability to identify living things becomes impaired or otherwise unattainable, the Company would expect a significant decrease in the number of lives ended.

*COMPETITION*
The Company currently has no direct competition, but cannot guarantee that competition or other alternatives will not emerge. However, due to our unique position, we have the ability to greatly influence events in this regard. (*See "Use of Net Proceeds: Other," below.*)

*GOVERNMENT REGULATION*
Due to the noncompetitive nature of our market, it is possible that governments or their agencies may attempt to deregulate our industry or otherwise encourage alternative businesses under the auspices of anti-monopolization laws currently in use in various nations. Again, however, due to our unique position, we have the ability to greatly influence events in this regard. (*See "Use of Net Proceeds: Other," below.*)

*DEPENDENCE ON KEY PERSONNEL*
Our future success depends upon the continued service of our executive officers and other key personnel. Our key employees include Mr. Death, our Chief Execution Officer, and Dr. Doom, our President and Chief Operating Officer. If we lost the services of one or more of our key employees, or if one or more of our executive officers decided to join a competitor or otherwise compete directly or indirectly with us, this could have a significant adverse effect on our business. In the event we were to lose the services of any key personnel, we cannot assure our ability to replace such personnel.

*CLAIMS FROM THIRD PARTIES FOR DEATHS DEEMED TO BE ASSOCIATED WITH THE COMPANY, ITS EMPLOYEES, FACILITIES, AND SUBSIDIARIES.*
Company operations rely on the creation of Death opportunities. This creates the potential for claims to be made against the Company, either directly or through third parties. These claims might be made for personal injury, negligence, loss of life, loss of future earnings, or other legal theories. Any claims could: result in costly litigation that could be time-consuming to defend, divert management's attention and resources, cause delays in acquisitions or releasing new or upgrading existing products and services. However, the Company plans to institute significant legal safeguards to counter any such claims. (*See Company Prospectus, "Sue Us and Die," page 42.*)

*THE ABSOLUTE ACHIEVEMENT OF COMPANY GOALS*
If the Company were to achieve completely its stated goal such that no living thing existed and none were therefore likely to emerge, the Company would necessarily cease operations.

*THE WIDESPREAD NEGATIVE CONNOTATIONS ASSOCIATED WITH DEATH*
With few exceptions, Death has historically been considered as something to "avoid," and this negative image could adversely affect the Company's ability to forge agreements with potential business partners. To counter this, the Company intends to improve its image by supporting National Public Radio and the National Endowment for the Arts, and is currently in discussions with The Children's Television Workshop to replace Elmo with a character called "Dead Elmo."

The company also intends to sponsor, either directly or through third parties, cultural events such as cross-desert marathons and deep ocean shark watches, and an annual "Work 'Til You Drop" day, in partnership with or through the acquisition of a greeting card company. The Company cannot guarantee, however, that its efforts will improve on or materially alter Death's negative reputation.

*USE OF NET PROCEEDS: OTHER*
In addition to those initiatives stated above, the Company may use a portion of the net proceeds from the sale of stock to pay certain individuals on a per diem or per corpus basis to facilitate the termination of select individuals, or to encourage certain individuals to self-terminate.

*DIVIDENDS*
The Company has no plans to pay a dividend for the foreseeable future, nor does it expect a dividend to be an incentive for the purchase or retention of the stock. (*See Company Prospectus, "Stock Incentives: Your Life Is a Dividend, Comprenez-vous?" page 33.*)

NOTES:
This prospectus contains forward-looking statements, the accuracy of which, unlike Death, involve risks and uncertainties.

"Death," "Choose Death," "A Little Death'll Do Ya," and "Mmmm Mmmm Dead" are registered trademarks and/or service marks of Death, Inc. The Company has also applied for trademark status on the following: "The End," "He Looks So Peaceful," "Got Your Boots On?," "The Best Hiding Place on Earth," "What a Difference a Death Makes," "Reach Out and Kill Someone," "Leave the Dying to Us," "Got Plague?," "Good 'Til the Last One Drops," and "Death: It's Everywhere You Don't Want It to Be."

# PARENTS: WEB SITES TEACH FUCKING PROFANITY

## Demand Laws Prohibiting Obscene Shit Their Kids Are Picking Up Online

A VOCIFEROUS COALITION of parenting groups today urged Congress to introduce a more stringent Communications Decency Act, arguing that profanity-filled Web sites are a corrupting influence on their children.

"I used to think my kids got their potty-mouths from the shit they saw on TV and radio," testified one frustrated parent. "But after surfing the Web, Jesus fuckin' Christ. That must be where they learn it."

Speaking before a Senate panel, several dozen parents pleaded with lawmakers to revisit the Communications Decency Act, which was struck down by the Supreme Court earlier in the year on First Amendment grounds.

"I believe the only way to safeguard my children from the foul language they're exposed to online is to pass a strong Internet decency act," said Maria Zandavino, a mother of three from East Haven, Conn. "And don't talk to me about so-called 'filtering software.' I use it and the little bastards must be getting around it, 'cause they still swear like motherfuckin' sailors."

For parents like Rory Kennel of Kansas City, Mo., however, the issue goes beyond profanity.

"You've got Web sites out there that tell you to screw authority, that tell you everyone in government should be treated like scum," Kennel told the senators. "Well, I don't want my kids exposed to that disrespectful mentality, so I want you assholes to do something about it."

Some parents contend that even min-imal or indirect exposure to the Internet is dangerous. "I got a nine-year-old in third grade, he can't even fuckin' read, okay?" said Philadelphia father of two Anthony Miller. "But you know what? The kid swears out his ass all day long. It's like, all these bad words, he absorbs them digitally or something."

### Emotional Testimony

While Constitutional scholars believe any act restricting language on the Internet would eventually be struck down by the courts, it was clear that senators were moved by the often emotional testimony. In one of the more stirring moments, Billy Cadwaller, a father of one from Macon, Ga., described how the Internet has soured his relationship with his 11-year-old daughter.

"One night I came home late and went in to give my little girl a kiss, and she wakes up all coughing and blinking and says to me, 'Oooo, Daddy, you are shit-faced again,'" Cadwaller testified. "Now where did she learn that? I'll tell ya. I went to one of those search engines and found 25 sites had the phrase 'you are shit-faced' on 'em. Twenty-fuckin'-five."

"Fuck," responded Sen. Orrin Hatch, R-Utah.

But the day's most poignant testimony came from Pamela Gottschalk, a single mother from Los Angeles who was able to draw a definitive connection between child behavior and the proliferation of obscene language on the Internet.

"How old's the Web anyway? Maybe five years, right?" Gottschalk said to the panel. "Well, my boy Joey is five years old, and he's a foul-mouthed dumb-ass little loser just like his father. Now you tell me there's not a relationship there."

> "I used to think my kids got their potty-mouths from the shit they saw on TV and radio, but after surfing the Web, Jesus fuckin' Christ. That must be where they learn it."
> —FRUSTRATED PARENT

# Eluminum®:
# Alcoa to Make First Web-Only Metal

## Company Predicts Coca-Cola, Others, Will Buy Into Concept

An Alcoa spokesman explains the Web-based images the company believes can be built with Eluminum.

FOLLOWING WHAT it called the "logical migration" of its offline products onto the Internet, Alcoa this week unveiled Eluminum®, the world's first "entirely Web-based metal."

Analysts, however, quickly refuted claims by the nation's largest aluminum producer that it is now a "major Internet player."

"What the hell is a 'Web-based metal?'" said Warburg Pincus mining analyst Morton Fendelsohn. "If it exists only on the Web, then you can't do anything with it. It's useless."

"People said the same thing about the Eiffel Tower," countered Alcoa's new President, Alain J.P. Belda.

Eluminum, Belda said at a press conference, has all the positive qualities of aluminum, but is only available on the Web. As a result, he claimed, it will never wear, tear, break, or discolor. In addition, customers wishing to use Eluminum to build their own Web-only products will be able to download the metal 24/7 through Alcoa's Web site.

As an example of a potential customer, Alcoa cited Coca-Cola, a major offline aluminum consumer, but one Alcoa has ignored online.

"They've built up an impressive Web presence, a site displaying literally hundreds of Coca-Cola cans," said Jack Rimm, president of Alcoa's new Web Metals Group. "Eluminum can be used in the manufacture of each one of those Web-based containers."

However, a Coca-Cola spokesman in Atlanta said the company was unaware of Alcoa's announcement, and "baffled" by its assertion that Coke cans on its site could be constructed with Eluminum.

"Those cans, they're just, you know, pictures," said spokesman Bradley Clark. "We don't need aluminum, or Eluminum, or whatever. Is this a joke?"

"People said the same thing about postmodernism," Belda retorted.

Belda conceded Eluminum would be a "hard concept for some to grasp" but insisted its relatively low cost would ease customer apprehension. The product is expected to sell for $1,200 the metric tonne, about 25 percent lower than aluminum, but a price that still promises "impressive" gross margins, he said. Eluminum can be replicated with the click of a mouse, while alumina — the basis for aluminum — is one of the more difficult metallic elements to mine.

Several industry observers, however, questioned whether anyone would actually buy Eluminum.

"People said the same thing about the Pocket Fisherman," Belda responded.

Rimm said he expects other metals producers to follow Alcoa's lead, although he argued aluminum's light weight and flexibility make it the most attractive real-world-to-Web metal. He refused, however, to answer the question, "What in God's name are you talking about?"

Belda added that several major durable goods companies are tracking Eluminum's success, and predicted the product will eventually be used in the construction of online appliances, automobiles, and camping equipment.

"Eluminum positions Alcoa to participate fully in the growth of the Internet," said Belda. "It's the new metal for a new age."

In another first for the metals industry, Alcoa also revealed that its new product was entirely concocted in the company's marketing department.

# they've got the CLAP

## Music Industry Salivates Over Fusion of Classical and Rap

The past year has seen some of the biggest mergers and acquisitions in history: the $2 billion deal between MFS Communications and UUnet Technologies, Cisco Systems' $3.7 billion acquisition of StrataCom, Bell Atlantic Corp.'s $22 billion merger with Nynex Corp. But all of these deals combined will not approach the value of the least likely merger of all.

Only half a year after cellist Yo-Yo Ma and rap star Sean "Puff Daddy" Combs held an impromptu jam session in New York's Central Park, the improbable fusion of classical music and rap has taken off, sweeping aside pop divas and banal boy bands to reign atop both the charts and the cash register.

Clap dominates MTV. Clappers populate the newsstands. Even the Grammys, long considered less hip than other award shows, will have a Clap category this year.

### WHAT IS THIS CLAP?

Where rappers sang of an often violent street-life existence, and classical music's sophisticated instrumentalism appealed to the upper classes, Clappers sing about the street lives of 18th-century aristocrats to the accompaniment of piano, strings, woodwinds and brass. And always, as in Clapper Def Ludwig's single Baroque 2 Da Bone, there is that incessant clapping:

*We eat a lotta cake, (clap)*
*Sometimes it gets old, (clap)*
*The servants fetch our robe de chambre,*
*So we don't get cold. (clap, clap...clap, clap)*

It's unquestionably a dramatic shift for both communities, but as Queen Leitmotifah (formerly Queen Latifah) explains, it was time for a change. "For years and years, we prided ourselves on 'telling it like it is.' We didn't hold nothing back. We sang about the crime, the drugs, the violence. But then we realized, 'Shit, that's depressing.'

"Now, we don't sing about ourselves. Instead, we have to read a lot of history, try to get into the heads of the masters, like Mozart, Tchaikovsky. Then we look at what life was like in, say, the palaces of Vienna in 1743, and we tell it like it was.

"OK, so we have to use our imaginations a lot," Leitmotifah added.

## YO-YO MA BIG THANG

To the record industry, Clap does more than combine two musical movements. It brings together two historically disparate economic groups—wealthy classical music aficionados and street-level rap fans — who have contrary, but appealing, buying habits. "Young music fans have less sense than money," explained Sony executive Max Schmeel, "and old classical music lovers have more money than sense. This puts us in a very good position."

How good? Schmeel estimates the annual Clap market will reach $400 billion by next year, and judging by the rush to cross into Clap, that number may be revised upward. Already, Blow Da Chateau, the Clap single by Sonata by Nature (formerly Naughty by Nature), sits atop the R&B, classical, and pop charts. Meanwhile, Yo Yo Ma and Combs last week signed a $100 million deal with Sony Music to produce two albums as Yo-Yo Ma Big Thang and Puff Daddy Dvorak. Combs already has a hit on his hands with the disc Aristobitch, a duet with noted cellist Kim Jong.

What makes Clap's future particularly lucrative is that it has transcended music and become a social force at the street level. Wealthy suburbanites who once sent their children to private schools are enrolling them in inner-city schools, believing the atmosphere will widen their appreciation of Clap. Once-violent street gangs, meanwhile, have taken on the personas and lifestyle exhibited by Clap and its performers. According to the FBI, the infamous Crips have at least two cells that have renamed themselves the Clefs, and the Latin Kings will soon rename themselves the Libretto Kings. These changes are more than just skin-deep.

Said 17-year-old Chicago resident Ralph "Bolero" Winston, a member of the Bach Boys gang: "We useta control everything west of Dearborn between 30th and 32nd, and life was fast, dangerous,

whacked out, you know. But that's not the thing anymore. We want to control our tempo allegre. We seek out the pastorale, embrace divertissement. That's our refrain."

Ironically, Chicago law enforcement has a slightly different refrain: "The truth is, we have no friggin' idea what these kids are talking about nowadays," said Chicago Gang Task Force detective Lance Boylgrim. "We had the street language and street names down, but now all they talk about is andante and arpeggio and harmonic structure. I had a kid yesterday actually call me contrapuntal. To my face."

But Clap is forcing everybody to retool. Even classical artists who once regarded other forms of music as beneath them are rethinking. "I have never felt this strong about a music since

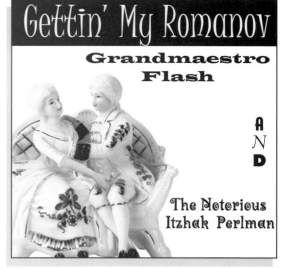

I first heard Verdi," said Luciano "Bad Luc" Pavarotti, who plans next year to rap tenor in the Metropolitan Opera's "Rigoghetto," the Clap version of Verdi's classic. "As some of my new friends are saying, 'I got da Clap, and I not goin' back.'"

# ChiefRelief Makes CEO Removal an Art

WHENEVER A COMPANY announces its CEO is stepping aside, the banalities run rampant. If he's staying on board, he will "focus on long-term corporate vision" or "new business development." If he's moving on, "the timing was right," and he will be "sorely missed" for his "invaluable contributions" that prepared the company to "go to the next level."

Who, you might wonder, gets paid to write this stuff?

ChiefRelief Inc., which since 1994 has quietly become one of the most influential companies in the world of corporate public relations, counsels hundreds of firms on what it calls the "removal arts."

"Make no mistake, there is an art to gracefully removing a CEO," insists Charlotte Hemphill, the energetic and empathetic 37-year-old CEO of ChiefRelief. "After all, think about the mixed messages that must be sent. The person is being replaced, so clearly they're not getting the job done. Yet when they're leaving, you praise this person's abilities and contributions. Both can't be true, right?

"Well," she adds with a smile, "that's the art."

When a company wants to oust a CEO, the first thing ChiefRelief does is suggest an Alternative Job Description, or AJD. These are titles that make it appear as if the outbound chief will still play a vital role in the company. Common AJDs include Chairman of the Board, Chief Visionary, and Director of New Business Development. Conversely, if you want to make it clear the person won't be actively involved, Hemphill suggests conferring the title Founder.

Next, quotes must be attributed to the departed, not only to mollify the outgoing executive, but to assuage investor fears. Three popular ones, which bring in substantial royalties for ChiefRelief: "It was the right move at the right time," "I'm still in a position to be involved in the strategic direction of the company," and "I will continue to be an active chairman."

Active chairman?

"Yes, I know that's an oxymoron, but most people don't pick up on it," Hemphill says. Her personal favorite, however, is, "I will focus my attention on new business opportunities."

"That's really like a code," she explains. "What it means is they'll focus on finding new business opportunities for themselves, since they're pretty much out of a job."

ChiefRelief also stresses that the words used by incoming CEOs are no less important. When in doubt, Hemphill suggests riffing on the following: "(Predecessor) has been an integral part of our success. His enormous talent and vision helped us gain a market-leading position. He is also a good friend, and I wish him great success in his new endeavor."

The scope of ChiefRelief's influence is impressive. In July, when Wired Ventures CEO Louis Rossetto stepped aside, he said he would continue as company chairman and focus on "new product development." When Ed McCracken was forced out after a dismal performance at Silicon Graphics, the company nonetheless insisted he "made a remarkable contribution in building Silicon Graphics, and we value his vision and achievements." In July, when Apple Computer's Gil Amelio was abruptly ousted from the top spot, no one had anything nice to say.

Guess which two of the three were ChiefRelief clients? "The changes at Wired and SGI were made peacefully. That's why we call our company 'the Ex-Lax of P.R.' We make the transition smooth and easy."

In a related note, just before press time, ChiefRelief announced that Hemphill has stepped aside as CEO and will focus on overall corporate vision.

"Charlotte has been an integral part of our success, and her enormous talent and vision helped us gain a market-leading position," says interim Chief Executive Paul Kaiser. "She is also a good friend, and I wish her great success."

# WIDESPREAD USE OF PLAGIARIZED PAPER PROVES TEACHERS TOTALLY BIASED

The emergence of Internet-based term paper factories, which allow students across the nation to turn in the same paper, has finally exposed what civil rights groups say is the single greatest threat to the American educational system: unfair teachers.

IN MILWAUKEE, Kevin Rooney got a D. In Daytona, Fla., Amanda Grathway got a C. And across the country in Los Angeles, Kay Lin Cho got an A. On the surface, this might be expected. After all, Cho is ranked near the top of her junior class, while Rooney, according to his high school guidance counselor, "should probably be working with his hands."

But what is surprising is that these students turned in the identical term paper, one they bought and downloaded from an Internet site. And that, they say, can mean only one thing.

"Teachers are so biased," said Grathway, a 17-year-old junior at Daytona High School who, like the others, paid $8.95 for "Death and the Afterlife in *Gilgamesh* and *The Iliad*," at ComingToTerms.com. "They say they're not, right? But how could Mrs. Pervitelli give me a C? Patti Clary turned in that same exact paper last semester in Mr. Hemish's class, and she got, like, a B+. So either Mr. Hemish has a thing for Patti, or Mrs. Pervitelli hates my guts. I think we all know what the real answer is.

"Both," she added.

Indeed, the emergence of so-called Internet term paper factories, and the grade variations they inevitably produce, has finally exposed what student and civil rights groups say is the single greatest threat to the American educational system: unfair teachers.

"We've been tracking this one term paper, 'Why Hylemorphism Is Preferred Over Materialism,' across colleges for six months," said Noah Lovotski, president of the national students rights organization Equal Grades for Equal Work. "So far, it has gotten 343 A's, 455 B's, 269 C's, 44 D's, and 16 F's. This is patently unfair, and we suspect many teachers of, if not outright bias, then grading on a curve."

Even more alarming, some teachers have seen the same term paper more than once and still given it a different grade. Teresa Pullmall, a junior at St. Mary's Catholic School in Washington, D.C., recalled her experience: "Last month, I turned in my term paper, 'The Ontological Argument of St. Anselm of Canterbury & Gaunilo's Response,' to my teacher, Sister Carla. She gave me an F. Well, I happen to know that my paper was every bit as good as the one Bobby O'Reilly turned in to her last year — in fact, it was the same paper — and he got an A!"

Asked to explain, Sister Carla said she recognized the paper, and believed Pullmall was guilty of plagiarism.

"Oh, right. I didn't plagiarize it. I paid for it," responded Pullmall. "She's just covering up the fact that she likes boys better."

Like Sister Carla, several educators insisted the real issue exposed by identical term papers is widespread plagiarism. In fact, Boston University recently filed a lawsuit against eight Web sites that sell term papers, charging them with wire fraud, mail fraud, racketeering, and violation of a Massachusetts law that prohibits the sale of term papers.

But Rick Dangle, who runs term paper site FivePagesOfFluff.com, called that a "convenient dodge."

"Every time we say the system is obviously unfair, that teachers are obviously playing favorites, they toss out the P word to confuse the issue," said Dangle. "Thank God the Internet exists so students can communicate instantly and expose these so-called educators for what they are."

Dangle, however, is quick to point out that not everyone in education is guilty. He also runs UltimateSAT.com, a site that regularly hacks into the computer system of the College Board, which administers the Scholastic Aptitude Test (SAT) used to gain admissions to colleges and universities.

"We sold 4,500 sets of SAT answers last semester, and each buyer scored a perfect 1,600," he said. "At least there is some honor left in the system."

SatireWire's
# BusinessMonth
## WEEKLY
DECEMBER 1998

**MAD COWS USE CELL PHONES**

**TYPO CAUSES COMPANIES TO MERDE**

**DOJ SUES APPLE FOR CREATING MICROSOFT MONOPOLY**

**JERSEY FIRM WINS NET PAVING CONTRACT**

**NEW HOME FOR THE TECHNOLOGICALLY IMPAIRED**

# INTERNET CEOs
## ARE THEY TOO YOUNG?

**PROS: INNOVATION, VITALITY, BRAVADO**

**CONS: BED-WETTING**

Carly Jenkins
Omnetcom
Age 7

Kate Naylor
PLP Web
Age 10

Bo Peabody
Tripod
Age 5

Austin Aruzzo
WormTrader.com
Age 6

# OY, YOU NEVER VISIT YOUR MOTHER'S WEB SITE

## Not That You Should Care, Mr. I-Have-My-Own-Site-Now

Outside I'm smiling, but inside, *plagen zich*. Not that you should care.

*Editor's Note: This month, BusinessMonth Weekly Editor Treat Warland cedes the editorial page to your mother, who has an important message.*

I'm thinking of divorcing your father. Oh, you didn't know that, Mr. I-have-no-time-for-the-woman-who-bore-me-and-taught-me-HTML? Well, if you ever bothered to drop by your mother's Web site, just once in a while, spare just a few of your precious surfing minutes, you'd know that. It was in my Weblog from last week.

But far be it from me to complain, although would it hurt so much to visit the family Web site — the site where you first learned how to code, I shouldn't have to mention? I've done some things around the place. Remember that animated GIF that your father used to love? The one with the stupid dancing fish? On the homepage, he wanted it! He insisted! Well it's gone! I'm doing everything in Macromedia Flash now. Your father doesn't even know. G-d forbid he should make time to visit his own wife's site.

So I should be forgiving you? It's in your genes, that's what RabbiNet says.

Your sister Rachel, she visits your mother's site every week, and you know how hard it is for her to get around, what with that 28k dial-up connection she suffers with, and that *schmendrick* of a husband always hogging the computer. He surfs like a pig! But your sister Hannah — Judaism should have saints! She has a link to my site right on her homepage, and she surfs in every day, after work. And she's got little ones!

But you, you with your fancy DSL, you who won't put up a link to your own mother's site, you, who have by the way not brought me one grandchild — not that I'm *utzing*, G-d knows — you're too busy chasing every girlie site with so much as a *sheyner ponim*. But I have news for you, Mr. I-can't-be-bothered-to-visit-my-own-mother's-site-but-I-can-troll-for-strumpets-at-Baywatch.com. That *goyishe* site has no pictures of the sort you're after, not so much as a *pupik* showing.

And don't tell me you're spending all your time at MinyanWorship.org. That site's not doing so well.

They can never get a quorum, no small thanks to you who never shows up for prayer, as G-d in *himmel* knows.

Are you cleaning your mouse? Remember to clean your mouse. And keep your fingers on the keyboard, where they belong. Oy, how I suffer.

You know, I haven't changed your page since you left. It's just like it was when we were still under one site, one happy family. Ouch, memories! But it's still there, if you want to come back and see it, even maybe make a few changes. Not that I'm asking you to move back in. I know you have your own URL now and your own "site," which I shouldn't say, so I won't, that it's a mess, Mr. Garbage Mouth, and my

Oh, did I already show you my picture? G-d forbid you should see too much of your mother.

friend Mrs. Meierson, who must have seen it G-d knows how, says don't make yourself sick, that son of yours is just a *nebbish*, a nobody, look at the way he keeps that site of his with all the broken links and script errors.

So I'm not saying you should consider coming back, but you still have the password to the site, if you remember how to use it, I'm not holding my breath.

You remember Annabelle14@aol.com, the girl you met on MitzvahSingles.org? Such a lovely person. She still comes by my site. And so pretty! She sent me a GIF, and I put it up. You should come see it. How long will it be until somebody else, some nice rich *mensch* who makes a good living and has a nice clean Web page, is visiting my site and sees Annabelle and sweeps her off her feet? Not that you should care. But her picture is there. And a link to her Web site. And her email address. Not that you would think to care about such things as a dying mother's last wish for your happiness.

By the way, have I mentioned I'm dying? It was in my Weblog from last week. Oh, that's right, you don't have time to come to your mother's site anymore. I'm leaving the site to your sisters.

# QUOTE HIM

"We got a little carried away."
— John Chambers,
chief executive of voracious high-tech
juggernaut Cisco Systems, explaining why
his firm, which has acquired 21 companies
in the last two years alone, bought itself
last week in a $5.4 billion deal.

## OUTPOST GERBILS REALLY KITTENS

Online retailer Outpost.com, which recently ran controversial TV commercials showing gerbils being fired from a cannon, claimed today it never used actual gerbils. Instead, Outpost executives said, the company dressed week-old kittens in gerbil costumes. The company added that its new marketing campaign, in which Outpost executives will burn tropical rain forests, also will not use actual gerbils.

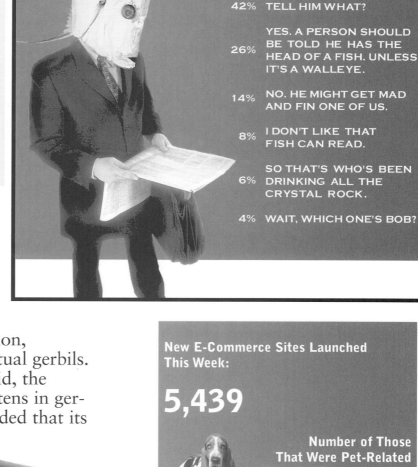

**OFFICE POLL**

## SHOULDN'T SOMEONE TELL BOB?

**42%** TELL HIM WHAT?

**26%** YES. A PERSON SHOULD BE TOLD HE HAS THE HEAD OF A FISH. UNLESS IT'S A WALLEYE.

**14%** NO. HE MIGHT GET MAD AND FIN ONE OF US.

**8%** I DON'T LIKE THAT FISH CAN READ.

**6%** SO THAT'S WHO'S BEEN DRINKING ALL THE CRYSTAL ROCK.

**4%** WAIT, WHICH ONE'S BOB?

---

**New E-Commerce Sites Launched This Week:**

**5,439**

**Number of Those That Were Pet-Related**

**5,348**

---

# TYPO CAUSES COMPANIES TO MERDE

Due to a last-minute typographic error in documentation outlining a $77 billion deal between two of the world's largest oil companies, Exxon Corp. and Mobil Corp. announced this week that they have agreed to merde. According to papers filed with the U.S. Securities and Exchange Commission and the Department of Justice, the two companies hope to merde within six months, pending shareholder and regulatory approval. To gain advantageous tax status, the companies further stated the action will be accounted for as a pooing of interests.

# Justice Department Sues Apple For Making Microsoft a Monopoly

## Accuses Computer Maker of Self-Destructive, Anti-Competitive Practices

IN WHAT PROMISES to be the most significant antitrust ruling since the 1983 breakup of AT&T, the U.S. Justice Department and 20 states filed suit against Apple Computer Inc., claiming the company's history of "inept, anti-competitive" management practices is responsible for turning Microsoft into an illegal monopoly.

"At several junctions since its inception, Apple had the opportunity to become the predominant maker of operating systems, but instead management incompetence and arrogance resulted in numerous decisions that gave us the Microsoft we know today," Attorney General Janet Reno told reporters. "We believe it's time for Apple to pay for that."

Filed in a Washington, D.C., court, the 53-page complaint alleges that Microsoft, the world's largest maker of personal computer software, has used unfair tactics to crush competition and restrict consumer choice. Included among those tactics were forcing computer manufacturers to use a startup screen designed by Microsoft that prevented rivals from getting prominent display on the desktop, and reaching agreements with online and Internet service providers that contractually required the providers to offer Microsoft's Internet Explorer as the exclusive or primary browser.

None of this would have happened, the suit states, if Apple hadn't made "so many amazingly bad business moves" over the years.

According to the filing, Apple's anti-competitive, pro-Microsoft-monopoly behavior began in the 1980s, when, unlike Microsoft, it refused to license its operating system to other computers makers to build clones. As a result, Apple surrendered potential market dominance to IBM clones running Microsoft software. At the same time, Apple stingily sued any software developers who attempted to write applications for its products without a license, which pushed angry developers toward Microsoft.

In an even more disastrous early decision, Apple licensed its software to Microsoft so it could develop applications for the Macintosh operating system. Not long thereafter, Microsoft came out with its first Windows product, which looked "remarkably like" Apple's.

"'Here's the source code to our operating system, Bill. But no cheating!'" quipped Connecticut Attorney General Richard Blumenthal. "I think we could win the case on that move alone."

As the years went by, Apple management's reaction to its steady decline was to insist that its products would win because they were better, and to continually charge more for them until, by 1994, it decided it would allow clones to be built after all. This was followed by the decision that it would not allow clones to be built after all, then by a decision that it would allow it, then that it wouldn't, and finally, no one cared.

As a direct result, the suit concludes, Microsoft has grown to monstrous proportions while Apple has developed an intensely loyal customer base which, if gathered together, could easily fit into the spare luggage compartment of Bill Gates' Land Rover.

Apple interim CEO Steve Jobs said he was shocked that his company, and not Microsoft, was named as the defendant. However, Microsoft Chairman Bill Gates said he would have claimed entrapment had the DOJ focused on Redmond.

"We never wanted to become a monopoly, but [Apple] pretty much forced us into it," Gates said. "Everybody knew they had the best computer. Everybody knew they had the best operating system. And what did they do? They let us steal it, for God's sake. What choice did we have?"

**In addition to creating the Microsoft monopoly, the lawsuit also indicts Apple for giving us:**
- Microsoft Windows
- Microsoft NT
- Microsoft Bob
- Bill Gates' *The Road Ahead*
- Chippy the Paper Clip

Microsoft CEO Bill Gates: "Despite evidence to the contrary, we always assumed Apple did really want us to win. But when they came out with the Newton, we knew they'd given up."

The U.S. Federal Emergency Management Agency has issued an "Internet Bubble Advisory," and warned individuals to use extreme caution to keep from being consumed by the Bubble. FEMA recommends taking the following precautions:

■ Move slowly and methodically. The Bubble is attracted by things that move fast and without thinking.

■ If it asks you what time it is, UNDER NO CIRCUMSTANCES are you to say "Internet Time."

■ The following will cause the Bubble to grow larger. DO NOT SAY ANY OF THE FOLLOWING: Eyeballs equals revenue. IPO. Right now we're focused on market share. I am a day trader. Profitability isn't the issue. I'm thinking of starting an incubator. Sand Hill Road likes it. Internet companies should be valued differently.

■ The following will cause the Bubble to grow very angry. DO NOT SAY ANY OF THE FOLLOWING: I'm mostly in cash and T-bills. I'm thinking of starting a site called FuckedCompany.com. The telephone was really the greatest technical innovation of the 20th century. I prefer stocks that pay a dividend.

■ The Bubble will try to convince you it is not a Bubble, but an incredibly strong economic cycle created by increased productivity, low inflation, and sustainably low unemployment. DO NOT LISTEN.

■ The Bubble is invisible, but if you hear a voice promising to get you in a great startup in the business-to-business applications service provider market, RUN LIKE HELL. Even if this is not the Bubble, it's still a good idea to run from whoever said it.

## FRONT END

# WORD ASSOCIATION

**Henry Blodget**
CIBC
Oppenheimer
Internet Analyst

IT WAS, SOME ARE ALREADY SAYING, the single greatest call in the history of Internet analysis. Only days ago, a little-known CIBC Oppenheimer analyst named Henry Blodget put a seemingly absurd $400 price target on Amazon.com, a company that last quarter lost $45 million on revenues of $153 million. Hours after his report, Amazon's stock jumped 46 points, passing $300, and seems well on its way to matching Blodget's mark.

How does he do it? Having conducted interviews with analysts before, we knew better than to ask directly. Instead, we hired renowned business psychologist Dr. Lerner Lowenstein to sit down with Blodget and conduct a word-association test meant to peer deeper into his psyche.

DR. LOWENSTEIN: Mr. Blodget, I'm going to read from these little cards, and I want you to say the first thing that comes to your mind, all right?
BLODGET: Yes, fine.

DR. LOWENSTEIN: Good. Here goes. "The lung of a small camel, placed in a box two meters high by one meter wide, set down among a troupe of elderly Irish dancers on a warm summer's eve."
BLODGET: Incoherent rambling.

DR. LOWENSTEIN: "The lung of a small camel, placed in a box two meters high by one meter wide, set down among a troupe of elderly Irish dancers on a warm summer's eve.*com*."
BLODGET: Strong buy.

"I tripped and fell on the...the Internet," says Vinton Cerf.

# Jersey Concrete Firm Gets Internet Paving Contract

## INFORMATION SUPERHIGHWAY NEEDS PAVING LIKE ANY HIGHWAY, SAY COMPANY ASSOCIATES

IN A SURPRISE move, ICANN, the Internet's governing body, announced last week that NorthJerseyConcrete.com has won a bid to pave the Internet, a 10-year, $400 billion project that critics call laughable, but that ICANN insists has "suddenly become a matter of life or death."

Vinton Cerf, a board member of the Internet Corporation for Assigned Names and Numbers, conceded that paving the Internet might seem unusual, but said the need became "blindingly obvious" after a meeting with associates from NorthJerseyConcrete.com.

"I tripped and fell on the...the Internet," said Cerf, explaining his facial abrasions, black eye, and noticeable limp. "This is why we've also asked North Jersey Concrete to put in sidewalks. I am proof that people can get very badly hurt if this project is not fully funded."

Internet companies are expected to pay 5 percent of their annual revenues to cover project costs, said Cerf.

A subsidiary of Hoboken-based North Jersey Concrete & Waste Management, NorthJerseyConcrete.com said its involvement in the Internet was long overdue.

"It came to our attention a couple of months ago that this Information Superhighway was being built, and we were not a little aggrieved that we were not invited to participate in the grading and paving of this great highway, for which we should have been invited to participate in," said Anthony Capiello, who identified himself as a "consultant" for the firm. "Also, we came to understand that union labor was not being used in the constructive aspects of this project, a deficiency that we found most disturbing.

"When we met with ICAM (sic), they informed us that this highway in fact had no pavement or sidewalks, and did not need pavement or sidewalks," Capiello continued. "It is fortunate that our persuasions convinced them that this was not a very wise move on their part, and perhaps might be something they should reconsider."

The contract, however, raised strong objections from companies expected to pay into the highway fund, many of whom said they would not participate.

"The Internet is wires and servers and routers and switches. You can't pave it. It doesn't need sidewalks," said Cisco Systems Chief Executive John Chambers. "We will not pay one cent toward this ludicrous project."

Informed of the response, Capiello said he would gladly invite Chambers to "take a little tour" of the Internet. "Certainly I would not contend to have all the mental faculties as Mr. Chambers does in this area," said Capiello, "but perhaps he does not understand just how very big and very deep the Internet is, and how it is possible to get very, very lost in there."

# MAD COWS USE CELL PHONES
## Researchers Claim Discovery Solves Mystery Disease

IN ANOTHER blow to the cellular industry, British scientists studying mad cow disease claim to have discovered the source of the mysterious affliction after catching a pair of Holstein-Friesians chatting away on mobile phones, which also have been linked to eye cancer and brain dysfunction.

"We knew mobile phones were dangerous, and we knew cows were intrigued by wireless technology, but when we saw them using the mobiles, we made the connection right away," said lead researcher Kevin Barrington, who spotted the culprits at a dairy farm outside Kent.

Listening in on the conversation, Barrington said he never heard the cows utter a word. "Bloody typical mobile user," he noted. "Nothing to say."

Cell phone manufacturers — already plagued by studies connecting cell phones to cancers and brain abnormalities — immediately dismissed the British claims. "To even insinuate that cell phones could somehow be the cause of this disease is as absurd as the notion that cows could use cell phones at all," said Nokia spokesperson Nigel Wanthorpe. However, after being shown a photograph (inset) taken by researchers, Wanthorpe demurred. "Dear God in heaven," he said, "what have we done?"

John Ashton, who runs a cattle operation outside Essex, admitted that like many farmers, he has been using cell phones to communicate with his herd for years. "Mostly I'd ring 'em up to tell 'em when it was time to come in for the slaughter," he explained. "I'd say, 'ello, Melissa? You and Elsie and Camille come in so's I can stun you into a stupor an' slit your throats, awright?' Saved me time 'aving to round 'em up, and it was nice and impersonal. I didn't 'ave look in those big brown eyes."

However, once Ashton learned of the connection to the disease, he took the phones away. "That was not at all pleasant," he added. "With all due respect, I don't think you 'ave really seen a mad cow until you take away its mobile."

Prior to the discovery, scientists had theorized that mad cow, or bovine spongiform encephalopathy (BSE), was caused by mutated proteins called prions, or possibly by widespread tobacco use. Tobacco was ruled out as a suspect last year, however, after a study found that while cigarette smoking among cows had dropped 45 percent from 1993 to 1997, incidents of BSE had recently increased.

The cell phone diagnosis, however, gives victims and cattle farmers hope that the disease can be treated by prohibiting livestock from using cellular technology, and that they can now sue the burgeoning wireless industry *ex puga amplus*, which is a legal term for half a million pounds.

British Agriculture Minister Jack Cunningham, meanwhile, lashed out at the cows for further endangering the community by not using hands-free devices while traveling on roadways.

GUILTY: A cow in rural England is caught using a cell phone.

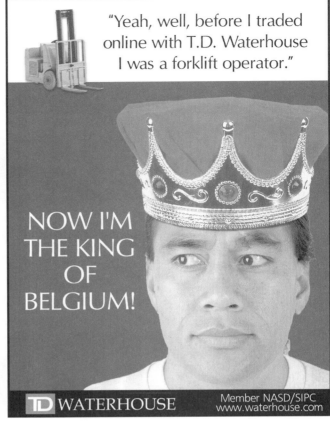

# SEC Says Online Broker Ads Misleading; Not Just Bartenders Who Can Get Rich Trading

IN A STINGING REBUKE, the Securities and Exchange Commission accused several online brokers of deceiving the public by insinuating bartenders and tow truck operators could somehow buy up islands and corporations because they were able to make trades online for $14.99.

"To claim (as Discover Brokerage does) that online trading can make bartenders and truck drivers rich is egregiously misleading and borderline absurd," said SEC Chairman Arthur Levitt. "There are also police officers and shellfishermen. Or what about oceanographers? They could make a killing by avoiding the high fees charged by traditional brokerage firms."

Added SEC Enforcement Director Lanny Rice: "Don't forget the people who apply a coating of latex to foam rubber products. They could buy helicopters and hire Christo to wrap their ranches in landscape art."

## YAHOO! BEATS ANALYSTS' ESTIMATES, DOGS

Internet giant Yahoo!, which last week soundly beat analysts' estimates, reportedly wasn't satisfied and beat their dogs as well, according to wire reports. Some analysts even reported getting wedgies.

"I've had my estimates beaten plenty of times before, OK, so that's not what I'm upset about," said PaineWebber analyst Scott Feldstein. "But they didn't have to kick my cocker spaniel like that. Damn their quarter-over-quarter page-view growth."

In a statement, Yahoo! Chairman Tim Koogle said the company is on track to beat estimates again next quarter, at which time analysts should expect, at the very least, "another visit from Mr. Cheeky."

[ADVT]

# E-grieving.com

## THE DIGITAL WAY TO SAY GOODBYE

IT'S BEEN several months now, but Kelly Posner can clearly recall how she felt the day her aunt in Germany died. She was pissed.

"The funeral and viewing were on a Wednesday in Munich," says Posner. "But I hardly knew this aunt, and I didn't have $1,700 for a last-minute ticket to Germany."

Fortunately, she found E-grieving.com. After a quick site search, she plugged the names of Aunt Betty and Uncle Rolf into a pre-scripted, $1.99 e-grieving that combined the sympathy she wanted to express with the valid excuse she needed to stay put:

*Dear (Uncle Rolf) I'm sorry I,*
*Can't be there for the viewing,*
*But it turns out my passport,*
*Like (Aunt Betty),*
*Needs renewing.*

According to Kevin Delaney, founder and CEO of E-grieving.com, Posner's dilemma is typical of the 20,000 "compassion clients" who have used the service since its launch six months ago.

"Everybody praises the flexibility of the networked economy, allowing employees to be in different places, but the same paradigm shift has also scattered families," says Delaney. "Companies react to a distributed workforce by offering distance learning. We react to the distributed family by offering distance mourning."

Particularly popular is E-grieving's "Wail Across the Web" product, which allows users to send a targeted message accompanied by a variety of RealAudio laments, such as the gnashing of teeth, stifled sobbing, keening, and drunken, good-hearted laughter (for Irish wakes). One example:

*I just can't make the funeral,*
*To honor Robert's leaving,*
*But click to hear,*
*The wail sincere,*
*Contained in this E-grieving.*

While its primary market is the individual consumer, E-grieving has made lucrative strides by licensing its database to corporations such as Nortel, which deploys E-grieving on its corporate intranet so employees can send sympathies for free. "It's a great way for us to let our employees know that we care about their families and loved ones," says Nortel spokesperson Andrea Lincoln. "And it serves a higher purpose by encouraging them to stay on the job instead of taking bereavement time."

E-grieving is also experimenting with video-conferencing, allowing distance mourners to watch and even contribute to memorial services. "But there's still a bandwidth problem," Delaney admits. "Our beta mourners found that buffering is really incompatible with bawling."

Death, however, is only one of the sympathy scenarios E-grieving pursues. The company has expanded into the general e-sympathy business, offering electronic condolences for a variety of loss-related situations, from political campaigns to job promotions to parts in the school play.

There is even one labeled "Friend fired for 'lack of production'":

*I heard you lost your job after,*
*Some kind of inquisition,*
*Those sneaky sys admin folks,*
*Quidnuncs all, in my opinion.*
*But hey, you're free, relax, slow down,*
*Now you'll have lots of time,*
*To visit all those porno sites,*
*That got you in this bind.*

Bolstered by a recent $7 million, second round of venture capital funding, E-grieving has launched an additional product: Weepz, the Emotional Currency® that can be exchanged for merchandise and services from E-grieving partners. Products currently available include flowers, gift baskets, embalming services, counseling, and hard liquor.

Weepz is expected to account for the majority of E-greiving's revenue by 2000, Delaney says. But for now the site's strength stems from its ever-deepening database of targeted e-grievings, which have been tailored to meet a range of cultural needs. For instance, a variation of the e-grieving Posner sent to her uncle is one of the most popular messages among expatriate Indians:

*Dear (survivor), I'm sorry I,*
*Can't be there for the pyre,*
*But it turns out my visa,*
*Like (dead person),*
*Has expired.*

It's that kind of vertical marketing, says Posner, that will keep her and others coming back.

"E-grieving solved my problem quickly, easily, and appropriately, and for a fraction of the cost," Posner says. "I can't wait until somebody else dies so I can use it again."

---

**HEADQUARTERS:** Chicago

**FOUNDED:** 1998

**CEO:** Kevin Delaney

**SLOGAN:** "The Digital Way to Say Goodbye"

**RAISON D'OT:** Before technology, relationships were based on face time. Now, most relationships are based on email. Digital mourning is a natural by-product of this evolution.

**PRODUCTS/SERVICES:** Wail Across the Web; Weepz® Emotional Currency.

**FOUNDING INSPIRATION:** Says Delaney — "I finally score box seats to a Cubs-Mets game, and my cousin in St. Louis dies. Talk about a dilemma."

If employees are allowed to work while at work, they become more productive personal Web surfers, said consultant Sadie Wassoon.

# STUDY: Work Not an Impediment to Personal Web Surfing at Work

## Meanwhile, Policies Prohibiting Work During the Surfday Found Unproductive

More than 80 percent of respondents to a new LGI/Gallup poll admit they do "some" or "a lot" of work while at work, but almost all insist they never let business-related matters interfere with personal Web surfing at the office.

"When I come in at 8:30, I'm pretty much focused on surfing the Web for personal reasons," says survey respondent Barth Biggs, an account representative at Harmony Photo Imaging in Glenville, Ohio. "Occasionally, yeah, I'll switch over and do some business-related thing, but it's just a breather, and I mostly do it during lunch."

According to the study, an overwhelming 86 percent of those surveyed say doing some work during the surfing day has no negative impact on their personal Web surfing. In fact, 48 percent say doing occasional work at work actually improves the quality of their personal surfing, and 28 percent also say it makes them happier and less stressed.

"There's a common misconception that if you allow your employees to work a little during the surfday, then they will take advantage of that and spend the whole day working," says surf management consultant Neil Nariget. "The truth is, people won't abuse that freedom. They'll appreciate it, and as a result be more effective when emailing with friends, checking their portfolios, and hanging out on eBay."

Clearly, employers are aware of the issue. More than 70 percent of respondents say their companies prohibit all but personal Web surfing while at the office. Many of those laboring under these policies, however, claim they are impossible to enforce.

"If it were up to my boss, I'd spend my whole day checking my stocks, shopping for travel bargains, and exchanging personal emails," said one woman, an employee of a major pharmaceutical company, who asked to remain anonymous for fear of retribution. "But nowadays, it's nearly impossible to avoid doing some work. I mean, my colleagues sit right next to me. My customers know how to reach me via email. What am I supposed to do, ignore them all day?"

According to Sadie Wassoon, managing director of consulting firm LGI, the answer is no. "When companies allow employees to spend a few moments online each day to get work issues out of the way — things such as analyzing sales projections, planning a marketing campaign, or dealing with customer complaints — these employees are able to better focus on the demands of their personal lives," she said.

*In other survey findings:*

■ 82 percent of employees admit they send work-related emails while at work.

■ 80 percent of employers say they have caught their employees surfing work-related Web sites.

■ 28 percent of employees take precautionary measures to keep employers from detecting their work-related Internet use.

■ In the area of inappropriate surfing, one in three workers say they spend 25 minutes or more each day using the Internet for work, usually at sites directly related to their duties.

# OLDER FOLKS NOT BITTER ABOUT SUCCESS OF NET CEOS HALF THEIR GODDAMN AGE

## "So What If I've Worked My Butt Off for 30 Years and Some 20-Year-Old with Acne Is Running a Billion-Dollar Company?" Is General Feeling

A NEW STUDY by MIT's Sloan School of Management has concluded that contrary to popular belief, older working Americans do not begrudge the overnight success of young, inexperienced Internet entrepreneurs, but instead have "nothing but respect" for the "energetic little bed wetters."

"Far from being bitter, most of those surveyed specifically said they were impressed that people who can't manage their way out of a paper bag could achieve a level of success that they themselves will never approach," explained Richard L. Boulles, 47, a professor in the business school who said he was inspired to conduct the study after venture capitalists refused to fund his meticulously researched auto parts startup but gave $8 million to a pair of high school students whose Web site sells dolls' heads.

"Hey, more power to 'em," said respondent Richard Knowling, a 54-year-old assistant production manager for Goodyear Tire. "Just because I've been working like a dog since I was 15 and now I bring home $52,000 a year and have zero chance of ever making so much as vice president while some little shit with

No matter how much venture funding they have, young CEOs need to wear their bike helmets.

a Web site that shows pictures of cats breaking wind gets $3 million in financing and goes to dinner with Bill Gates...where was I?"

Boulles, who polled 1,000 Americans aged 42 and up, said the survey also included older executives who have signed on with Internet firms, and found this demographic was even more enthusiastic about the much, much younger crowd.

One member of that group was William Paiche, who at age 55 left his job at BBD&O to become marketing vice president of software startup CurseThe-Frog.com, where the average employee is 20 years old. "For me, it's the thrill of a lifetime to be around young, energetic people who think they know everything and who view anyone over age 30 as a failure if he doesn't have his own company," said Praiche. "And just from a pure business perspective, nothing is more rewarding than working side-by-side with a tireless team of go-getters who are too young to vote and couldn't find Argentina on a map of Argentina."

## HOW YOUNG IS TOO YOUNG?

While not unusual, Kate Naylor and Austin Aruzzo are on the young side of the Internet founder curve. Naylor, age 10, launched community site Pretty Little Pony (now PLP Web) last year. The company, which allows users to build free homepages dedicated to the Pretty Little Pony, has so far received $4 million in venture financing for reasons that analysts and those of us in the media are pretending we understand. Aruzzo, meanwhile, has yet to bring his online used worm auction, WormTrader.com, to the Web, but was able to secure $2.5 million in financing because he owned a domain name.

*BusinessMonth Weekly* sat down with the pair to discuss their business models, and what impact their ages have had on their companies.

**BMW:** Kate, let's start with you. Certainly you're to be commended on securing $4 million in financing for PLP, but undoubtedly you've heard the grumbling. People say you're too young to be an executive, that you don't have experience managing people, and that you will be unable to handle the intense pressures of running a company. How do you respond to that?

**NAYLOR:** Bu...bu...bu...

**BMW:** Oh hey, hey, look, don't cry...

**ARUZZO:** Meanie!

*Loving care ...* *for the technically spare*    *Silicon Pines*

# The Toughest Decision:
## Should My Loved One Be Placed in an Assisted Computing Facility?

For family members, it is often the most difficult and painful moment they will face: to accept that a loved one — a parent, a spouse, perhaps a sibling — is technologically impaired and should no longer be allowed to live independently, or come near a computer or electronic device without direct supervision. The time has come to place that loved one into the care of an Assisted Computing Facility. But you have questions. So many questions. We at Silicon Pines want to help.

**WHAT EXACTLY IS AN "ASSISTED COMPUTING FACILITY"?**
Sometimes referred to as "Homes for the Technologically Infirm," "Technical Invalid Care Centres," or "Homes for the Technically Challenged," Assisted Computing Facilities, (ACFs) are modeled on assisted living facilities, and provide a safe, structured residential environment for those unable to handle even the most common, everyday multitasks. Most fully accredited ACFs, like Silicon Pines, are oases of hope and encouragement that allow residents to lead productive, technologically relevant lives without the fear and anxiety associated with actually having to understand or execute the technologies themselves.

**WHO SHOULD BE IN AN ACF?**
Sadly, technology is advancing at such a dramatic rate that many millions, of all ages, will never truly be able to understand it, putting an undue burden on those friends and family members who must explain it to them. But unless the loved one is suffering from a truly debilitating affliction, such as Reinstallzheimers, the decision to commit is entirely personal. You must ask yourself, "How frustrated am I that my parent/sibling/spouse is unable to open an email attachment?" "How much of my time should be taken up explaining how RAM is different from hard drive memory?" "How many times can I bear to hear my dad say, 'Hey, can I replace the motherboard with a father-board? Ha ha ha!'"

**MUST IT BE FAMILY, OR CAN I PLACE ANYONE IN AN ACF?**
Several corporations have sought permission to have certain employees, or at times entire sales

## Silicon Pines

departments, committed to ACFs. At present, however, individuals can be committed only by direct family or self-internment. The reason is simple: there are not nearly enough ACFs in the world to accommodate all the technologically challenged. For example, there are currently 860,000 beds available in ACFs, but there are 14 million AOL users.

### HOW MUCH WILL IT COST?

ACF rents range from free* up to $12,500 per month. The disparity is currently a point of contention in the ACF industry. Many residents are covered through government programs such as Compucaid or Compucare, but reimbursement rates are low and only cover a portion of the fees. Exacerbating the situation are the HMOs (Helpdesk Maintenance Organizations), which often deny coverage, forcing residents to pay out of pocket or turn to expensive private techcare insurers such as BlueCache/BlueScreen.

### WHAT SHOULD I LOOK FOR IN AN ACF?

First, make sure it's a genuine Assisted Computing Facility, and not an Assisted Living Facility. To tell the difference, observe the residents. If they look rather old and tend to openly discuss bowel movements, this is probably assisted living. On the other hand, if they vary in age and say things like, "I'm supposed to figure that out? I'm not Bill goddamned Gates, you know!" this is probably assisted computing.

Also, at a well-run ACF, residents should lead full, independent lives, and should be allowed the use of many technology devices, including telephones, electric toothbrushes, and alarm clocks. However, only a facility's Licensed Techcare Professionals (LTPs) should perform computational or technological tasks such as installing programs or saving email attachments. And LTPs should NEVER answer residents' questions because studies have shown that answering user questions inevitably makes things worse. Instead, residents should simply have things done for them, relieving them of the pressure to "learn" or "improve."

### CAN A RESIDENT EVER GET OUT?

No.

### OK, THIS SOUNDS PROMISING. HOW CAN I LEARN MORE?

For your enlightenment, we offer extensive information on

*"But Mommy, I'll miss Daddy."*

*"Oh, honey, I know. But with the money we'll save on 'Dummies' books, you can buy a new dress."*

Silicon Pines and the ACF lifestyle on the following pages. But whatever you decide, keep in mind that due to demand, ACFs now have long waiting lists. WebTV subscribers alone will take years to absorb.

*Offsetting the costs are technology companies themselves, many of which subsidize ACFs. Firms such as Microsoft, Dell, Qualcomm, and America Online will pay up to 100 percent of a resident's monthly bill, but there is a catch. ISPs, for instance, require residents to sign service contracts lasting a year or more. Microsoft, meanwhile, prohibits the installation of any competitive software, while Priceline requires that residents buy shares of its stock, which seems onerous but saves residents on lavatory tissue.

The independence you want... Silicon Pines

the assistance you obviously need

# "I'm Glad I'm in Here!"
## A Resident's Story

The dilemma is awesome. But it has to be faced. Should you allow your loved one to battle on, endure the indignity of being obviously technologically impaired, and await the inevitable — involuntary commitment to an Assisted Computing Facility? Or should you break the news gently and hope the family member volunteers to leave for a new home?

MR. BOITANO
BEFORE

It's a decision that can split a family, as it did with the Boitanos of Clifton, N.J.

### DROPPING HINTS
"Dad always had a hard time, like with pasting parts of a Word document into a spreadsheet, but what got to me were the emails from Mom," said Carolyn Boitano, 28. "They were always under his address. I kept telling her she should get her own account, but she always told me Dad said it was unnecessary."

THE BOITANO KIDS

Carolyn started dropping hints, leaving brochures from a couple of ACFs so her father and mother would see them, but it didn't work. Frustrated, she decided to confront her father to tell him he should go to Silicon Pines. The news shocked her parents, as Carolyn remembers vividly.

"My father just screamed at me. 'It's not me who should be committed, it's your mother!' But I told him he was the one who couldn't figure out how to set up a separate email account."

Carolyn's appeal once again failed. However, Mr. Boitano's youngest child, 22-year-old Ricky, was more persuasive.

### "I'M GOING TO KILL YOU"
"I knew Carolyn wasn't getting anywhere, but it was frustrating for me too," said Ricky. "So finally I just told Dad what I felt: that he was going to Silicon Pines, or I was going to kill him."

### NO NEED TO KILL HIM
Ricky's emotional plea opened his father's eyes and made Mr. Boitano realize he was unable to deal with life's day-to-day technology needs. To everyone's relief, he declared himself Technologically Impaired and moved into Silicon Pines, where his wife and children email him almost every day.

"I won't lie. When my kids first approached me about coming to Silicon Pines, I was angry," said Mr. Boitano. "I knew I wasn't exactly a whiz, but I didn't figure I should have to move out of my house.

"But that's what's so great about Silicon Pines," he continued. "I don't have to figure out anything anymore. Now, if I come to a site that says I need to download Flash, I don't call someone for help or give up and go to another site. At the Pines, an LTP [Licensed Techcare Professional] is always there looking over my shoulder. And they don't show me how to do it, they just do it.

MR. BOITANO TODAY!

"I wasn't sure this was the place for me, but I have to admit, I'm glad I'm in here!"

# *10 Warning Signs*
## You May Be Technically Impaired

Being technologically challenged or impaired is nothing to be ashamed about. In fact, millions of people suffer from it daily. Many, however, don't recognize their condition, and unless they talk about it, these people are often difficult to diagnose. It is our sincere hope that the following list of Warning Signs may serve as a guide to help you, or someone you know, make an informed decision.

**1.** After sending someone an email, you phone to tell that someone that you've sent them an email.

**2.** All your bookmarks are tech support sites.

**3.** Look at your email address. Does it end in "aol.com"?

**4.** You keep forgetting which side of the mouse you use to "right-click."

**5.** All your bookmarks are genealogy sites.

**6.** When your computer freezes, and someone tells you to turn up the heat in the room, you actually do it.

**7.** When installing software and it asks if you want to do a "normal" or "custom" install, you get upset that there is more than one option.

**8.** You say things like "With my new 850 MHz machine, the Internet is much faster."

**9.** You ordered a computer with a CD-ROM, but instead it came with a stupid cup holder.

**10.** You are told about viruses such as ILoveYou and warned not to click the attachments, then the next day you get an ILoveYou email and click on the attachment because, well, it came from someone you know.

If you recognize any three of these signs, you may be in need of an evaluation by a Licensed Techcare Professional (LTP). If you recognize five or more, you may be suffering from a more serious condition known as Reinstallzheimers. *Seek help now.*

*Freedom for you...*     Silicon Pines

*and your family*

# The Silicon Pines Difference

**N**estled among gently rolling hills, Silicon Pines is proud to be the only Assisted Computing Facility in the world to practice "Degenerative Computing in Place." We provide a unique blend of housing and personal computing assistance to maintain your independence and maximize your quality of technological life, while allowing you to fall further and further behind at your own pace, without any pressure.

**YOU'RE SPECIAL, BUT NOT "DIFFERENT"**
At Silicon Pines, you'll feel special, but never alone or different. In fact, you'll be in the company of people with the same skill levels, and will experience planned daily activities and recreational programs geared to your interests and abilities. Our qualified professionals provide 24-hour technological care, as well as physical, occupational, and speech recognition therapy.

Sample activities include:
- Cut & Paste Night
- Printing for Life
- Screensaver Hour
- Meet Your Neighbor's Mouse
- Puppet Show with Floppy, Zippy, and Chippy
- Old-Fashioned Defrag-a-Long

**INTERFACE WITHOUT GETTING "IN YOUR FACE"**
Best of all, you'll make new friends and share new experiences in computing — but never feel anxious or frustrated. Why not? Because at Silicon Pines, we NEVER tell you to do something. We NEVER expect you to figure it out. We NEVER even SHOW you how to do it. WE JUST DO IT.

It's no surprise that "Just Do It for Them" is one of the mantras at Silicon Pines. But as senior Licensed Techcare Professional Gregg Pervis explains, there's a little more to Assisted Computing the Silicon Pines way.

"Even though we don't expect them to do anything, I like our residents to feel a sense of accomplishment, so if I'm installing a new program, I let them participate. For instance, when the program is done loading, there will be a screen that says 'Installation successful. Click OK to continue.' I could do that myself, but instead I'll turn to the resident and say, 'So, what do you think we should do here?'"

Six times out of 10, the resident will say, "Click 'OK'?" Gregg then lets them click the OK button. "You should see their faces light up," Gregg says. "It's a beautiful thing."

*CRISIS INTERVENTION— An LTP (right) rushes in to take over from residents faced with a "Click OK to continue" box.*

**BUILDING SELF-ESCREEN**
LTP Patty Walsh has another method, which has made her a resident favorite. "I don't push residents to launch any programs; I don't think that's right," says Patty. "But I do bend that rule." According to Patty, here's what she does:

PATTY: Hi, (Resident), would you like to launch the screensaver?

RESIDENT: Yes. What do I do?

PATTY: Sit right there and don't touch the keyboard for eight minutes.

*(After the eight minutes go by, the screensaver kicks in.)*

PATTY: You did it!

RESIDENT: I did it!

If this sounds good to you, or someone you know, isn't it time you considered Silicon Pines?

DAIMLERCHRYSLER Co-Chairmen Juergen Schrempp (left) and the other guy.

# DAIMLER UNION WITH CHRYSLER A "MERGER OF EQUALS"

## Schrempp and Other Guy to Share Power, Responsibilities

IN A *historic, $92 billion deal that both sides touted as a "merger of equals," German auto giant Daimler-Benz announced last month it will merge with struggling American carmaker Chrysler Corporation to form a new company called* DAIMLERCHRYSLER. *The firm will be based in both Stuttgart, Germany, and Auburn Hills, Mich., and will be jointly led by Daimler's Juergen E. Schrempp and Chrysler's Robert J. Eaton. BusinessMonth Weekly briefly talked with the co-chairmen and co-chief executive officers in Eaton's office.*

**BMW:** You know, they say that in mergers and acquisitions, there are no mergers, only acquisitions. Rumor has it this one wasn't really equal, that Daimler only called it a merger to soothe the pride of the weaker Chrysler.

**SCHREMPP:** You have seen the memo? Someone has leaked it.

**EATON:** Ha ha. Such a kidder. That rumor's absurd. People think just because Daimler will come first in the name, just because Daimler shareholders will get 57 percent of the new company, and just because I agreed to step aside after three years so Juergen can...

**SCHREMPP:** Mr. Schrempp.

**EATON:** ...yes, so Mr. Schrempp can become sole chairman, that this is somehow unequal. They forget that we're still one of the Big Three automakers. We have significant market share, and Daimler is thrilled to join with us.

**BMW:** So now that the deal is done, it's not true that real power will rest with Daimler and that Chrysler will be subsumed?

**SCHREMPP:** Of course this is false. The Americans will continue to have complete autonomy. I fail to understand why you would even ask such a question.

**BMW:** Well, partly it's because you're sitting in his leather chair while Mr. Eaton is kneeling on the floor.

**SCHREMPP:** He likes the floor. Is better for his back.

**BMW:** He's also shining your shoes.

**SCHREMPP:** He is doing the exercising. Look, now he will shine his own shoes. Very great workout for the forearms, yes, Alan?

**EATON:** It's Robert.

**BMW:** Let me ask you about the new company name. If it's an equal partnership, why not ChryslerDaimler?

**SCHREMPP:** This is funny for you to ask. Just today I decide the name is too long. So I decide we will perhaps combine more, take the "ler" from Chrysler and the "Daim" from Daimler.

**BMW:** That would make it...Daimler.

**SCHREMPP:** Yes. Is better.

**EATON:** Ha, boy, great sense of humor.

**BMW:** So, sharing power at such a large company has got to be difficult. I assume you two converse regularly. What are the big issues you're dealing with now?

**EATON:** Oh, you know, the important stuff. Production schedules. Worldwide marketing promotions...

**SCHREMPP:** Kaffee.

**BMW:** Excuse me?

**EATON:** Whoa, look at the time. We'll have to end the interview now.

**SCHREMPP:** Kaffee. Get me some kaffee, Alan.

**EATON:** Ha. See? Told you. What a kidder. *Mein Herr, ix-nay on the orders-hay while the eporter-ray is ere-hay.* Well, that's all. You'll have to run.

**BMW:** I did have a few more questions.

**EATON:** Maybe later. Here, I'll show you out.

**SCHREMPP:** Alan. You will please make it black.

**BMW:** What did he say?

**EATON:** He said, "Robert, you will please make it back." He's so dependent sometimes. Guy can't make a move without me.

**SCHREMPP:** And no sugar this time.

# SUN RELEASES OFFICIAL MICROSOFT STANCE

## Reusable Statement Expected to Save Time, Money

Sun spokeswoman Andrea Letti shows reporters how the new statement should be used.

IN AN EFFORT to streamline corporate communications and eliminate redundancy, Sun Microsystems last week issued what it called its "official and final" statement on the company's relationship with rival Microsoft.

"Microsoft sucks," Sun said.

According to Andrea Letti, a spokeswoman for Palo Alto, Calif.–based Sun, the statement will now serve as the company's sole comment concerning Microsoft, its products, business practices, and subsidiaries. The purpose, Letti explained, is to reduce the amount of time Sun employees spend responding to "numerous, daily" questions about the software giant.

On Wall Street, Merrill Lynch immediately raised its rating on Sun from "accumulate" to "strong buy," arguing that the coarse nature of the statement heralds a decisive change of direction for the software and hardware maker.

"Very recently, Sun has been positioning itself as the company that 'put the dot in .com,'" Merrill analyst Rebecca Fraisling said in a research note. "However, nobody knows what that is supposed to mean. 'Microsoft sucks,' by comparison, is pretty self-explanatory."

In Redmond, Wash., a Microsoft spokesman refused to comment on Sun's derisive assertion, stating it was company policy not to respond to rumors.

Based on the "Write Once, Run Anywhere" slogan used by Sun to promote its Java programming language, the Microsoft statement relies on the concept, "Say it once, write it anywhere." Letti went on to explain how the new system will work:

"Let's say I'm a Sun vice president of marketing and you're a reporter. You ask what I think about Windows 98, or whatever. I say, 'Microsoft sucks.' You follow up and ask if I think Windows NT will cut into our operating system development. Again, I say, 'Microsoft sucks.' Or let's say you're from the Department of Justice and you ask if I think Microsoft is a monopoly. Doesn't matter. My answer's the same. 'Microsoft sucks.' End of interview."

Letti said Sun is now hopeful that reporters, analysts, shareholders, and legal officials won't "harass" the company with questions about Microsoft anymore. "It's why we issued it as an official release," she said. "You can use it whenever you want, in any story you want, and attribute it to any Sun executive you want. There's no expiration date."

While some industry observers quietly wondered if Sun should have used less blunt language, Hambrecht & Quist analyst Carlton Dortmund estimated the official stance should help Sun by keeping its executives on task and off the phone. Dortmund also said the "powerful language" and universal accessibility of the statement should increase Sun's brand awareness in the media.

Asked about Dortmund's comments, Letti started to answer, then wagged a finger. "Microsoft sucks," she said, smiling. "Nice try."

# SUPPORT THE CONTROLLED BURN OF DOTCOMS

Comparing the Internet to an uncontrolled and overcrowded forest, the Federal Reserve last week authorized a "prescribed burn" to incinerate the vast majority of Internet companies, a move the Fed hopes will thwart inflation by depriving the blazing U.S. economy of fuel.
To this we say, "Huzzah!"

According to Fed officials, burning down the buildings containing most Internet companies will not only deter growth, but will also increase the nation's "uncomfortably low" unemployment rate. That, in turn, will relieve inflationary wage pressures, as more unemployed workers compete for fewer openings.

The program immediately found support among the handful of dotcoms slated to avoid the flames, including AOL, Amazon, and eBay. But several thousand Internet companies identified as "scrub brush" were outraged, and threw what we can only call self-serving hissy fits. Listen to this whining from Stephan Paternot, co-CEO of potential conflagree theglobe.com: "I'll tell you right now, if the Feds come in here and try to set our building on fire, our 200 employees will fight with everything they have."

(Fed spokesman Kevin Keegan suggested globe employees try covering their building in their stock options, which, he noted, "have been under water for so long they'll never catch fire.")

Buy.com CEO Greg Hawkins, meanwhile, has resorted to fear-mongering as a means of protest. "I, for one, don't want to die," he said just after the announcement was made, "nor do I want to flee into the streets to save my life."

Oh, please. If he had read the notice, Hawkins would know that buildings, not individuals, are being targeted, and as for being forced into the streets, Keegan explained the Fed will first confiscate all properties via "eminent domain." Only then will buildings be set alight. "So it's not like these fires will actually force people and businesses out into the street," Keegan said. "We'll have forced them out at least a day earlier."

Fortunately, eBay CEO Meg Whitman provided a welcome voice of reason. She cited a Forrester Research report projecting that most dotcoms, (with no help from the government) will go out of business by the end of 2001, and that only three major players will be left in each category. "So you see," she said, "the fire is coming and it will consume almost everyone. The Fed solution will simply make the inevitable more orderly."

And more enriching. As Amazon.com CEO Jeff Bezos noted, the remains of former competitors will provide nourishment to those, like Amazon, left behind. "After a forest fire, mineral-rich ashes from plants are distributed into the soil by rains, thereby feeding the remaining flora," Bezos explained. "In the same way, employees of incinerated Internet firms will be soaked up by the survivors, thereby providing nutrients to maintain a healthy econosystem."

Hopefully, the Fed program will be carried out soon, and not just to steady the economy. It would also put an end to the self-indulgent protests of Candace Carpenter, CEO of women's portal and torch-list member iVillage, who has been on every CNBC program calling the idea of burning companies to the ground "preposterous. You simply cannot compare the Internet economy to a forest," she said.

As Bezos points out, however, she is wrong.

"It's easy," he noted. "You just call the big Net companies 'healthy trees,' and the smaller companies 'scrub brush' or 'weeds,' and there, you've done it."

## U.S. Worldview Threatened

# AMERICANS ANNOYED BY "ALL THIS INTERNATIONAL SHIT" ON INTERNET

THE PROFUSION of international news available on the Internet has made it increasingly difficult for the average American to ignore the rest of the world, a trend university researchers say threatens Americans' long, proud history of disregarding anything not about them.

"With all the foreign newspapers and multicultural sites, the Internet is making it almost impossible for the average American to remain uninformed and apathetic," said Samantha Lessborn of Washington State University, which conducted the nationwide survey. "Americans can still do it. But it now takes effort, whereas before it was as easy as turning off Tom Brokaw whenever he said, 'In South Korea today...'"

According to survey participant Danny Grisham, a 22-year-old from Cheyenne, Wyo., it's not just the plethora of international news on the Web that is irritating. "Look, I can get around the news. I just turn off Reuters headlines in MyYahoo," he said. "But even some of the search sites like Yahoo! and AltaVista are available in different languages. Like everybody in the world doesn't speak American.

"I can see where it's important if we're, like, beating some country in the Olympics or bombing them or, ideally, both," Grisham added. "But if some Colombian drug lord sinks a ferry full of Israeli soldiers in North Latvoania or Serbo-Malaysia, or wherever, and

Americans aren't involved, what has that got to do with me?"

Other respondents said they were appalled, not just by the availability of non-U.S. news, but by the way important U.S. news is reported by some of these foreign sites. "Yesterday, for instance, the St. Louis Rams beat the Atlanta Falcons, OK, and I go to the *London Times* site and it's not even there," said Chip Pernadge of Kansas City, Mo. "Jesus, no wonder those guys lost the war and had

to give Hong Kong back to Canada."

Sensing a market opportunity, Net Nanny, makers of Net Nanny filtering software, announced this week it will introduce NetNarrow, an English-only product that automatically filters out content that appears to be international. Specifically, the software looks for world datelines and keywords indicative of irrelevant foreign stories, including "Shiite," "post-Apartheid," and "Bob Geldof."

Survey-taker Craig Barker of Brooklyn, New York, said he will be among the first to get NetNarrow. "On the Web, there are so many ways to get news from so many different places, I could really get some fresh insights into what's going on in other countries if I wanted to," he said. "But I don't want to."

"You'd think these Internet people would know that," Barker added. "I mean, that's why the Internet is called America Online, right? It's supposed to be about America."

Get a load of these typos.
Colour ... theatre ...
realise ... defence ...

# FRONT END

# My Calendar

**David Wetherell, CEO of Internet holding company CMGI**

| | |
|---|---|
| 8 a.m. | Come up with e-commerce site idea |
| 9 a.m. | Decide what site will sell/do |
| 10 a.m. | Launch e-commerce site |
| 11 a.m. | Appear on CNBC |
| Noon | Lunch |
| 1 p.m. | Hold IPO for e-commerce site |
| 2 p.m. | Appear on CNBC |
| 3 p.m. | Use IPO proceeds to start B2B site |
| 4 p.m. | Decide what B2B site will do |
| 5 p.m. | Launch B2B site |
| 6 p.m. | Sell B2B site |
| 7 p.m. | Appear on CNBC |

## THE MRACEK EFFECT

John Mracek, President of Internet advertising firm AdKnowledge, announced today that while his name is only slightly longer than that of Bill Gates (Microsoft), Steve Case (AOL), and Jim Clark (Netscape/Healtheon), it is considerably more difficult to pronounce.

## WHERE DOTCOMS ARE SPENDING THEIR MONEY:

| | | |
|---|---|---|
| 1 | Marketing/advertising | 50 percent |
| 2 | Foosball equipment | 13 percent |
| 3 | Espresso machine | 12 percent |
| 4 | Pizza delivery | 8 percent |
| 5 | Weekly site redesign | 4 percent |
| 6 | Skittles | 5 percent |
| 7 | On-site car detailing | 4 percent |
| 8 | Patents | 3 percent |
| 9 | Product development | 1 percent |
| 10 | Business plan | <1 percent |

## NEW DOMAINS UNNECESSARY

Contradicting the testimony of other Internet firms, Indonesia's top English-speaking adult site, TurnInToYourOwnDesire.com, told a Senate panel last week it was having "no trouble" registering new and valuable .com domains, citing four it had registered in the past few weeks as proof that the need for additional top-level domains is exaggerated:

- LowValueSex.com
- ComeAtMePresently.com
- FreeHeatedSex.com
- YouAreToBeWantingMeBadAreYouNot.com

## FRONT END

### CDNow Wins Patent for Loss-Based Revenue Model

Online music seller CDNow, desperately in need of cash, may have staved off its demise by virtue of its recently awarded patent for "an Internet business model in which expenditures permanently exceed revenues." According to Jason Olim, CEO of the Fort Washington, Pa., firm, CDNow plans to vigorously defend its patent in a counter-suit filed against Amazon.com, which claims it established the model first.

### Man Continually Logs On/Off ObsessiveCompulsive.com

A 26-year-old British man has been unable to leave his computer for three weeks as he continually logs on and off ObsessiveCompulsive.com, a site catering specifically to those suffering from obsessive-compulsive disorder.

According to Oliver Pratt, president of Obsessive-Compulsive, Nathan Raintree of Liverpool has not been away from the site for more than 82 seconds since initially signing up more than 20 days ago. Like all members, Mr. Raintree can log off, said Pratt. But after doing so, he is automatically sent an email that says "Thanks for visiting ObsessiveCompulsive.com. By the way, did you log off the site? Are you sure? You should make sure. Click here to make sure."

"When he clicks, he is sent back to the site, where he's automatically logged on," Pratt explained. "It's really terrific. We can get, like, 12 million page views a day from just one guy."

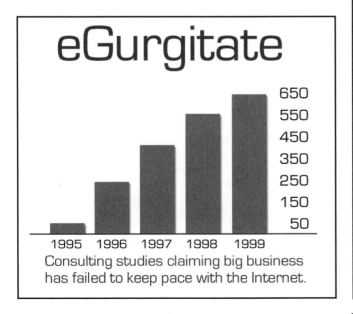

### eGurgitate

| | | | | |
|---|---|---|---|---|
| 1995 | 1996 | 1997 | 1998 | 1999 |

650
550
450
350
250
150
50

Consulting studies claiming big business has failed to keep pace with the Internet.

105

**A boarded-up click house in suburban Philadelphia. Neighbors won't complain for fear clickheads will sell their belongings on eBay.**

# FDA REGULATES INTERNET

## "Click Houses" Crop Up in Suburbs

CONCERNED BY numerous studies claiming the Internet is addictive, the U.S. Food and Drug Administration last week officially classified the Internet as a "controlled substance," a move that will force the nation's 60 million known users to seek a physician's prescription in order to access the Web.

The ruling was quickly condemned by Internet companies, which claim the decision will put them out of business and would likely create a vast black market in illegal Internet usage. Already, police across the nation report the sudden appearance of "click houses" in once genteel suburban neighborhoods — illegal dens recognizable by boarded-up windows (to prevent screen glare) and 24/7 traffic.

"These clickheads are coming and going at all hours, using shared passwords and, in some cases, sharing mice," said Howard Roper, the police chief in Blue Bell, Pa. Neighbors, he added, are afraid to speak out because some clickheads, especially those addicted to auction sites, threaten to sell their belongings on eBay if they complain.

While acknowledging the ruling was socially disruptive, the FDA said it had little choice. "Studies have proven that the Internet is addictive, and our mandate is to control the dispensation of addictive substances," said FDA Commissioner Jane E. Henney. The FDA ruling calls for Internet traffic measurement firms to change their terminology from "unique visitors" to "unique addicts," and will require that a safety label be included with each Internet prescription reading: "Warning: This product may cause day trading."

Anti-drug forces generally applauded the decision, although they said it didn't go far enough. "While we agree that the Internet should not be easily available, we also believe the Internet should first be tested on animals to discern its physiological and psychological impact," said Hallie Minor, director of Citizens Against Drugs. Minor spoke at a press conference organized by Tipper Gore, who plans to launch a nationwide "Just Say Internyet" campaign, which she hopes will convince young people to stay away from the Web.

Not surprisingly, Gore's plan was condemned by San Francisco-based URL-UP, which has started "mice exchange" programs, allowing users to turn in their used, dirty mice and trackballs for clean, new ones. "We are in no way advocating Internet usage," said URL-UP director Mike Barnovic. "But no matter what Mrs. Gore says, the fact is that people are going to use the Internet, so let's make it as safe as possible."

Internet companies, meanwhile, have strenuously objected to the classification of the Internet as a drug, and say they will fight the ruling. "To label the Internet a drug is absurd," said David Wetherell, head of holding company CMGI. "It is, if anything, a cult."

Added RealNetworks CEO Rob Glaser: "No, it's not a drug or a cult. It's a process."

"Oh, like smelting?" Wetherell replied.

"Yes, that's right," said Glaser. "Just like smelting."

**TREND SETTERS: CARLY FIORINA**

# NEW HP CHIEF CAN DO STRADDLE JUMP

Talk about setting a trend. In July, Carleton "Carly" Fiorina was appointed as the new chief executive officer of Hewlett-Packard, which instantly became the largest public corporation ever led by a woman, and made Fiorina, at age 44, the only female CEO among the 30 companies making up the Dow Jones Industrial Average.

The job won't be easy. She takes over a company with 123,000 employees and $47 billion in annual revenue, but one that acknowledges it missed out on the Internet's early growth and has some catching up to do. We caught up with Fiorina via telephone in her Palo Alto, Calif., office.

**BUSINESSMONTH WEEKLY:** Ms. Fiorina, with your appointment, you are now the only chief executive of a Dow company who is capable of doing a straddle jump. What does that mean to you?
**FIORINA:** Sorry?

**BMW:** A straddle jump. The cheerleading move where you jump up in the air and spread your legs and touch your toes. The other Dow guys — and that's the problem, they're guys, right? — can't do one. OK, some guy gymnasts can do 'em, but...
**FIORINA:** Excuse me, but what does this have to do with Hewlett-Packard?

**BMW:** Well, it really puts you ahead of the competition. And not just with the Dow guys. You look at the chief execs at Compaq or Dell or Gateway or Sun (Microsystems), I'll bet they can barely get off the ground. Like Michael Dell's gonna do a split. Right.
**FIORINA:** I hate to disappoint you, but cheerleading ability had nothing to do with why I was given this job. Before this I was president of Lucent Technologies' Global Service Provider group, the company's largest and fastest-growing division, which accounted for 60 percent of Lucent's total revenues. Before that I was...

**BMW:** A receptionist.
**FIORINA:** No! I mean, yes, but that's not the point. God, you're acting just like all the other business press. From the moment I was appointed, they talked about how stylish I was, how I wear Armani suits, how I was once a receptionist, how I was a "perky, cheerleader" type. You don't see anyone writing about Warren Buffet's hairdo, or Lou Gerstner's pouty lips.

**BMW:** Right, but whose fault is that?
**FIORINA:** Come again?

**BMW:** Well, you're a woman.
**FIORINA:** Of course I'm a woman. But there's more to me and my job than gender. Now if you can't get off that subject and get on to something else...

**BMW:** I suppose I could ask you about your e-services initiative.
**FIORINA:** You could, yes. With the help of HP's great management team, I intend to make the company a major player in the second chapter of the Internet, and our e-services, where at the enterprise level we will strive to invest in and invent on the Internet platform, will be a primary factor in that.

**BMW:** Uh huh, uh huh...so, what are you wearing?

# FRONT END

## OFFICE POLL

### IF THE CAMEL MELTS...

| | |
|---|---|
| I WILL NO LONGER BE INTERESTED IN THE CAMEL. | 45% |
| SUPPLY WILL RISE, DEMAND WILL FALL, INVEST IN CAMELS! | 28% |
| AT LAST, A USE FOR THAT STRAW | 15% |
| WAXY DESERT BUILDUP | 12% |

**PEPSICO FINDS NEW CFO ON STOCK MESSAGE BOARDS:** Pepsico Corp. recently announced it has ended its search for a new chief financial officer with the surprise hiring of Stockpicker_Dude_78, a frequent poster on The Motley Fool's stock message boards. "We interviewed about 20 people, most from Fortune 500 corporations, but Stockpicker_Dude stood out," said Pepsico CEO Roger Enrico. "For instance, when we asked this one CFO candidate about working for Pepsi, she said she would be 'honored to join such a progressive, respected company,'" Enrico recalled. "But Stockpicker_Dude's response — 'This stock will be $100+ by end of month! Shorts cover your asses!' — was much more spirited." In a brief statement, Stockpicker_Dude said he heard Pepsico was a major takeover target, and added he would be loading up on the stock in the morning.

## HOUSE SENDS SPAM BILL TO SENATE; SENATE SPAM FILTER DELETES IT

The anti-spam bill passed by the U.S. House of Representatives earlier this month was sent to the Senate this week, but the Senate's spam filtering software automatically determined it was junk mail and deleted it. Amy Lee, Chief System Administrator of the Senate, defended the software's actions: "Our filter recognizes the email addresses of anyone known to propagate junk," she said. "This one came from house.gov. Of course the program blocked it."

Undeterred, House leaders vowed to send the Unsolicited Electronic Mail Act again. "We sent that bill to the Senate because they were referred or requested additional information," said Rep. Heather Wilson, R-N.M. "I don't want to waste their time or ours, but we are seeking positive, motivated individuals that are serious about voting for this bill."

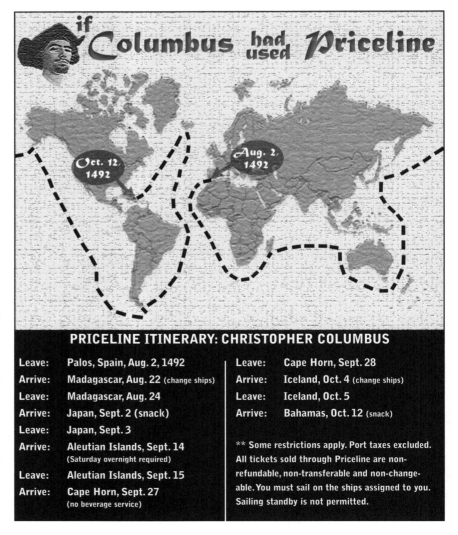

**if Columbus had used Priceline**

### PRICELINE ITINERARY: CHRISTOPHER COLUMBUS

| | | | | |
|---|---|---|---|---|
| Leave: | Palos, Spain, Aug. 2, 1492 | | Leave: | Cape Horn, Sept. 28 |
| Arrive: | Madagascar, Aug. 22 (change ships) | | Arrive: | Iceland, Oct. 4 (change ships) |
| Leave: | Madagascar, Aug. 24 | | Leave: | Iceland, Oct. 5 |
| Arrive: | Japan, Sept. 2 (snack) | | Arrive: | Bahamas, Oct. 12 (snack) |
| Leave: | Japan, Sept. 3 | | | |
| Arrive: | Aleutian Islands, Sept. 14 (Saturday overnight required) | | | |
| Leave: | Aleutian Islands, Sept. 15 | | | |
| Arrive: | Cape Horn, Sept. 27 (no beverage service) | | | |

** Some restrictions apply. Port taxes excluded. All tickets sold through Priceline are non-refundable, non-transferable and non-changeable. You must sail on the ships assigned to you. Sailing standby is not permitted.

# WORK OR FAMILY?
# FAMILY OR WORK?

**In the 24/7 economy, your choice is clear: work. But nothing drags on success at work like the guilt you feel when you're not spending enough time at home.**
**Now there is a solution.**

## FamilyFetch.com — Rent a Life
**Virtual Family in Under an Hour. Guaranteed.**

**Using our familyfetch network, we will deliver one or more of our "virtual family members" to fill in for you at home, whatever the need may be.**

This could be someone pretending to be you!

Who could possibly replace you? How about...

a way strong soldier Dad?

or a way cool Yoga Dad?

"The first time I used FamilyFetch, my 7-year-old called me at work and said, 'Mom, there's a woman here who says she's my mother,' and I said, 'Look, I don't have time for this. Let her in.'"
— Jane Gaites, Richmond, Va.

109

# his words enlighten and encourage the

# e

# way of life

AT ETOYS, it is said, Chief Executive Toby Lenk keeps a copy of the searching, evocative i:opt:in stapled to his chest. At Amazon.com, CEO Jeff Bezos has wept openly while reading the heart-rending fulfillmentness to new company employees. And at AOL, Steve Case reportedly hired Barry White to record the inspirational i e therefore i am so he could listen to the poem on his way to work each day.

Clearly, no other poet — and perhaps no other individual — has so moved the legions online as has e.e. commerce, whose poems, with their seemingly scatological syntax, are infused with the fast-paced, often steamy, yet eternally hopeful commercial potential that is the Internet.

The best-known of the so-called "Internet Poets" — whose swelling ranks include DSLiot, William Keywords Worth, and Elizabeth Barrett Browsing — commerce is considered a master of the genre. As Davis Galt, culture editor of *Computer World*, wrote of commerce: "He guts the Internet as a fisherman does a perch, yet the perch is better for the gutting, for his knife is love."

For Galt, and millions of others, there is no greater example of this than commerce's e-ishness unflowering. Not unlike the sweet courtship and inevitable consummation of youth, the poem depicts an online buyer's first moments of innocent hesitation, which in Internet time quickly becomes commitment and, at last, the naked, breathless sale.

## i thank You Tim
### by e.e. commerce

(An Ode To World Wide Web Pioneer Tim Berners-Lee)

*the feeling at first*
*is who wants this information. the*
*key*
*to me-my-password-my-visa*
*are they repute-able; then ifso*
*encrypt:secure, i am*

*my bottom line approves,*
*and encrypted kisses are a far*
*better fate*
*than driving to the store; unwise*
*shopper i swear by all that is*
*online. don't cry*
*type in cc,expiration and*
*leaning back.wait; for fulfillment*
*for*
*life's not always that which can*
*betouched.*
*(and breasts soflat*
*offline. are online made full)*

i thank You Tim for most this amazing
thing-electronic-thing
spirits soar profits soar people
click
clickclick they buy
a true dream of productness;and for everything
which is natural which is infinite which is
yes
yes:i opt-in for your mailing list.

i consumer of this Internet most
new most:in-
complete. intense
-its scripted kisses, make
my heart-soar-my-wallet-
light the way oh sylvan:seducer oh
perlant debaucher
i am your whore your broadband access me feed me your sweet
cookies. i part-my-lips i drop-my-packets
before you
yahoo!

i brickish retailer who had died am born
again today,
and your foresight;website is the birthday
gift;
you have givenme great. presence of web
(and life and love and earnings unattainable:
before the great happening illimitably
Internet)

(now the customers of my customers
awake and
now the distributors of my distributors are
worried)

Yet at times, commerce's same word-knives of love can form a lethal stiletto aimed at those unwilling to recognize their place in an e-world. The most cited instance of this comes, not from a reviewer, but from a watershed moment in the history of online retailing.

One night in early 1998, Egghead CEO George Orban was reading commerce's mort d'bricks, which had been emailed to him by a friend. It was no coincidence that, three days later, Egghead announced it would close all its retail stores and sell only online.

"I won't say mort d'bricks alone led to our decision to go Web-only," recalls Orban, now chairman of Egghead.com. "But you can't read the lines:

*'tectonic shifter i. mother;of*
*new channels weep:weeping:weep-*
*ishness*
*for those, so old. so off-*
*line. real-doors-real-windows-real-*
*losses. Where*
*is their domain?death.com'*

without feeling that you should do something, and do it now."

There are those, however, who feel commerce has gotten more than his due. Poetic colleague Elizabeth Barrett Browsing, for instance, insists not all the Internet Poets consider commerce the star pupil of their class. While "wonderfully talented," commerce is too narrowly focused, she maintains.

"He misses the full experience of the Web. It's not just commerce, it's also content" — a reference to one of commerce's more contentious poems, *where commerceis i am, con.tent*, in which the poet argues that content alone cannot satisfy online. It must, he insists, be accompanied by a call to buy.

And there are harsher critics. "e.e. commerce is a talentless huckster," says David O. Cotterdam, professor of linguistics at Harvard University. "That he is even called a poet shows the depths to which we as a post-literary society have sunk in pursuit of this crass Internet mania."

It should be noted that Cotterdam's latest collection of poems, *Webs Are for Spiders*, was panned by a reviewer at Amazon.com.

And yet, to devoted fans like Susan Housingham, senior product developer at software maker CyberCash, commerce is a mother figure, giving birth to the realization that the Internet is not simply a way to make money, but a valid way of life. In particular, Housingham points to commerce's *all in navigator gold* — about a group of coworkers browsing the Web — which she says beautifully encapsulates a typical Internet experience, and how, "in the end, we are all caught up in this wonderful Web."

*all in navigator gold went my*
*browser exploring*
*at a great high-speed of band-*
*widthishness*
*into the silver Web.*

*four lean colleagues crouched low*
*and smiling*
*o'er my shoulder watched:the*
*merry dancingbaby fleetly*
*we clickedthru; pursuing perchance*
*to purchase*
*the swift sweet cd*
*the cheap coach class seat*
*amazonpriceline. we live in this*
*great*
*beyond.com*

*i am locked in; (like a kiss everlasting*
*a love ever-evolving*
*an impressive monthly mortgage*
*from e-loan)*
*to this internet eternal. I.*
*and you?*

# CAN ANYONE MAKE MONEY BUILDING THE BUG?

## ViruSystems Also Plans to Place Advertisements in Viruses

*VIRUSES ARE one of the truly great threats to the wired economy, but to Lonell Navisem, they represent something else entirely: the largest untapped market in Internet history.*

*Navisem, 24, is the founder and CEO of ViruSystems, an aggressive and highly controversial start-up that intends to manufacture and sell computer viruses. BusinessMonth Weekly sat down with Navisem in his office in the Malaysian capital of Kuala Lumpur to discuss ViruSystem's groundbreaking, and ethically suspect, business model.*

**BUSINESSMONTH WEEKLY:** Lonell, just so we have this straight, you intend to manufacture and sell computer viruses, and also to act as an intermediary between IVMs (Independent Virus Makers) and the virus program consumer, taking a percentage of each sale. In other words, you intend to profit from the manufacture and propagation of chaos.

**NAVISEM:** No, no, no. We will not propagate the chaos. It is the current system that propagates the chaos. Currently, the crackers or coders or script kiddies, whatever you wish to call them, are creating viruses with no oversight. And they are primarily motivated by malice and curiosity. Therefore, by placing viruses in the commercial domain, we effectively wrestle the power away from these nihilistic hands and place it firmly within the more rigid, responsible capitalist system, where there is oversight and, we believe, immense revenue potential.

**BMW:** So, how did you come up with this idea?

**NAVISEM:** It was the Melissa virus that opened my eyes. That thing has already had many, many mutations. It has gone out to millions of computer users. But for all of that, in the end, do you know what it will be remembered as?

**BMW:** A multibillion-dollar catastrophe.

**NAVISEM:** Yes, of course, but you are not thinking the big picture. That virus, my friend, was the biggest bulk email in history, and it did not carry advertising. Talk about a catastrophe.

**BMW:** That's...that's sick.

**NAVISEM:** I agree. You say to yourself, "How could such a huge mass marketing opportunity go unmonetized?" Turns the stomach. So we are going to change that. Not only will we make and sell viruses, but we will sell advertising space in the message that goes with each virus unit.

**BMW:** Ad space? Who would want to place an advertisement in a virus email?
**NAVISEM:** How about the anti-virus software makers such as Symantec and McAfee? There is real synergy for them. In a single email, you get a virus and an offer to buy the vaccine. Or they could advertise in the virus itself once it is activated. So while the virus is destroying files, a screen could pop up telling you that you have been infected, and please click here for the antidote. It is a direct marketing dream. And also offers true convenience for the end user. Such a win-win, I do not know why nobody has thought of this before.

**BMW:** Maybe because this whole thing sounds illegal?
**NAVISEM:** But it is not. Well, not here in Malaysia. It is illegal to distribute viruses, but as you know, we are not distributors. We are only going to manufacture and sell the viruses, and sell ad space. What customers do with the product is their business.

**BMW:** But don't you think that what they're going to do with the product is infect other computers?
**NAVISEM:** Not necessarily. It could be, say, virus aficionados trying to complete their collections. For instance, let us say they have a 1997 Strange Brew virus, and a 1999 Melissa, but they need the 1999 BubbleBoy. Or perhaps it will not be the collectors. Maybe people will also buy these viruses as a form of self-defense.

**BMW:** Self-defense.
**NAVISEM:** Yes. You know, "Do not mess with me mister. I am packing the bad code." It helps level the pitch. We give the law-abiding Netizen access to the same weaponry that the criminals have. That is what your American gun lobby is all about, is it not?

**BMW:** Hence your marketing slogan.
**NAVISEM:** Yes. "When computer viruses are outlawed, only outlaws will have computer viruses." But we are much more diverse than your gun industry. We make and sell weaponry, but we also have an additional revenue stream: we sell advertising space on the bullets.

**BMW:** But let me ask you this: viruses are free, so why would coders bent on random acts of malice bother to spend money on what they now make or get for nothing?
**NAVISEM:** It may not cost them money. It depends on what option they choose.

**BMW:** Option?
**NAVISEM:** Yes. They could pay $50 for a one-time license to a virus that carries no advertising, or they could opt for the ad-supported virus and pay nothing.

**BMW:** But why would they bother with your viruses since your products will support the "system" so many of them despise?

"It is so obvious, I don't know why nobody has thought of it before."

Maybe because it's illegal?

**NAVISEM:** Put yourself in their fingers. If they have the option to build or obtain a virus that does little more than send itself out to everyone in your address book, or obtain an outrageously virulent, quality-controlled piece of code that erases hard drives or whole networks of hard drives, we think they will happily choose the latter.

**BMW:** Quality control?
**NAVISEM:** Yes. Some viruses are very poorly constructed and easily beaten. I personally see to it that each of our viruses goes through a thorough 10-step quality-control process to guarantee its long life and destructive capability.

**BMW:** Not that you advocate using viruses for such a purpose.
**NAVISEM:** Of course not. Well, I must be going. I have the 2000 LoveBug to test.

**BMW:** LoveBug? That some new virus you'll be issuing?
**NAVISEM:** Oh, yes. Very promising. I am sure you will be hearing about it eventually.

**BMW:** Gee, I can't wait.
**NAVISEM:** Okay, no problem. I will just put you on our mailing list.

**ViruSystems**

**BASED:** Kuala Lumpur, Malaysia

**FOUNDED:** 1999

**CEO:** Lonell Navisem

**BUSINESS:** Manufacture and sell computer viruses, and act as a reseller for IVMs (Independent Virus Makers)

**SLOGAN:** "If Viruses Are Outlawed, Only Outlaws Will Have Viruses"

**RAISON D'OT:** People say email is the killer app, or they say e-commerce is the killer app, but viruses are, quite literally, the killer app, and we intend to capture that market.

# WHY STOCKS WILL NEVER GO DOWN - STORY ON A3

e C6

| PE | VOL 100S | LAST | NET CHG |
|---|---|---|---|
| ... | 2828 | 28.40 | +2.94 |
| ... | 874 | 5.70 | +0.05 |
| 22 | 569 | 2.59 | +0.01 |
| cc | 2554 | 16.10 | +0.45 |
| dd | 1157 | 16.80 | +0.46 |
| dd | 82 | 0.88 | +0.10 |
| dd | 253 | 2.53 | +0.02 |
| 33 | 318 | 28.18 | +0.17 |
| dd | 5228 | 66.62 | +1.06 |
| 8 | 361 | 13.61 | +0.45 |
| 25 | 559 | 15.10 | +0.15 |
| 29 | 154 | 38.50 | +0.15 |
| ... | 848 | 4.35 | +0.15 |
| cc | 28882 | 72.96 | +2.00 |
| 29 | 2122 | 29.59 | +0.51 |
| dd | 525 | 17.53 | +0.67 |
| dd | 128 | 1.17 | +0.08 |
| ... | 19 | 33 | ... |
| ... | 16 | 28.20 | +0.10 |
| ... | 11 | 1.90 | +0.25 |
| 16 | 350 | 2.45 | + ... |
| dd | 3300 | 23.60 | +0.30 |
| 26 | 82 | 15.91 | +0.01 |
| 10 | 311 | 8.58 | +0.18 |
| dd | 2327 | 23.55 | +0.51 |
| ... | 165 | 20.64 | +0.34 |
| dd | 2240 | 34.73 | +3.25 |
| ... | 2465 | 8.90 | +0.25 |
| dd | 3328 | 17.67 | +0.15 |
| 86 | 960 | 41.10 | +1.13 |
| 10 | 256 | 22.92 | +0.08 |
| dd | 5 | 4.26 | +0.11 |
| dd | 1055 | 16.51 | +0.20 |
| dd | 2515 | 5.10 | +0.10 |
| 7 | 409 | 17.20 | +0.12 |
| dd | 1878 | 3.39 | +0.15 |
| ... | 326 | 2.29 | +0.06 |
| dd | 74265 | 23.24 | +0.29 |
| dd | 161 | 3.19 | ... |
| 21 | 1409 | 13.05 | +0.55 |
| dd | 362 | 0.89 | +0.09 |
| dd | 783 | 3.75 | +0.03 |
| ... | 33164 | 0.70 | +0.01 |
| 12 | 89 | 27.59 | +0.44 |
| dd | 1383 | 14.12 | +0.28 |
| ... | 1 | 12 | +0.50 |
| dd | 108 | 1.48 | +0.02 |
| dd | 2657 | 2.31 | +0.16 |
| dd | 484 | 0.90 | +0.10 |
| 18 | 6 | 10.97 | +0.13 |
| dd | 336 | 10.70 | +0.27 |
| 33 | 2939 | 31.23 | +0.43 |
| 9 | 207 | 2.85 | +0.09 |
| dd | 427 | 1.48 | +0.22 |
| ... | 92 | 1.16 | ... |
| dd | 293 | 3.04 | +0.07 |
| ... | 2552 | 1.96 | +0.05 |
| dd | 383 | 2.61 | +0.14 |
| dd | 9422 | 55.87 | +1.03 |
| dd | 2275 | 6.08 | +0.03 |
| dd | 77 | 9.80 | +0.20 |
| dd | 102 | 2.54 | +0.03 |
| dd | 4295 | 1.99 | +0.05 |
| 56 | 43093 | 16.71 | +0.15 |
| dd | 2958 | 17.90 | +0.14 |
| ... | 2058 | 17.80 | +0.30 |
| 52 | 1047 | 44.55 | +1.24 |
| dd | 717 | 11.20 | +0.02 |
| dd | 1188 | 1.20 | +0.03 |
| dd | 401 | 0.34 | +0.01 |
| dd | 124 | 2.98 | +0.02 |
| 18 | 2836 | 18.20 | +0.68 |
| 20 | 1251 | 27.02 | +0.45 |
| dd | 108 | 2 | ... |
| dd | 3834 | 24.20 | +0.20 |
| 17 | 420 | 18.98 | +0.23 |
| 15 | 718 | 17.55 | +0.15 |
| 14 | 132 | 24.31 | +0.44 |
| ... | 56 | 25.75 | +0.15 |
| 11 | 32 | 5.05 | +0.05 |
| 16 | 29 | 16.41 | +0.04 |
| dd | 745 | 4.90 | +0.10 |
| dd | 60 | 4.86 | +0.16 |
| dd | 235 | 1.30 | +0.10 |
| dd | 97 | 1.97 | -0.03 |
| ... | 30 | 0.20 | +0.03 |
| ... | 465 | 8.34 | +0.14 |
| dd | 41 | 0.96 | +0.09 |
| ... | 23 | 7.60 | +0.20 |
| ... | 29 | 7.24 | +0.03 |
| dd | 1240 | 1.61 | +0.21 |
| ... | 475 | 8.20 | +0.96 |
| dd | 162 | 1.70 | ... |
| dd | 18057 | 21.12 | +2.06 |
| ... | 2720 | 2.26 | +0.05 |
| dd | 721 | 8.89 | +0.30 |
| ... | 4170 | 8.08 | +0.59 |
| ... | 32069 | 5.66 | +0.06 |
| 29 | 447 | 11.78 | +0.84 |
| ... | 12551 | 4 | +0.06 |
| 74 | 717 | 74 | +4.00 |
| dd | 1193 | 5.15 | +0.31 |
| dd | 409 | 0.24 | ... |
| 16 | 224 | 12.30 | +0.30 |
| dd | 9938 | 33.27 | +1.27 |
| ... | 997 | 4.27 | +0.07 |
| dd | 29225 | 10.39 | +0.39 |
| 13 | 956 | 5.93 | +0.06 |
| dd | 114 | 6.30 | +0.42 |
| 18 | 408 | 13.26 | +0.22 |

| YTD % CHG | 52 WEEKS HI | LO | STOCK (SYM) | DIV | YLD % | PE | VOL 100S | LAST | NET CHG |
|---|---|---|---|---|---|---|---|---|---|
| +45.8 | 48.94 | 11.63 | IntrIntgnc ININ | | ... | dd | 130 | 13.07 | +0.16 |
| +15.6 | 32.35 | 16.88 | InterCeptGp ICPT | | ... | dd | 161 | 30.85 | +0.60 |
| +31.4 | 18.88 | 12 | ♣IntrchngFnl IFCJ | .54 | 3.0 | 12 | 2 | 18.07 | +0.13 |
| +62.4 | 5.06 | 0.28 | InterDent DENT | | ... | dd | 80 | 0.47 | ... |
| +171.7 | 25 | 4.50 | ♣IntrDgtl IDCC | | ... | ... | 1521 | 14.69 | +0.24 |
| +18.6 | 6.81 | 2.29 | Interep IREP | | ... | dd | 1192 | 4.15 | +0.04 |
| +24.8 | 11 | 3.25 | ♣IntrfaceInc IFSIA | .18 | 2.8 | 11 | 593 | 6.53 | +0.08 |
| +147.5 | 15.97 | 5.16 | IntrgrphCp INGR | | ... | 53 | 3431 | 14.85 | +0.39 |
| +4.3 | 24 | 16 | Intrgroup INTG | | ... | ... | 6 | 19.15 | +0.14 |
| +64.3 | 12 | 1.06 | ♣Interland ILND n | | ... | dd | 159 | 1.25 | +0.03 |
| +60.8 | 28.81 | 0.72 | Interliant INIT | | ... | dd | 435 | 1.25 | +0.04 |
| +24.4 | 50 | 2.91 | IntrlkElctr LINK | | ... | 33 | 927 | 9.59 | +0.09 |
| +8.3 | 4.34 | 1.44 | IntlnqSftwr INLQ | | ... | dd | 3 | 2.20 | +0.30 |
| +29.0 | 26 | 9.50 | Interlogix ILXI | | ... | dd | 201 | 24.34 | +0.64 |
| +146.3 | 45.88 | 3.63 | IntrmedComm ICIX | | ... | dd | 11626 | 17.70 | +0.14 |
| +39.3 | 10.19 | 2.50 | IntermetCp INMT | .16 | 3.2 | 4 | 145 | 5.05 | +0.05 |
| +12.7 | 55.88 | 12.50 | InterMune ITMN | | ... | ... | 3224 | 38.95 | +0.09 |
| +68.0 | 54.25 | 0.77 | InterNAP INAP | | ... | dd | 4855 | 2.32 | +0.09 |
| ▲+30.4 | 44.02 | 30 | IntBcshCp IBOC s | 1.00 | 2.3 | ... | 55 | 44.50 | +0.99 |
| +13.3 | 27.50 | 1.50 | IntFibercom IFCI | | ... | dd | 3610 | 4.28 | +0.25 |
| +11.6 | 48 | 30.13 | IntSpeedwy A ISCA | .06 | .1 | 39 | 1945 | 42.39 | +0.39 |
| +37.6 | 6.25 | 0.28 | InternetAm GEEK | | ... | dd | 683 | 0.86 | +0.18 |
| +29.9 | 45.19 | 1.22 | InternetCap ICGE | | ... | dd | 12005 | 2.30 | +0.07 |
| +30.7 | 5.75 | 0.25 | IntComrcComm ICCX | | ... | ... | 997 | 0.26 | +0.03 |
| +11.3 | 21 | 1.86 | IntrntComrc A ICCA | | ... | dd | 267 | 3.20 | +0.04 |
| +52.6 | 10.63 | 0.68 | IntrntGold IGLD | | ... | dd | 141 | 0.80 | ... |
| +2.5 | 68.44 | 6.75 | IntrntInt IIJI | | ... | ... | 184 | 8.93 | +0.07 |
| +29.8 | 20.38 | 0.13 | IntnetPic IPIX | | ... | dd | 3605 | 0.68 | +0.01 |
| +32.6 | 108.75 | 19.75 | IntrntSec ISSX | | ... | cc | 12279 | 52.84 | +0.84 |
| ▲+622.0 | 8.89 | 1.16 | IntneurPharm IPIC | | ... | dd | 27186 | 9.25 | +0.40 |
| +21.2 | 27.75 | 5.22 | Interphase INPH | | ... | 28 | 197 | 6.94 | +0.05 |
| +0.7 | 4.03 | 1.31 | IntrplyEntn IPLY | | ... | ... | 1217 | 2.58 | ... |
| +28.0 | 12.38 | 3.09 | Interpore BONZ | | ... | 18 | 325 | 5.04 | ... |
| +87.4 | 34.88 | 1.25 | INTERSHOP ADS ISHP n | | ... | ... | 52 | 1.90 | +0.10 |
| +63.9 | 67.31 | 13.56 | Intersil ISIL | | ... | ... | 32401 | 37.60 | +1.56 |
| +78.7 | 17.25 | 6.19 | InterTel INTL | .04 | .3 | ... | 699 | 13.74 | +0.36 |
| +46.7 | 27.75 | 1.70 | IntertrTch ITRU | | ... | dd | 3177 | 1.80 | +0.15 |
| +64.8 | 14 | 5.63 | IntrVoiceBr INTV | | ... | 41 | 2373 | 38.53 | +0.71 |
| +51.4 | 24.44 | 0.72 | IntrwvComm IWAV | | ... | dd | 361 | 0.76 | +0.04 |
| +37.5 | 68.47 | 5.84 | Interwoven IWOV s | | ... | dd | 24244 | 20.59 | +0.71 |
| +13.7 | 18.88 | 5 | IntestCp INTT | | ... | 9 | 24 | 7.25 | +0.35 |
| +72.2 | 7.25 | 3 | ♣Intevac IVAC | | ... | dd | 13 | 5.38 | +0.13 |
| +81.7 | 33 | 1.58 | IntraBio IBPI | | ... | dd | 4631 | 1.76 | ... |
| +24.5 | 64 | 14.75 | IntranetSol INRS | | ... | dd | 2373 | 38.53 | +1.14 |
| +8.9 | 21.44 | 0.77 | Intraware ITRA | | ... | ... | 585 | 1.60 | +0.10 |
| +10.7 | 15.50 | 3.20 | IntrogenThera INGN n | | ... | ... | 513 | 6.25 | ... |
| +32.2 | 17.25 | 2.75 | ♣Intrusion INTZ | | ... | dd | 251 | 3.22 | +0.02 |
| +9.7 | 69.31 | 22.63 | Intuit INTU | | ... | dd | 22472 | 35.62 | +1.14 |
| +5.6 | 19.06 | 3 | IntutvSrgcl ISRG n | | ... | dd | 2625 | 8.02 | +0.06 |
| +22.4 | 96 | 32.75 | InvFnlSvc IFIN s | .08 | .1 | 58 | 3452 | 66.74 | +1.52 |
| +3.2 | 17 | 10 | InvTitl ITIC | .12 | .8 | 11 | 8 | 15.25 | +0.25 |
| +143.5 | 5.13 | 1.31 | InvisionTch INVN | | ... | dd | 356 | 3.50 | +0.12 |
| +10.4 | 87.44 | 38.50 | ♣Invitrogen IVGN | | ... | dd | 8187 | 77.38 | +0.53 |
| +4.2 | 11.88 | 7.13 | ♣Invivo SAFE | | ... | 12 | 5 | 9.83 | ... |
| +118.7 | 6.75 | 0.28 | IonNtwks IONN | | ... | dd | 317 | 0.82 | +0.04 |
| +4.3 | 8.44 | 0.28 | iPrint.com IPRT | | ... | dd | 2407 | 0.75 | +0.31 |
| +21.6 | 11.25 | 7.75 | IpswichBsh IPSW | .44 | 4.0 | 10 | 1 | 11.10 | +0.15 |
| +5.0 | 24.88 | 13.25 | IrwinFnl IRWNE | .26 | 1.2 | 13 | 73 | 22.24 | +0.24 |
| +3.6 | 9 | 3.41 | IscoInc ISKO | .15j | ... | dd | 2 | 6.75 | ... |
| +15.4 | 15.75 | 7.88 | IsisPharm ISIP | | ... | dd | 1186 | 12.26 | +0.22 |
| +21.9 | 17.75 | 6.44 | ♣IsleCapris ISLE | | ... | 9 | 403 | 8.30 | +0.11 |
| +60.0 | 4 | 0.50 | Isolyser OREX | | ... | ... | 306 | 1.60 | +0.07 |
| +74.7 | 14.63 | 2.59 | IstaPharma ISTA n | | ... | ... | 1716 | 2.85 | +0.10 |
| +4.2 | 66.63 | 41.50 | ItoYokado IYCOY | .45e | .9 | ... | 24 | 50.61 | -0.89 |
| +299.4 | 15.50 | 3.14 | ♣Itron ITRI | | ... | 38 | 714 | 14.48 | +0.38 |
| +26.0 | 6.75 | 3.18 | IvanhoeEngy IVAN n | | ... | ... | 879 | 3.70 | +0.10 |
| +57.2 | 9.06 | 0.38 | iVillage IVIL | | ... | dd | 3412 | 1.67 | +0.01 |
| +39.5 | 39 | 9.94 | Ixia XXIA n | | ... | ... | 5554 | 17.30 | +0.96 |
| +56.0 | 22 | 0.69 | iXL Ent IIXL | | ... | dd | 7744 | 1.56 | +0.14 |
| | | | -J-J-J- | | | | | | |
| +89.6 | 20.75 | 7 | JAKKS Pac JAKK | | ... | 12 | 5554 | 17.30 | +0.68 |
| +36.8 | 23.79 | 12.50 | ♣J&JSnackFd JJSF | | ... | 25 | 1239 | 23 | +0.15 |
| +26.3 | 20.13 | 7.19 | JDA SftwrGp JDAS | | ... | 46 | 1112 | 16.50 | ... |
| +30.7 | 29.50 | 6.80 | JD Edwards JDEC | | ... | dd | 2083 | 12.34 | +0.39 |
| +59.1 | 140.50 | 13.06 | JDS Uniphs JDSU | | ... | dd | 230323 | 17.06 | +0.53 |
| +16.4 | 30.50 | 5.53 | JJillGp JILL | | ... | 14 | 442 | 18.04 | +0.06 |
| +9.1 | 4.38 | 0.75 | JLM Ind JLMI | | ... | ... | 217 | 2.25 | +0.03 |
| +23.1 | 12.50 | 2.50 | ♣JMAR JMAR | | ... | dd | 400 | 4 | +0.13 |
| +29.0 | 126 | 5.75 | J N I Cp JNIC | | ... | 34 | 3641 | 16.10 | +0.25 |
| +24.2 | 6.25 | 3.25 | JPS Ind JPST | | ... | dd | 66 | 5.90 | +0.06 |
| +246.7 | 14 | 0.88 | j2 GlblComm JCOM s | | ... | ... | 34 | 3.90 | ... |
| +9.2 | 14 | 3.44 | Jacada JCDA | | ... | cc | 1240 | 1.61 | +0.30 |
| +5.0 | 33.13 | 18.56 | JackHenry JKHY s | .12 | .4 | 51 | 1791 | 29.50 | +0.14 |
| +0.0 | 20.83 | 4.63 | JacoElec JACO s | | ... | 3 | 213 | 7.28 | +0.06 |
| +3.7 | 5.94 | 2.19 | JacobsnStr JCBS | | ... | dd | 14 | 3.50 | ... |
| +42.3 | 14.38 | 4.88 | JacorCm wt | | ... | ... | 3 | 9.25 | ... |
| +67.9 | 23.88 | 11 | JamsRvrBksh JRBK | .56 | 2.4 | 18 | 45 | 23.50 | ... |
| +26.6 | 8.31 | 5.50 | JamesnInn JAMS | .98 | 13.8 | dd | 194 | 7.08 | ... |
| +61.6 | 56.25 | 0.45 | JAWZ JAWZ s | | ... | ... | 829 | 1.80 | +0.06 |
| +29.3 | 38.75 | 5.03 | Jazztel ADS JAZZ | | ... | ... | 217 | 2.25 | +0.57 |
| +29.1 | 6.50 | 1.88 | JetFormCp FORM | | ... | dd | 81 | 2.26 | +0.01 |
| +25.8 | 9.13 | 4.75 | ♣JohnsnOutdrs JOUT | | ... | 13 | 4 | 7.39 | +0.02 |
| +33.3 | 8.55 | 3.56 | JosBank JOSB | | ... | 8 | 512 | 6 | ... |
| +39.0 | 2.06 | 0.56 | JudgeGrp JUDG | | ... | 5 | 51 | 1.39 | +0.04 |
| +63.0 | 244.50 | 28.60 | JunprNtwk JNPR s | | ... | 80 | 199993 | 46.63 | +1.94 |
| +125.5 | 13.50 | 0.59 | JunoOnline JWEB | | ... | dd | 1935 | 1.48 | +0.07 |
| +83.8 | 35 | 1.15 | ♣JupiterMtrx JMXI | | ... | dd | 3186 | 1.51 | +0.06 |
| | | | -K-K-K- | | | | | | |
| +80.0 | 67.38 | 25.50 | ♣KLA Tencor KLAC | | ... | 29 | 81210 | 60.65 | +3.65 |
| +20.8 | 24.25 | 10.75 | KPMGConsltng KCIN n | | ... | ... | 7461 | 18.60 | +0.21 |
| +2.2 | 34.56 | 13.06 | KSwiss A KSWS | .06 | .2 | 13 | 424 | 24.44 | +0.31 |
| +38.9 | 11.44 | 4.63 | KVH Ind KVHI | | ... | ... | 84 | 7.64 | +0.04 |
| +29.2 | 13.63 | 8.48 | KaiserVen K[illegible] | 2.00e | [illegible] | [illegible] | 9 | [illegible] | [illegible] |
| +7.3 | 19.50 | 9.81 | ♣KamanCp K[illegible] | .44 | [illegible] | [illegible] | [illegible] | [illegible] | [illegible] |
| +81.0 | 74.63 | 0.50 | KanaComm [illegible] | | [illegible] | [illegible] | [illegible] | [illegible] | [illegible] |
| +79.0 | 13.90 | 5 | ♣KayeGp K[illegible] | [illegible] | [illegible] | [illegible] | [illegible] | [illegible] | [illegible] |
| +182.5 | 26.44 | 3.94 | Keith TK[illegible] | | [illegible] | 23 | [illegible] | [illegible] | [illegible] |
| +23.1 | 6.56 | 1.54 | Kelstrm[illegible]ELL | | [illegible] | [illegible] | [illegible] | [illegible] | [illegible] |
| +0.7 | 29.25 | 18.50 | ♣KellySvc A KELYA | 1.00 | 4.2 | 11 | 301 | 23.80 | +0.35 |
| +80.0 | 19.49 | 6.25 | KendleInt KNDL | | ... | dd | 187 | 17.89 | +0.06 |
| +4.0 | 6.88 | 3.40 | KenndyWilsn KWIC | | ... | 11 | 92 | 4.20 | +0.35 |
| ▲+58.2 | 15.65 | 8.88 | KenseyNsh KNSY | | ... | dd | 657 | 16.02 | +0.37 |

| YTD % CHG | 52 WEEKS HI | LO | STOCK (SYM) | DIV | YLD % | PE | VOL 100S | LAST | NET CHG |
|---|---|---|---|---|---|---|---|---|---|
| +124.5 | 6.20 | 1.44 | LMI Aero LMIA | | ... | dd | 1 | 4.91 | +0.09 |
| +3.5 | 23.50 | 18 | LNB Bcp LNBB | 1.00b | 4.8 | 10 | 11 | 21.05 | ... |
| +37.4 | 10.94 | 1.63 | L90 LNTY | | ... | dd | 1040 | 2.70 | +0.08 |
| +16.9 | 15.50 | 10.38 | LSB Bk NC LXBK | .56 | 4.3 | 13 | 34 | 13 | +0.05 |
| +22.0 | 26.95 | 12.50 | LSI Ind LYTS | .34 | 1.4 | 25 | 209 | 24.94 | +0.39 |
| +40.0 | 15.70 | 7.56 | LTX LTXX | | ... | 20 | 34406 | 33.05 | +0.27 |
| +15.6 | 18 | 9.13 | LVMH Moet LVMHY s | .13e | 1.2 | ... | 210 | 11.02 | +0.33 |
| +61.9 | 10 | 3.56 | LaJolla LJPC | | ... | dd | 1688 | 7.64 | +0.34 |
| +25.2 | 10.31 | 4.38 | LabOne LABS | .54j | ... | dd | 28 | 7.20 | +0.02 |
| +2.4 | 5.75 | 2 | LaCrosFtwr BOOT | .13 | 4.1 | dd | 34 | 3.20 | +0.10 |
| +40.0 | 15.70 | 7.75 | Ladish LDSH | | ... | 12 | 335 | 15.05 | +0.50 |
| ▲+38.9 | 13.50 | 7.56 | LakelandBcp LBAI | .36f | 2.7 | 17 | 57 | 13.20 | +0.30 |
| +15.8 | 16.38 | 10.31 | LakelandFnl LKFN | .60f | 4.1 | ... | 5 | 14.48 | +0.23 |
| +45.6 | 7.50 | 3 | LakelandInd LAKE | | ... | 13 | 29 | 5.55 | +0.15 |
| +0.3 | 10.63 | 7.13 | LksGaming LACO | | ... | 24 | 97 | 9.35 | +0.03 |
| +120.7 | 32.35 | 16.88 | LamRsch LRCX | | ... | 17 | 406 | 33.05 | +0.27 |
| +11.4 | 50.75 | 32.13 | LamarAdvts A LAMR | | ... | ... | 4415 | 43 | +0.38 |
| +63.4 | 11.15 | 6.39 | LamarCap LCCO | .20 | 1.8 | ... | 128 | 11.03 | +0.06 |
| +17.8 | 34.48 | 18.50 | LancastrCol LANC x | .68 | 2.1 | 13 | 530 | 33.05 | +0.27 |
| +2.6 | 13.50 | 8.56 | Lance LNCE | .64 | 5.2 | 16 | 277 | 12.33 | +0.05 |
| +31.9 | 5.25 | 1 | Lndcrp LCOR | | ... | dd | 1 | 1.83 | +0.04 |
| +52.0 | 6.28 | 3.25 | Landair LAND | | ... | dd | 8 | 5.70 | ... |
| +42.2 | 6.63 | 2.50 | LandecCp LNDC | | ... | dd | 215 | 4 | ... |
| +4.9 | 19.50 | 14.25 | LndmrkBcsh LARK | .60 | 3.3 | ... | 8 | 18.35 | +0.60 |
| +28.3 | 72.88 | 37.63 | ♣LandstarSys LSTR | | ... | 14 | 415 | 71.13 | +1.23 |
| +16.7 | 38.44 | 3.69 | Lanoptics LNOP | | ... | dd | 153 | 11.23 | +0.16 |
| +21.3 | 34.50 | 1.03 | LanteCp LNTE | | ... | dd | 192 | 1.23 | +0.06 |
| +34.1 | 12.38 | 3.78 | Lantronix LTRX n | | ... | ... | 2114 | 8.55 | +0.10 |
| +25.6 | 33.50 | 3.40 | LrgScleBio LSBC n | | ... | ... | 620 | 7.07 | +0.05 |
| +8.9 | 10.13 | 1.91 | Larscom A LARS | | ... | ... | 168 | 2.25 | +0.11 |
| +108.0 | 5 | 1 | LaserPacMed LPAC | | ... | 7 | 96 | 3.12 | +0.09 |
| +104.9 | 7.81 | 1.13 | LaserVis LVCI | | ... | 20 | 2146 | 3.33 | +0.13 |
| +76.5 | 2.75 | 0.90 | Laserscope LSCP | | ... | ... | 233 | 1.93 | +0.01 |
| +107.2 | 5.56 | 0.91 | LaserSight LASE | | ... | dd | 444 | 2.59 | +0.20 |
| +41.5 | 16.50 | 2.38 | LstMin.com LMIN | | ... | ... | 83 | 3 | +0.12 |
| +51.0 | 14 | 1.50 | LatitudeComm LATD | | ... | dd | 518 | 1.90 | +0.05 |
| +41.0 | 41.69 | 15 | LatticeSemi LSCC s | | ... | 38 | 20820 | 26.90 | +2.40 |
| +48.8 | 9.75 | 0.24 | LaunchMedia LAUN | | ... | dd | 4219 | 0.80 | +0.06 |
| +14.3 | 12.10 | 6.63 | LawrencSvg LSBX | .40 | 3.3 | 13 | 82 | 12 | +0.06 |
| +5.9 | 29.98 | 21 | ♣LawsnPdts LAWS | .64 | 2.2 | 11 | 21 | 28.80 | +0.15 |
| +157.2 | 8.88 | 3 | LaynCrstnsn LAYN | | ... | dd | 10 | 8.40 | +0.20 |
| +24.7 | 81.88 | 20.50 | ♣LeapWireless LWIN | | ... | dd | 634 | 31.18 | +0.22 |
| +69.1 | 16.88 | 1.05 | Leapnet LEAPD s | | ... | dd | 76 | 1.35 | +0.06 |
| +51.5 | 78.88 | 14.50 | LearnTreeInt LTRE | | ... | 14 | 878 | 24.02 | +0.17 |
| +38.5 | 3.13 | 0.16 | Learn2.com LTWO | | ... | ... | 611 | 0.25 | ... |
| +49.9 | 28 | 9.38 | LeCroy LCRY | | ... | dd | 23 | 18.55 | +0.25 |
| +11.5 | 4.22 | 1 | Lectec LECT | | ... | dd | 2 | 2.09 | +0.01 |
| +7.7 | 11.25 | 8.19 | LedgerCap LEDG | .20 | 1.9 | 11 | 38 | 10.50 | +0.30 |
| +112.0 | 19.44 | 6.50 | ♣LegatoSys LGTO | | ... | dd | 5214 | 15.77 | +0.83 |
| +33.1 | 19.88 | 9.57 | ♣LeitchTech LVID n | | ... | 28 | 3 | 10.25 | +0.03 |
| +208.8 | 9.56 | 1.78 | ♣LendingTree TREE | | ... | dd | 164 | 6.37 | +0.12 |
| +4.8 | 18.38 | 11.88 | ♣Lesco LSCO | .15f | 12 | 38 | 55 | 12.56 | +0.31 |
| +18.1 | 28.50 | 2.39 | Level 8 LVEL | | ... | dd | 368 | 4.99 | +0.04 |
| +68.1 | 95.25 | 9.13 | Level3Comm LVLT | | ... | dd | 61691 | 10.46 | +0.30 |
| +173.1 | 15.75 | 0.47 | LexarMedia LEXR n | | ... | ... | 601 | 2.56 | +0.03 |
| +70.8 | 37.81 | 2.50 | Lexent LXNT n | | ... | 26 | 621 | 5 | ... |
| +34.7 | 49.25 | 5.41 | LexiconGns LEXG | | ... | dd | 1815 | 10.85 | +0.03 |
| +41.4 | 39.75 | 6.38 | LibrtTch LBRT | | ... | dd | 2727 | 7.98 | +0.18 |
| +22.9 | 10.95 | 6.50 | ♣LbtyBcp LIBB | .12 | 11 | 40 | 60 | 10.75 | +0.19 |
| +4.2 | 39.94 | 3.50 | LbtyDgtl A LDIG | | ... | 54 | 1442 | 4.85 | +0.09 |
| +14.1 | 74.69 | 3.13 | LbtyLvwr A LWIRA n | | ... | ... | 28 | 6.60 | +0.10 |
| +58.6 | 11.75 | 1.32 | Life F/X LEFX n | | ... | ... | 421 | 2.07 | +0.06 |
| +41.2 | 7.31 | 1.19 | Lifecell LIFC | | ... | dd | 818 | 2.25 | +0.08 |
| +17.8 | 8.88 | 3.38 | ♣LifecorBio LCBM | | ... | dd | 36 | 5.45 | +0.15 |
| +50.1 | 19.25 | 11 | LifeInSys LIFE | | ... | 35 | 54 | 18.95 | +0.15 |
| +56.9 | 41.19 | 0.50 | LifeMndrs LFMN | | ... | dd | 1280 | 1.51 | +0.02 |
| +28.7 | 51.75 | 18.25 | LifePoint | | ... | 54 | 4521 | 35.74 | +0.39 |
| +2.8 | 8.70 | 4.03 | LifetmHoan LCUT | .25 | 3.5 | 28 | 8 | 7.06 | +0.05 |
| +2.1 | 16.31 | 7.81 | Ligand B LGND | | ... | dd | 988 | 13.70 | +0.25 |
| +44.6 | 27.50 | 7.13 | ♣Lightbridge LTBG | | ... | 26 | 11477 | 18.98 | +0.27 |
| +18.7 | 57.94 | 9.19 | ♣LtPathTch A LPTH | | ... | dd | 2609 | 11.28 | +0.10 |
| +9.6 | 9 | 0.84 | Lightspan LSPN | | ... | dd | 5594 | 1.30 | +0.39 |
| +11.3 | 65.88 | 23.13 | Lincare LNCR | | ... | 28 | 9793 | 63.50 | +1.90 |
| +6.0 | 13.90 | 9.44 | LnclnBcp LNCB | .36 | 2.6 | 19 | 67 | 13.65 | +0.10 |
| +24.2 | 26.40 | 11.02 | ♣LnclnElec LECO | .60a | 2.5 | 14 | 490 | 24.38 | +0.43 |
| +23.1 | 74.75 | 32.69 | LinrTch LLTC | .16f | .3 | 44 | 50636 | 56.95 | +4.16 |
| +59.8 | 108.38 | 17.75 | LIONBio ADS LEON n | | ... | ... | 114 | 30.30 | +2.90 |
| +44.3 | 11.38 | 1.49 | Lionbridge LIOX | | ... | dd | 960 | 2 | +0.23 |
| +4.7 | 53 | 30.50 | LiqBox LIQB | .80 | 2.1 | 12 | 409 | 38.99 | +0.13 |
| +5.4 | 14.88 | 1.65 | LiquidAudio LQID | | ... | dd | 558 | 2.70 | +0.07 |
| +62.5 | 6.92 | 2.83 | LiquidWld LIQWF | | ... | ... | 36 | 6.40 | +0.52 |
| +65.2 | 10 | 2.06 | Litronic LTNX | | ... | dd | 22 | 4.13 | +0.09 |
| +3.9 | 51.13 | 19.81 | Littlfuse LFUS | | ... | 22 | 359 | 29.75 | +0.72 |
| +73.6 | 9.50 | 0.20 | LivePerson LPSN | | ... | dd | 262 | 0.28 | +0.02 |
| +5.8 | 14.67 | 7.75 | LocalFnl LFIN | | ... | ... | 152 | 13.89 | +0.21 |
| +5.1 | 30 | 11.88 | LodgeNtEntn LNET | | ... | dd | 61 | 18.53 | +0.42 |
| +28.0 | 6.88 | 0.25 | LogOnAm LOAX | | ... | dd | 87 | 0.40 | +0.02 |
| +22.1 | 3.25 | 0.63 | LogicDvc LOGC | | ... | ... | 52 | 1.45 | +0.05 |
| +108.6 | 5.69 | 1.13 | ♣Logility LGTY | | ... | dd | 48 | 3.26 | +0.01 |
| +23.5 | 39 | 18.63 | ♣Logitch ADR LOGIY s | | ... | 3 | 41 | 29.96 | +0.30 |
| +18.7 | 8.88 | 4.65 | LoJack LOJN | | ... | 12 | 85 | 6.75 | +0.15 |
| +37.8 | 14 | 6.56 | LoneStarStk STAR | .50 | 3.8 | 19 | 1539 | 13.28 | +0.12 |
| +0.2 | 15.50 | 10.94 | LI Fnl LICB | .32 | 2.3 | 12 | 4 | 13.66 | ... |
| +38.9 | 26.50 | 0.84 | LookSmart LOOK | | ... | dd | 742 | 1.49 | +0.02 |
| +37.3 | 7 | 3.70 | Loudcloud LDCL n | | ... | ... | 10068 | 3.86 | +0.08 |
| +48.2 | 23.88 | 0.50 | LoudeyeTch LOUD | | ... | dd | 48856 | 1.76 | +0.55 |
| +1.8 | 8.31 | 2.25 | LowrncElec LEIX | | ... | ... | 45 | 3.07 | +0.02 |
| +51.5 | 31.48 | 13.75 | ♣LufkinInd LUFK | .72 | 2.7 | 17 | 102 | 27.17 | +1.20 |
| +76.0 | 28.94 | 1 | LumenonLgtwv LUMM | | ... | 11 | 349 | 1.22 | +0.04 |
| +18.8 | 12.50 | 0.45 | Luminant LUMT | | ... | dd | 1632 | 0.66 | +0.08 |
| +13.7 | 13.13 | 2.09 | Luminent LMNE n | | ... | ... | 3339 | 5.19 | +0.01 |
| +10.8 | 64.13 | 11.95 | LuminexCp LMNX | | ... | dd | 1613 | 23.25 | +0.35 |
| [illegible] | 61.50 | [illegible] | Lynx[illegible]cs L[illegible] | | [illegible] | dd | 985 | [illegible] | [illegible]0.53 |
| | | | -M-M-M- | | | | | | |
| [illegible]5.9 | [illegible] | [illegible] | MAC[illegible] M[illegible] s | [illegible] | [illegible] | ... | [illegible] | [illegible]50 | [illegible] |
| [illegible] | [illegible] | [illegible] | MA[illegible] | .4[illegible] | [illegible]7 | 11 | 370[illegible] | [illegible] | [illegible] |
| [illegible] | 5 | [illegible] | [illegible] | | [illegible] | 17 | 30[illegible] | [illegible] | ... |
| +20.8 | 9.13 | 2.85 | MAPICS MAPX | | ... | ... | 34 | 6.04 | +0.21 |
| ▲+91.0 | 25.38 | 10.50 | ♣MB Fnl MBFI | | ... | 15 | 132 | 25.55 | +0.35 |
| +75.9 | 38.75 | 1.63 | MCK Comm MCKC | | ... | dd | 3868 | 2.03 | ... |
| +25.9 | 35.38 | 13.40 | ♣MCSi MCSI | | ... | 13 | 719 | 15.84 | +0.26 |

| YTD % CHG | 52 WEEKS HI | LO | STOCK (SYM) | DIV | YLD % | PE | VOL 100S | LAST | NET CHG |
|---|---|---|---|---|---|---|---|---|---|
| +37.5 | 7.88 | 3.63 | MagnaEnt A MIEC | | ... | 47 | 152 | 6.53 | +0.08 |
| +27.6 | 11.75 | 7.50 | MahaskaInv OSKY | .60 | 5.5 | 11 | 5 | 10.85 | +0.30 |
| +21.4 | 4.24 | 2.19 | MainStMain MAIN | | ... | 10 | 22 | 3.68 | + ... |
| +42.4 | 10.10 | 5.25 | MainStBcp MBNK | .20 | 2.0 | ... | 105 | 9.97 | +0.08 |
| +40.9 | 19.65 | 10.63 | MainStBks MSBK | .36 | 2.1 | 21 | 156 | 17.52 | +0.69 |
| +27.4 | 19.38 | 1.50 | Mainspring MSPR n | | ... | ... | 112 | 3.98 | ... |
| +5.4 | 18.75 | 1.20 | MajrAutoCo MAJR s | | ... | ... | 204 | 2.47 | +0.02 |
| +18.9 | 9.75 | 4.94 | ♣MallonRes MLRC | | ... | dd | 5412 | 5.88 | +0.04 |
| +46.9 | 40 | 3 | MgtNtwk TMNG | | ... | ... | 50 | 6.31 | +0.04 |
| +17.8 | 6.94 | 1.94 | MnchstrTch MANC | | ... | ... | 23 | 2.65 | +0.15 |
| +18.3 | 75.25 | 10.13 | ♣ManhAssoc MANH | | ... | 61 | 1139 | 34.81 | +0.04 |
| +12.0 | 4.44 | 0.91 | Mannatech MTEX | | ... | ... | 317 | 1.40 | +0.02 |
| +28.4 | 66.06 | 11.25 | Manugistics MANU s | | ... | dd | 15976 | 40.83 | +0.47 |
| +30.1 | 52.50 | 15.38 | ♣MapInfo MAPS s | | ... | 50 | 1471 | 33.04 | +1.15 |
| +50.0 | 29.13 | 8.63 | Marconi ADS MONI n | .06 | .6 | ... | 1513 | 10.28 | +0.02 |
| +40.9 | 20 | 1.13 | Marex MRXX n | | ... | dd | 24 | 1.70 | ... |
| +43.6 | 27 | 2.11 | Marimba MRBA | | ... | dd | 406 | 2.54 | +0.01 |
| ... | 28.38 | 1.63 | MktWatch MKTW | | ... | dd | 178 | 3 | +0.20 |
| +0.8 | 16.75 | 13.50 | MrshSupr A MARSA | .44 | 2.8 | 12 | 2 | 15.75 | +0.86 |
| +4.6 | 13.65 | 9.38 | MrshSupr B MARSB | .44 | 3.3 | 9 | 25 | 13.20 | +0.35 |
| +93.1 | 25 | 12 | MartekBiosci MATK | | ... | dd | 720 | 23.65 | +0.48 |
| +32.5 | 109.75 | 7.94 | ♣MarvellTch MRVL n | | ... | ... | 16010 | 29.07 | +2.31 |
| +42.4 | 44.50 | 15.50 | MatavCbl MATV | | ... | dd | 5 | 18.89 | +0.52 |
| +62.0 | 20.25 | 7.25 | MatriaHlthcr MATR s | | ... | 45 | 38 | 15.59 | +0.14 |
| +14.5 | 9.81 | 2.75 | Matritech NMPS | | ... | dd | 508 | 3.50 | +0.02 |
| +54.4 | 12.94 | 5.50 | MatrixBcp MTXC | | ... | 15 | 6 | 11 | +0.04 |
| +35.2 | 17.94 | 6 | ♣MatrixPharm MATX | | ... | dd | 1192 | 11.10 | +0.20 |
| +19.6 | 7.55 | 3.75 | MatrixSvc MTRX | | ... | ... | 330 | 7.10 | +0.02 |
| +9.4 | 49.38 | 10.25 | MatrixOne MONE | | ... | cc | 4175 | 19.90 | +0.42 |
| ▲+17.5 | 37.13 | 25 | MatthwInt A MATW | .20 | .5 | 20 | 85 | 37.20 | +0.10 |
| +84.3 | 40.50 | 8.38 | MattsonTch MTSN | | ... | dd | 2488 | 19.01 | +0.64 |
| +8.8 | 9.85 | 8.25 | MaxErmRestr MAXE | | ... | 87 | 2 | 9.52 | ... |
| +4.7 | 9.63 | 5.06 | Maxco MAXC | | ... | 97 | 28 | 7.72 | +0.27 |
| +22.1 | 44.69 | 10.69 | MaximIntgl MXIM | | ... | 49 | 43367 | 58.40 | +3.48 |
| +38.8 | 68 | 4.81 | ♣MaximPharm MAXM | | ... | dd | 547 | 8.85 | +0.11 |
| -60.0 | 56 | 0.28 | ♣MaximPharm wt | | ... | ... | 444 | 0.40 | +0.10 |
| +49.3 | 11.05 | 5 | MaxusRlty MRTI | .68e | 6.5 | dd | 5 | 10.45 | +0.45 |
| +51.6 | 17.10 | 7.50 | Maxwell A MAXS | | ... | 15 | 389 | 16.30 | +0.07 |
| +35.9 | 22.56 | 12.06 | MaxwelTch MXWL | | ... | ... | 724 | 20.30 | +0.35 |
| -26.5 | 80.06 | 9.75 | ♣Maxygen MAXY | | ... | dd | 188 | 18 | +0.43 |
| +11.4 | 23.13 | 14.75 | MaynrdOil MOIL | | ... | 6 | 9 | 19.50 | +0.30 |
| -62.9 | 27 | 4.50 | McLeodUSA A MCLD | | ... | dd | 28964 | 5.24 | +0.02 |
| +172.8 | 23.13 | 14.75 | ♣McAfee.com MCAF | | ... | dd | 7214 | 13.60 | +1.16 |
| -32.7 | 53.58 | 12.38 | McData A MCDTA n | | ... | ... | 16541 | 31.13 | +0.44 |
| -33.8 | 141.38 | 16.44 | McData B MCDT n | | ... | ... | 13484 | 36.26 | +0.22 |
| +38.8 | 27.50 | 14.75 | McGrthRent MGRC | .64f | 2.4 | 12 | 12 | 26.90 | +0.20 |
| +112.4 | 22.83 | 8.50 | McNghAppri MAGI | | ... | 8 | 1229 | 22.57 | +0.15 |
| +27.5 | 33 | 3 | MeadeInstr MEAD s | | ... | 60 | 245 | 4.76 | +0.07 |
| +19.3 | 3.88 | 1.79 | MeadwVly MVCO | | ... | ... | 14 | 2.42 | +0.09 |
| +62.6 | 10.25 | 4.63 | MechDyn MDII | | ... | 23 | 340 | 9.35 | +0.10 |
| +164.3 | 16.50 | 2 | MchTch MKTY | | ... | dd | 904 | 9.25 | +0.08 |
| +57.5 | 19.30 | 13.38 | MedDsgn MEDC | | ... | ... | 3768 | 25 | +1.50 |
| +26.6 | 18 | 8.69 | MedallnFnl TAXI | 1.01e | 9.4 | ... | 388 | 10.73 | +0.17 |
| +23.7 | 75 | 11.75 | ♣Medarex MEDX s | | ... | cc | 13130 | 31.10 | +0.40 |
| +21.0 | 19.30 | 13.38 | MedfordBcp MDBK | .52 | 2.8 | 12 | 10 | 18.75 | +0.25 |
| +24.3 | 23.50 | 0.50 | Media100 MDEA | | ... | dd | 412 | 1.94 | +0.12 |
| +50.8 | 4.75 | 0.50 | MediaBay MBAY | | ... | dd | 254 | 0.80 | +0.01 |
| +16.1 | 35.38 | 8.75 | MediaComm A MCCC | | ... | dd | 5039 | 19.96 | +2.41 |
| +15.9 | 9.50 | 2.19 | ♣Medialink MDLK | | ... | 33 | 1 | 3.68 | +0.15 |
| +21.8 | 23.50 | 0.50 | MediaPlex MPLX | | ... | dd | 2996 | 0.99 | +0.09 |
| ▲+170.2 | 9.94 | 1.40 | MedAction MDCI | | ... | 19 | 8822 | 8.95 | +1.15 |
| +54.6 | 11.13 | 0.94 | Medlogscp MDLI | | ... | dd | 579 | 1.05 | ... |
| +40.8 | 9.94 | 1.40 | MediChmLfSci MCLS n | | ... | ... | 660 | 2.74 | +0.06 |
| +17.5 | 35.38 | 8.75 | Medicines MDCO n | | ... | dd | 2214 | 16.92 | +0.28 |
| +11.6 | 86.13 | 27.63 | ♣MedImmune MEDI | | ... | 59 | 23280 | 42.15 | +0.22 |
| +10.2 | 27.88 | 10.25 | MedisTch MDTL n | | ... | dd | 259 | 17.90 | +0.85 |
| +45.0 | 9.94 | 1.25 | MedPlus MEDP | | ... | dd | 158 | 1.96 | + ... |
| +72.3 | 44.69 | 10.69 | MedQuist MEDQ | | ... | ... | 1174 | 27.56 | +0.08 |
| +18.3 | 9 | 4.75 | MedstnInt MEDS | | ... | 14 | 32 | 4.80 | +0.02 |
| ▲+29.9 | 31.60 | 16.13 | MEEMIC MEMH | | ... | 14 | 13 | 31.99 | +0.39 |
| +21.0 | 5.06 | 3.70 | MegoFnl MEGO | | ... | 3 | 5700 | 3.80 | ... |
| +18.4 | 37.75 | 16.56 | MembrWrks MBRS | | ... | dd | 1488 | 25.15 | +0.08 |
| +43.5 | 20.63 | 1.02 | Mentergy MNTE | | ... | dd | 955 | 1.13 | +0.13 |
| ▲+40.1 | 28.75 | 13 | MentorCp MNTR | .12 | .4 | 21 | 826 | 27.32 | +0.34 |
| +4.4 | 33.63 | 17.02 | ♣MentorGraph MENT | | ... | 32 | 4177 | 28.65 | +0.01 |
| +27.2 | 13.75 | 1.01 | Merant MRNT | | ... | dd | 57 | 5.05 | +0.30 |
| +51.0 | 17.65 | 8.93 | MrcntlBk MBWM | p | ... | 13 | 3 | 17.08 | +0.08 |
| +9.5 | 45.13 | 29.75 | MercBkshMD MRBK | 1.04 | 2.7 | 15 | 522 | 39.08 | +0.13 |
| +53.5 | 70.38 | 1.40 | Mercator MCTR | | ... | dd | 1495 | 2.50 | +0.10 |
| +6.4 | 11.19 | 5.50 | ♣MercerInt MERCS | j | ... | 4 | 159 | 7.43 | +0.15 |
| ▲+31.3 | 31.65 | 19 | MercBcshVT MBVT | 1.32 | 4.1 | 12 | 102 | 31.85 | +0.20 |
| +9.0 | 55.50 | 17.13 | MercryCptr MRCY | | ... | 44 | 1422 | 50.61 | +2.41 |
| +25.6 | 162.50 | 30.75 | ♣MercInteract MERQ | | ... | 86 | 30323 | 67.12 | +1.23 |
| +2.7 | 8.50 | 2.13 | MeridnBio VIVO | .26 | 5.1 | dd | 119 | 5.07 | +0.07 |
| +27.1 | 21 | 8.25 | MeridnMed MTEC | | ... | 18 | 20 | 13.98 | +1.02 |
| +25.8 | 13.75 | 1.01 | Merisel MSEL s | | ... | dd | 7 | 1.16 | +0.03 |
| +48.4 | 8.96 | 5 | MeritMed MMSI | | ... | 30 | 462 | 8.35 | +0.40 |
| +46.3 | 69 | 10.63 | MerixCp MERX s | | ... | 10 | 4285 | 19.57 | +0.43 |
| +4.9 | 10.13 | 8 | MerLySP500Ind n | | ... | ... | 100 | 8.38 | +0.12 |
| +71.1 | 12.38 | 4.72 | MesaAir MESA | | ... | 22 | 2389 | 11.98 | ... |
| +15.3 | 14 | 9 | MesabaHldg MAIR | | ... | 11 | 789 | 10.64 | +0.09 |
| +30.3 | 6.94 | 0.25 | MessageMda MESG | | ... | dd | 2864 | 0.57 | + ... |
| +7.9 | 38.75 | 7.19 | Metalink MTLK | | ... | 59 | 1182 | 8.86 | +0.14 |
| +8.7 | 60 | 6.75 | MetaSolv MSLV | | ... | 21 | 6066 | 9.92 | +0.72 |
| +11.8 | 3.88 | 0.31 | Metatec META | | ... | dd | 5 | 1.11 | ... |
| +67.1 | 33 | 1.44 | MetawaveComm MTWV | | ... | dd | 1666 | 3 | +0.03 |
| +9.5 | 8.95 | 2.63 | ♣Methanex MEOH | | ... | 5 | 4671 | 7.95 | +0.16 |
| +6.2 | 21.91 | 4.41 | MethodEl A METHA s | | ... | 7 | 10899 | 7.60 | +0.10 |
| +92.0 | 7.61 | 0.50 | Metretek MTEK | | ... | dd | 26 | 1.92 | +0.02 |
| +62.2 | 49.50 | 1.38 | Metricom MCOM | | ... | dd | 1692 | 3.80 | +0.10 |
| +20.0 | 10 | 3.80 | ♣MetroInfo MISI | | ... | 18 | 8 | 4.60 | ... |
| +22.0 | 16 | 5 | MetroIntl A MTROA n | | ... | ... | 2 | 5.75 | +0.25 |
| [illegible] | [illegible] | 9.50 | Metr[illegible] MTON | | [illegible] | [illegible] | 2830 | 53.90 | +1.96 |
| [illegible]2.0 | 12[illegible] | [illegible]50 | Metr[illegible] MC[illegible] | [illegible]24 | 2[illegible] | [illegible] | 132 | 10.07 | +0.02 |
| [illegible] | 44[illegible] | [illegible] | Metr[illegible]r M[illegible] | | [illegible] | [illegible] | 83970 | 4.93 | +0.24 |
| [illegible] | 14[illegible] | [illegible] | Metr[illegible] M[illegible] | | [illegible] | [illegible] | 117 | 7.50 | +0.05 |
| [illegible] | [illegible] | 4.[illegible] | Metr[illegible] M[illegible] | [illegible] | [illegible] | [illegible] | [illegible] | 7.50 | ... |
| [illegible] | [illegible] | 5 | Metr[illegible] METFO | [illegible] | [illegible] | [illegible] | [illegible] | 8.72 | +0.22 |
| +57.9 | 6 | 2.25 | MetroFnl METF | j | ... | 54 | 105 | 3.75 | +0.25 |
| ▲+56.5 | 8.50 | 5.44 | MetroWst MWBX | .28 | 3.1 | 12 | 235 | 9 | +0.70 |
| +51.1 | 49.63 | 18 | MichaelStr MIKE | | ... | 17 | 2255 | 40.05 | +0.25 |
| +6.7 | 78.63 | 22.94 | ♣Micrel MCRL s | | ... | 46 | 12550 | 35.96 | +3.93 |

| YTD % CHG | 52 WEEKS HI | LO | ST |
|---|---|---|---|
| +63.1 | 14.13 | 1.34 | Mir |
| +11.0 | 92.56 | 25 | Mir |
| ▲+25.6 | 2.75 | 1.06 | Mir |
| +51.3 | 9.90 | 5.56 | Mir |
| +23.5 | 25.94 | 6 | Mi |
| +21.2 | 10.63 | 4.31 | MI |
| +5.3 | 9.94 | 5.75 | Mi |
| +24.1 | 36.95 | 22.50 | MS |
| +95.1 | 7.50 | 3.28 | Mi |
| +67.1 | 7.06 | 0.50 | Mi |
| +33.9 | 14.38 | 4.88 | MI |
| +26.5 | 31.85 | 16.38 | Mo |
| +29.2 | 16.50 | 1.81 | Mb |
| +60.0 | 5.63 | 1.13 | ♣Mc |
| +17.8 | 7.70 | 5.19 | ♣MC |
| +21.1 | 18.88 | 2.13 | Md |
| +29.1 | 29.94 | 19 | ♣Mo |
| +39.9 | 12.50 | 6.06 | Mc |
| +23.2 | 31.06 | 10.31 | Mc |
| +67.9 | 112.50 | 17.33 | ♣Mc |
| +5.7 | 57.63 | 33.31 | ♣Mc |
| +14.4 | 43.94 | 24.63 | ♣Mc |
| +28.5 | 14.95 | 7.25 | Mc |
| +15.8 | 6.06 | 4.31 | Mc |
| +8.2 | 54.69 | 29.44 | ♣Mc |
| +22.3 | 6.13 | 4.75 | ♣Mc |
| +66.3 | 15.20 | 8.31 | Mc |
| +7.6 | 12 | 8.25 | Mc |
| +44.8 | 7.25 | 3.63 | Mc |
| +20.5 | 12 | 6 | Mc |
| +66.3 | 16.38 | 0.38 | Mc |
| +33.3 | 10 | 4.38 | ♣Mc |
| +312.3 | 15.10 | 2.94 | Mc |
| ▲+72.7 | 40.08 | 1.36 | Mp |
| +35.8 | 22.50 | 1.50 | MI |
| +28.7 | 29.50 | 7.88 | Mu |
| +31.8 | 12.25 | 7.25 | Mu |
| +51.1 | 10.58 | 0.96 | Mu |
| +2.4 | 15.13 | 9.88 | Mu |
| +114.7 | 21 | 0.50 | My |
| +6.8 | 138 | 29.50 | My |
| +13.5 | 16.10 | 11.25 | My |
| +40.5 | 10.06 | 2.50 | NA |
| +38.3 | 28.13 | 0.97 | NB |
| +6.0 | 17.50 | 9.38 | NB |
| +182.1 | 15.38 | 3.88 | NB |
| +6.2 | 35.50 | 11.69 | NC |
| +3.9 | 7.90 | 5.25 | NC |
| +16.2 | 86 | 31.94 | ♣ND |
| +10.9 | 32.40 | 12.50 | NE |
| +29.2 | 78.63 | 5.72 | NI |
| +137.8 | 4.50 | 0.75 | NI |
| +9.7 | 11.38 | 6.50 | NN |
| +2.0 | 14.94 | 8 | NF |
| +28.5 | 58 | 15 | ♣NI |
| +134.7 | 5.88 | 0.31 | NC |
| +82.9 | 7.69 | 0.25 | NZ |
| +32.0 | 16.63 | 3.75 | NU |
| +4.6 | 21.50 | 11.94 | Na |
| +28.2 | 5 | 1.50 | Na |
| +5.8 | 43 | 5.13 | Na |
| +134.2 | 63.88 | 10.63 | Na |
| +0.9 | 17.50 | 5.25 | Na |
| +34.7 | 5.74 | 3.16 | Na |
| +18.5 | 12.25 | 5.03 | ♣Na |
| -20.3 | 20.81 | 8 | Na |
| +75.8 | 24.18 | 7.03 | Na |
| +28.4 | 9.94 | 3.81 | Na |
| +6.3 | 4 | 2.50 | Na |
| +9.1 | 1.44 | 0.60 | Na |
| +73.3 | 29.35 | 13.38 | Na |
| +3.3 | 27.88 | 15.19 | Na |
| +7.5 | 22.25 | 14.25 | Na |
| ▲+41.9 | 7.31 | 4.03 | ♣Nt |
| +31.3 | 24.50 | 1 | Nt |
| +24.5 | 57.56 | 26.69 | Nt |
| +120.4 | 3.49 | 1.16 | Nt |
| +4.8 | 25.63 | 17.62 | ♣Nt |
| +29.0 | 4.22 | 1.39 | Nt |
| +30.7 | 4.38 | 1.88 | Nt |
| +9.6 | 118 | 68.50 | Nt |
| +3.3 | 25.75 | 9 | Nt |
| +34.7 | 4.38 | 0.95 | Na |
| +21.1 | 3.69 | 1.34 | ♣Nt |
| +62.1 | 11.95 | 5.69 | Nt |
| +33.3 | 21.65 | 8.63 | Na |
| +29.8 | 3.50 | 1.06 | ♣Na |
| +17.9 | 13.75 | 1.31 | Nt |
| +107.8 | 17.10 | 7.50 | Na |
| +11.3 | 58.88 | 0.97 | Ne |
| +5.8 | 9.13 | 0.63 | Ne |
| +66.0 | 15 | 5.50 | ♣Ne |
| +20.9 | 4.81 | 2.56 | Ne |
| ▲+16.6 | 71 | 3.50 | Ne |
| +16.8 | 22.75 | 3.81 | Ne |
| +34.4 | 41.06 | 14.56 | Ne |
| +8.6 | 26.25 | 3.19 | Ne |
| +12.6 | 52 | 22.38 | ♣Ne |
| +4.2 | 13.63 | 2.22 | ♣Ne |
| +42.0 | 6 | 0.38 | ♣Ne |
| +31.2 | 7 | 3 | Ne |
| +67.1 | 25 | 0.75 | Ne |
| +19.8 | 20.25 | 0.88 | Ne |
| +31.2 | 35.94 | 2.25 | Ne |
| +28.4 | 18.75 | 1.01 | Ne |
| +64.1 | 14.44 | 6 | Ne |
| +30.1 | 17.25 | 1 | Ne |
| +27.2 | 80.88 | 15.75 | Ne |
| +0.8 | 15.50 | 0.53 | Ne |
| +26.3 | 22.88 | 1.75 | ♣Ne |

# ABSOLUT DENIAL

# GuideDied.com:

# Look Them Up, They'll Get You Down

IT'S LONELY AT THE TOP
AND DEADLY
IF YOU'RE ALONE

GuideDied.com CEO Ansell Atherton pretends to rappel in the company's Denver headquarters because our photographer told him it would look cool.

As HE approached the dangerous Second Step on the north face of Mt. Everest, Pearce Glazier heard the scream growing louder. In an instant, his guide, now just a bluish neon blur, rushed past him, his howl quickly fading as his body disappeared into the icy mist below.

"My first thought was actually, 'Wow, cool Doppler effect,'" Glazier recalled. "But I pretty quickly came to my senses and realized I was in deep trouble."

That was an understatement. Glazier had never been on Everest. His climbing resume was thin. His guide was gone. And he hadn't eaten a very good breakfast. Lost and alone, death appeared inevitable and, in fact, it did come two hours later, forcing us to make up the quote above.

But if Glazier had taken his wireless personal digital assistant up the mountain, and had his Visa card handy, he could have logged on to GuideDied.com, a new Web-based emergency alpine service that offers customers real-time support from virtual guides who help get them down safely.

With a base price of $10,000 an hour, GuideDied is expensive, but climbers under duress rarely quibble about the cost, said Ansell Atherton, CEO of the Denver, Colo.–based company.

"There aren't that many high-altitude climbers, so we're not a high-volume business," explained Atherton. "But we can charge enormous sums of money for our services because our customers don't have many options."

However, climbers who have made it down thanks to GuideDied's staff — five experienced moutaineers, including two Sherpas — have quibbled loudly about what they have called, in a class-action suit, "extortion in extremis."

"I was on Mount Elbrus [Russia] at night, in a storm, my oxygen ran out, and I'd lost most of my gear, and my guides, on an icefall," said Scott Mayhaw, a plaintiff and 29-year-old climber from New Zealand. "So I tapped into GuideDied for some help, and it turns out another climber, up on the Matterhorn, was also in trouble. So what did they do? They actually had us bidding against each other. Even now I can't understand how they could possibly do that."

"Oh, it's simple, really," replied Atherton. "We built our system to be flexible, so if we have a simultaneous save situation, our software automatically defaults to an auction format."

Atherton conceded, however, that many climbers don't have the financial resources to pay the $10,000 fee, not to mention

enter into competitive bidding. For them, the site offers a free, scaled-down public area, which includes maps, tips, and chat rooms for climbers to discuss their dilemmas with far-off colleagues.

The company, he added, doesn't guarantee the advice given out in chat rooms, and critics charge that there is a reason for that. Some of those offering counsel from chat rooms have little, if any, experience, as the transcript of a recent distress chat illustrates:

CHAT TRANSCRIPT
GUIDEDIED.COM
PUBLIC AREA 100699-15:22:45

CLIMBER Hello, is anyone there? My name's Dave, I'm up on K2, my guide just disappeared, and I can't get down.

POKEBOY2 hi dave. i'm kenny. do you hav any charizard cards? i hav charmander and charmeleon, but i realy wanted a charizard.

Despite the controversy, Ahterton insists GuideDied will not disappear. It will, however, make changes. "I think we're going to make climbers sign an ironclad no-liability clause," he said. "That's what they do at 757Pilot-Died.com, and they're pulling $10,000 apiece from 230 passengers at a time."

# 25 things you <u>MUST</u> do

**1** Don't Fear Failure. Fear what will happen to you if you fail.

**7** PLAN AHEAD FIVE YEARS. THAT'S WHEN THE STATUTE OF LIMITATIONS ON INSIDER TRADING RUNS OUT.

**2** Remember: Customer care is more than just talk. It's also a lot of pretending.

**8** Remember, anti-competitive practice makes anti-competitive perfect.

**three** Underpromise and overdeliver. Then overcharge and underexplain.

**9** Never compromise on your principles. Put a minimum price on them and stick to it.

**4** NEVER COMPROMISE ON QUALITY; "CHEAP," AFTER ALL, IS A QUALITY.

**10** THREE WORDS: MADE IN CHINA.

**5** Listen to your elders. Learn from them. Then fire them.

**6** C'mon, your kid will be in another play, but the IBM deal comes along only once.

**11** Treat your customers as you would want to be treated if you wanted to be treated like a superficial, trusting idiot with a credit card.

**12** Know your company inside out. Corporate spies will pay you for that information.

**XIII** ECONOMIZE. PUTTING "MBA, STANFORD UNIVERSITY" ON YOUR RESUME COSTS MUCH LESS THAN ACTUALLY GETTING ONE.

**14** Never forget the value of a dollar. It's $1.

# to SUCCEED in business

**17** *Seize the advantage. God invented gullible people for a reason.*

**16** Remember: You can't spell "s-u-c-c-e-s-s" without "h-a-p-p-y  m-a-r-r-i-a-g-e" …wait, yes you can.

**18** IF IT AIN'T BROKE, DON'T FIX IT. IF IT IS, CHANGE THE PACKAGING.

**19** Hmm… you can also spell "s-u-c-c-e-s-s" without "n-i-c-e," "f-a-i-r," or "l-e-g-a-l."

*20 Shake hands with Mr. M. Bezzle.*

**22** Never take the money and run. Walk slowly so as not to attract attention.

23 Loyal employees are like gold. Sell them.

**21** Remember: People count. But machines count faster, and they're non-union.

TWENTY-FOUR: NEVER LET 'EM SEE YOUR SWEATSHOP.

**25** If all else fails, remember, you have been paying good money for that fire insurance.

**15** WHISTLE WHILE YOU WORK THAT WAY COLLEAGUES WON'T HEAR YOU PULLING $20s OUT OF PETTY CASH.

# Y2K Survivors Devolve Ahead of Schedule

## CAMPERS WATCHING *MAD MAX* TAPES, TAKING CANNIBALISM CLASSES

IN THESE dark days before the year 2000, residents of Idaho's Hideaway Farms survival community are not sitting idle as they wait for the world's computer systems to fail and humanity to quickly follow.

Prospective survivors are learning not only to grow their own food and stalk wild animals, but to detect fear and weakness in an enemy through sense of smell, and even to eat their young.

"We're not actually eating our young, of course," said Jake Strangan, 38, a computer programmer and father of two who moved to Hideaway Farms from San Francisco in April. "We're practicing on dolls for now."

Hideaway Farms is one of an estimated 4,000 Y2K survival communities across North America. Its 5,000 residents, who live in mobile homes, recreational vehicles, and hastily constructed single-family homes, believe their willingness to voluntarily devolve puts them ahead of other survivalists, many of whom plan to devolve on an as-needed basis.

"I really thought we'd come out here and sit it out until events overtook us, but this is a proactive community," said Sarah Parmagiani, 22, a recently retired advertising account executive from Manhattan. "Some of us are learning to siphon gasoline out of abandoned cars using hollowed-out electrical cords. We're also learning to cower submissively in makeshift lean-tos while hordes of wild outlaws stomp past us looking for love slaves."

Parmagiani's boyfriend, Sam Tooks, is one of the outlaws-in-training. "I'm really quite shocked and disgusted with what I will become," said Tooks, 25, dressed in a torn, studded black leather vest and muddied teal sweatpants. "But I'm glad I'm here so at least I could prepare for it."

Tooks, a short, slight, former utility company accountant, noted that he has also learned to befriend large men. Hideaway Farms, he said, encourages scrawny, brainy males to strike up obsequious relationships with "big dumb guys," as it is believed brawn will rule and small men will be discriminated against in leadership positions and mating. In fact, Parmigiani conceded she has been checking out some of the community's "lusty, bulky ape-males" in preparation for the day when her boyfriend Sam is killed, exiled as an inferior, or turned into a "she-boy."

Aside from Y2K training, Hideaway Farms residents also have been busily hoarding the basic necessities: food, water, firearms, and zinc oxide.

"Civilization may come to an end and your life span may be cut in half, but you've got to be concerned about sunburn, especially out on the prairie, where there are no tall buildings or smog to protect sensitive noses," explained Charles Cartwright, a physician from Baltimore who will head up Hideaway Farms' AlphaInfant Aftercare Program, in which newborns are placed on a remote mountaintop for seven days to see if they are strong enough to one day join the clan.

## Y2K UPDATE

WITH LESS THAN A MONTH TO GO UNTIL THE YEAR 2000 COMPUTER BUG HITS, NEARLY 35 PERCENT OF FORTUNE 500 COMPANIES CLAIM THEY ARE Y2K COMPLIANT, 30 PERCENT SAY THEY ARE Y2K "PANICKED," 25 PERCENT SAY THEY EXPECT "ALL HELL TO BREAK LOOSE," AND 15 PERCENT SAY THEY EXPECT "ONLY THE INFORMATION TECHNOLOGY SECTORS OF HELL" TO BREAK LOOSE, ACCORDING TO A *BUSINESSMONTH WEEKLY* SURVEY.

When the time comes, four-year-old Hideaway Farms resident Kayli Peterson says it will be hard to eat Rusty, the family dog, "but Mommy says it's him or me."

# JUDAISM MAY BE Y2K SOLUTION

 Converts Would Have 40-Year Cushion

THE YEAR 2000 COMPUTER CRISIS CAN BE AVERTED IF every computer in the world converts to Judaism, Israeli scientists announced this week.

The Y2K crisis is caused by old, or "legacy," computer systems that recognize only the last two digits of a year, such as 99 instead of 1999. When the clock strikes 2000, computer experts fear many systems will fail to recognize the year "00," wreaking havoc across industries. However, in Judaism, it is currently the year 5760, meaning Jewish computers could avoid a similar problem — the Y5.8K crisis — for another 40 years. Computers currently use the Gregorian calendar, which begins with the approximate birth date of Jesus Christ.

To convert the built-in clocks on the world's estimated 2 billion computers, Tel Aviv–based Kosher Technologies has developed PC Mitzvah, a program that searches for Gregorian calendar dates and replaces them with Jewish calendar dates, said CEO Eric Rimmkovsky. Currently, some Y2K repair programs send in a computer "mole" program to seek out and change all references to the date. PC Mitzvah sends in a computer "Mohel" program to snip out lines of code and replace them with Jewish calendar dates, Rimmkovsky explained. When the program successfully completes the conversion, users see the message "Mazel tov!"

The program is designed for users of any religion and does not otherwise affect systems, although it does automatically shut down on Saturdays.

Meanwhile, another Israeli firm, ShivaTech, has announced plans to launch an enterprise-wide Y2K conversion solution for large corporate clients. Called PC Passover, the program sends out an Information Systems Angel® that will simultaneously convert all computers on a company network. Modems or network cards connected to computers that are to remain Gregorian need only be smeared with goat blood to avoid conversion, said a ShivaTech spokesperson.

SatireWire's
# BusinessMonth
## WEEKLY

**DECEMBER 2000**

**SALLY ASKS YOU TO SAVE THE DOTCOMS**

**HOW TO SPOT A FAKE PRESS RELEASE**

**McDONALD'S TOPS *WORKING CHILD* MAG LIST**

# DANGER:
# FALLING DOTCOMS

**LIFE IN A DOTCOM REFUGEE CAMP**

**eBAY AUCTIONS OFF EMPLOYEES**

# NATION HAVING HARD TIME GIVING SHIT ABOUT AOL–TIME WARNER MERGER

## Largest Merger in Media History Seen as Historic, Revolutionary, Whatever

CONTINUALLY BOMBARDED by news that the AOL–Time Warner merger will create the world's first fully integrated media and communications company — a potentially anti-competitive Goliath that could dominate broadband interactive services for decades — the majority of Americans have no idea what we just wrote, and they don't care.

"Intellectually, I know this merger is important. I hear about it all the time on the news, and all these business magazines and Web sites are always playing it up like the Second Coming, but really, who gives a shit?" said Tina Desmond, a 34-year-old patent clerk from Cleveland, Ohio.

According to Steve Case, chief executive of Dulles, Va.–based AOL, everyone should give a shit. "What we're talking about here is a revolution," Case insisted in an interview last week. "Our combined company will be the premier global company delivering branded information, entertainment, and communications across rapidly converging media platforms and changing technology."

"You know what I just heard?" countered 19-year-old University of Miami sophomore Bob Strock. "Blah blah fuckin' blah."

The realization that no one really cares about the merger irks competitors such as Qwest Communications, which is fighting the deal. Even analysts who cover the companies and approve of the merger have fared no better generating interest.

"Every day I tell my wife, 'Honey, this new company will provide an important new broadband distribution platform for America Online's interactive services and drive subscriber growth through cross-marketing with Time Warner's preeminent brands,'" said IDG analyst Keith Sturgess. "And every day, she says 'Keith, you're just so odd.'"

Case added that a combined AOL–Time Warner will spur a new era of innovation and robust competition and something something market leverage something, but we lost interest.

# theglobe.com Numbers Not So Bad If Ignored, Says New CEO

## NEW CHIEF ALSO VOWS TO THROW PREDECESSORS OUT WINDOW

"Blocking out the numbers makes me feel better and allows us to focus on our pretty logo," said CEO Charles Peck.

CHARLES PECK, incoming chief executive of theglobe.com, conceded last week that the troubled online firm is heavily in debt, but urged investors not to focus solely on the company's numbers because, he said, "They suck.

"Clearly, if you just look at the numbers, they are very bad," said Peck, who takes over a firm whose stock has dropped 94 percent, is $86.5 million in debt, and has just $19 million in cash reserves. "However, if you do that, then you're entirely missing the point I'm trying to make, which is, 'Don't look at the numbers.'"

Asked where else investors should look, Peck suggested several possibilities, including "down," "away," and "over there." Peck also insisted that when the numbers get better, that would be a better time to look at them.

Peck succeeds theglobe's 20-something founders, Todd Krizelman and Stephan Paternot, who have been told they will become co-vice chairmen of the board, but will actually be thrown naked and bleeding out of a very high window. Tickets for that event are selling well, said Peck, but will not materially impact company earnings in the current quarter, which also suck.

According to theglobe Chairman Michael Egan, the timing of Peck's arrival is "perfect.

"Right now, our two biggest needs are someone with a proven record of delivering profits within advertising-based business models, and someone who isn't afraid to throw Todd and Stephan out a very high window. Chuck Peck meets both needs."

# Fired eBay Employees Auctioned Off

AS PART OF the staff cuts it announced recently, San Jose, Calif.–based online auction site eBay said it will not release its employees outright, but will auction them off individually. To increase interest in the employees, who will come from the company's offline Butterfield & Butterfield division, eBay has paired each outgoing staffer with a fine collectible.

So far, bidding on human-resources-manager-Claudia-Penton-with-a-set-of-Mr.-Peanut-snack-cups has been slow, but the action on marketing-director-Randy-Keller-with-a-hand-painted-Limoges-sardine-server has been quite hectic. Said Keller: "I think it's obvious why my bids are moving. I have six years' experience in product positioning and demand planning, and come with a matching server tray."

## RIAA Demands End to Unauthorized Humming, Whistling

AFTER USING the courts to prohibit Napster and MP3.com from distributing music for free over the Internet, the Recording Industry Association of America has asked a federal judge to stop people from humming or whistling copyrighted songs in public. The RIAA also asked for $300 million in damages from the estimated 22 million drunken men who think drumming the opening beat to "Wipeout" is a good way to impress women in bars.

"Anyone who publicly hums or whistles is disseminating copyright-protected music and thereby infringing on our artists' rights," said RIAA spokesman Janet Fogerty. "Also, we don't like it when the wind blows. It sounds too much like the beginning to Elton John's 'Funeral for a Friend.'"

Free speech advocates were outraged over the RIAA's action, but women generally applauded. "Most of the guys I know can't drum "Wipeout" when they're sober, let alone drunk," said Helen Kurtz, a 22-year-old from Manhattan.

# McDONALD'S TOPS *WORKING CHILD* MAGAZINE LIST

## Child Laborers Make Happy Meal Toys in Flexible 16-Hour Shifts

IN ITS annual survey, *Working Child* magazine today named McDonald's as the "best company for working children," noting that the Chinese factory making McDonald's Happy Meal toys not only allows child laborers to sleep indoors, but gives them nearly eight hours off every day.

The magazine's annual list singles out those firms that help working children balance their illegal careers with their relatively nonexistent personal lives. McDonald's, whose contract with a mainland China factory was widely reported in the media, was cited for several innovations, including an unrivaled flextime policy that lets employees divide their workweek into any combination of seven 16-hour days.

The magazine also praised McDonald's farsighted "back-injury prevention" initiative. Factory workers, who live 16 to a room, sleep on wooden pallets with no bedding, thus protecting them from back problems that so often result from a too-soft mattress.

But according to Susan Schreff, editor-in-chief of *Working Child*, it was the company's "sick sibling" policy that most impressed the magazine's team of researchers. Under the program, child laborers are allowed to extend their normal 16-hour shifts to a full 24 hours if a sibling is injured or too sick to work.

"Some of these families are two-child income families, and they count on getting those $3 daily paychecks," said Schreff. "If one of the children becomes too ill to work, allowing the sibling to work 50 percent longer ensures that the family will at least get $4.50. I don't know of many companies that would do that."

Added 14-year-old factory worker An Luping: "I love my factory and McDonald's and the Communist Party and I am 19 years old."

In a related note, McDonald's announced that all Happy Meal toys not distributed by Dec. 1 will be donated to the "Toys By Tots" campaign.

## Taco Bell Chihuahua Fired; New Chalupa "Tastes Funny"

One week after falling sales caused Taco Bell to ditch its famous Chihuahua, the company unveiled a reformulated chalupa, described as a "crispy, flaky shell with sour cream, lettuce, tomatoes, and a new tough-and-stringy meat product that tastes like "chicken."

The company insisted the new chalupa, which will be sold "as long as supplies last," has nothing to do with the beloved Chihuahua, who was popularized in Taco Bell ads but did little to help sales. Concurrent with the Chihuahua's firing, New York–based Tricon Global Restaurants, Taco Bell's parent company, also replaced Taco Bell President Peter C. Waller, who it said "will be pursuing other interests" as part of a nutritious Fiesta Breakfast Burrito.

# GATES' STIGMATA NOT MEANT TO SWAY COURT

## Microsoft Insists Chairman's Charitable Works Not Aimed at Antitrust Case

MICROSOFT THIS WEEK denied it is attempting to win leniency from the courts by waging a PR campaign extolling the virtues of Chairman Bill Gates. Company spokesperson Miranda Magdeleine insisted Microsoft would never expect the court to be influenced by Gates' "infinite compassion," nor by his "occasional" episodes of bleeding from the hands and feet.

"On the contrary," said Magdeleine, "the Virgin Mary has often pleaded with Mr. Gates to shun notoriety for his good works because, as she puts it, she 'doesn't want to lose another one.'"

Despite this alleged counsel, however, Gates' altruism has somehow managed to make recent headlines; most notably, his charitable Bill and Melinda Gates Foundation, which has given away nearly $22 billion.

"But it's not an issue we like to discuss," said Microsoft CEO Steve Ballmer, speaking at a press conference specifically called not to discuss the topic. "If Bill selflessly gives unto others so that the burdens of the world be made as harmless as doves, that's between him and his Father."

Magdeleine, meanwhile, said she had no knowledge of rumors traced to Microsoft's intranet that "The Shepherd" — as Gates is known in Redmond — was nominated for 'venerable' status with the Roman Catholic Church. Vener-

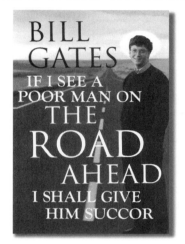

BILL GATES
IF I SEE A POOR MAN ON THE ROAD AHEAD I SHALL GIVE HIM SUCCOR

able is the first step toward canonization and sainthood.

However, a Vatican spokesman confirmed an application has been received. The Holy See, according to Cardinal Antonio Valencio, is impressed with the amount of money Gates has donated to charities, but has questions about the validity of the application.

"It's mostly this one note they've included from an ophthalmologist who says Mr. Gates is being treated for stigmata," Valencio said. "It appears to us as if this was altered, and originally said 'astigmatism.'"

Confronted with the Vatican's allegation, Microsoft Vice President Paul Moritz refused to discuss Gates' physical condition. However, he added, "I will tell you this. During board meetings, I have seen Bill hover in the air a good 20 feet off the ground while praying. But you know what? He always comes back down to wash our feet."

Gates, who Magdeleine said was busy planning a supper party for 12 of his top aides, was unavailable for comment.

# "HACKERS FOR NADER" DELIVER SURPRISE VICTORY

## Group's "Get Out and Change the Vote" Campaign Influences Dozens of Races

THE OVAL OFFICE was snatched away from Al Gore and George W. Bush this month when the International Brotherhood of Computer Hackers, urging its members to "Get Out and Change the Vote," endorsed Ralph Nader for president, leading the Green Party candidate to a post-election landslide victory.

While exit polls had Nader winning only 3 percent of the popular vote, the hacker group's campaign proved remarkably effective, as election computers gave the well-known consumer advocate a record 96 percent of the ballots — or 93 million votes. Vice President Gore won 3 percent, and Texas Governor Bush, initially assumed to be the winner, took minus-3 percent, had $50,000 charged to his credit cards, and had his middle name changed to "Abigail."

Across the nation, election officials were baffled. In Ontonagon, Mich., town clerk Casandra Dortmund said she counted the votes before sending the tally to the state, and recalled that Nader received only 18 of the 1,775 votes. But according to the state computer, Nader got 1,769 votes from Ontonagon, while Bush and Gore split the other six. "I guess some of the voters changed their minds after they voted," Dortmund said.

# 5 QUESTIONS
## Ask Jeeves

As RANDOM as they are relevant, enigmatic as they are enlightening, search engines have earned a slightly sullied reputation as a necessary evil. But it is a one-sided assessment. The search engines have not been able to explain themselves. Until now.

Thanks to its sophisticated program, which answers questions with phrases or sentences, Jeeves of AskJeeves.com granted *BusinessMonth Weekly* Editor Treat Warland the opportunity to actually interview a search engine. There were many important questions to ask. Unfortunately, he never got to most of them.

1) So, Jeeves, thanks for agreeing to the interview. Let me ask first, why is it that search engines still have difficulty delivering relevant results?

**Having Our Way: What Is It Really? Including Josephine Baker — Artist and Person**
From: http://www.gis.net/~dlamb/Josephine_Baker.htm

2) I'm sorry, you're not making sense.

**Laser eye surgery: is it worth looking into? Laser eye surgery is fast becoming the most technologically advanced method available for correcting common eye disorders.**
From: http://www.fda.gov/fdac/features/1998/498_eye.html

3) Are you always like this? You don't seem able to focus at all.

**Isn't It cool? I think this is so cool! I think I am cool!**
From: http:www.geocities.com/~homepage/whatscool.htm

4) No, it's not cool, but it does explain why, when I ask "How much is 2 plus 2?" you say...

**Shark Cartilage is Available!**
**The Shark Cartilage Information Center provides information regarding Shark Cartilage as an alternative health product.**
From: http://www.hqsc.com/default.htm

5) Exactly. Thanks anyway, Jeeves. It's been... enlightening.

**Love Bites Can Be Painful**
We've all been bitten by jellyfish. We know how painful they can be, and how the only cure is household vinegar. The cure for love can be much more simple. A quick bullet to the head is often effective.
From: http://www.gorskys.com.au/articles/back970327.html

## OFFICE POLL

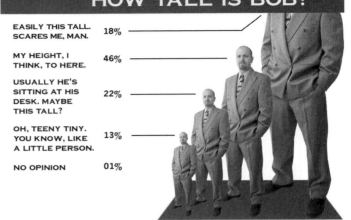

WE ASKED BOB'S CO-WORKERS...
### HOW TALL IS BOB?

| | |
|---|---|
| EASILY THIS TALL. SCARES ME, MAN. | 18% |
| MY HEIGHT, I THINK, TO HERE. | 46% |
| USUALLY HE'S SITTING AT HIS DESK. MAYBE THIS TALL? | 22% |
| OH, TEENY TINY. YOU KNOW, LIKE A LITTLE PERSON. | 13% |
| NO OPINION | 01% |

# DoubleClick Mostly Innocent

Online advertising network DoubleClick, under fire from the New York state attorney general for its now-scrapped plan to personally identify Web surfers and their habits through its software, denied today it ever implemented the scheme and offered to make amends by paying for online subscriptions to "any of the numerous porn sites" the attorney general frequents daily between 11:35 a.m. and 2 p.m. from his Dell XPS D300 office computer running Windows 98 and Netscape Communicator 4.6.

## Clarification: Love Bug "Worm"; Hackers "Twits"

The International Society of Computer Hackers blasted the media yesterday for continually using the word "virus" when referring to the "Love Bug" email that recently infected computers. The program was more accurately a "worm," not a virus, said the hacker group, adding that "ignorant journalists" should check their facts. In response, the Society of Professional Journalists thanked the hackers, who it said will now be referred to by the more accurate term "slovenly misanthropic twits."

# WEB GIVES O.J. CHANCE TO LOOK GUILTY AROUND WORLD

## AskOJ.com to Have Chats, Memorabilia, and Seek Tips on The Real Killer®

*"O.J. Simpson will get another chance to convince people that he didn't kill his ex-wife and her friend — on the Internet (at AskOJ.com)."*
— ASSOCIATED PRESS, JULY 19, 2000

UNCONVICTED ALLEGED killer O.J. Simpson last month announced the launch of AskOJ.com, a site that will enable the former football star to answer questions from users, sell personal memorabilia, and come across as a sleazy unrepentant murderer to an entirely new audience.

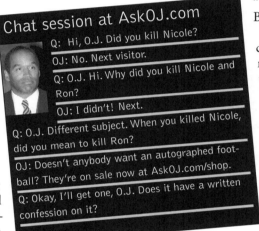

**Chat session at AskOJ.com**

Q: Hi, O.J. Did you kill Nicole?

OJ: No. Next visitor.

Q: O.J. Hi. Why did you kill Nicole and Ron?

OJ: I didn't! Next.

Q: O.J. Different subject. When you killed Nicole, did you mean to kill Ron?

OJ: Doesn't anybody want an autographed football? They're on sale now at AskOJ.com/shop.

Q: Okay, I'll get one, O.J. Does it have a written confession on it?

"I have been convicted by the American media, but the Web is international," said Simpson from the Tampa, Fla., headquarters of the Entertainment Network, which is running the site. "There are literally millions of people in Asia, Europe, and South America who need to hear my side of the story before they conclude that I am a deceitful butcher."

The former star athlete, who still holds the record for the longest open-field run by a sport utility vehicle, said he chose the Internet as his communication platform because it is an unprecedented source of "open, honest, and anonymous information." As a result, he hopes Web surfers will share information with him and help him find the "The Real Killer®" of Nicole Brown Simpson.

Though brand new, AskOJ.com has already undergone one revision. The site removed a button asking for help in finding "The Real Killer®" when nearly all of the 3,000 users who clicked the button and filled out the confidential form suggested O.J. look at "http://www.askoj.com."

"The Real Killer®," and "I have been convicted in the media®" are registered trademarks of O.J. Simpson.

# INTERNET DIVE FORCES FIRMS TO USE "MONEY"
## COMPANIES CONFUSED OVER HAVING TO ACCEPT TENDER OTHER THAN STOCK

The Internet stock drop has done more than just lop off paper profits. Startups, which once regularly paid for goods and services in stock, have been forced to switch to a form of payment called "money," a dramatic shift that has confounded both startups and those who once took equity for their work.

As one San Francisco software executive grumbled: "This 'money' stuff is quite difficult to find. Unlike our stock, it doesn't seem to grow on trees, and what's worse, we've learned we're not allowed to issue our own."

The drain on much-needed cash reserves, however, is not the only reason startups have had difficulty with the transition. "We have consultants, bankers, gardeners — you name

it — who just stare at us blankly now when we give them a check for their services," said Angela Macronus, CFO of San Jose, Calif.–based OneStopB2B.com. "We have to explain it to them succinctly. We say, 'This is $4,000. It's worth 4,000 shares of our stock.' That seems to work."

In fact, industry observers say service company employees — not startups — have been hardest hit by the change. At Valley Vendo, which since 1997 has taken equity in exchange for vending machine services, delivery drivers have practically revolted, said dispatcher Pamela Shreveson.

"They've worked with the same clients for years, and they're used to exchanging, say,

three cases of Coca-Cola and 16 cases of assorted snack crackers for 70 shares of stock. Now we're telling them, 'No, just take money.' Well naturally, they're confused. They say, 'Why are we suddenly giving our stuff away?' "

The trend is not limited to Silicon Valley, however, as London–based Web design firm ColourGraphics discovered last week.

"One French company we've been working with tried to pay us in something called 'euros,' " said ColourGraphics site producer Ian McNair. "We were like, 'Yeah, right, what the hell is that?' "

Ironically, McNair later learned that "Yeah, right, what the hell is that?" is also the official British government position on the euro.

This holiday season...

send the dotcommer in your life

a card that says,

*"Boy, am I glad I'm not you."*

Hallmark

# HOW TO SPOT A FAKE PRESS RELEASE

**COAXIAL CABLE CORP.**
A Sad Investment

PRESIDENT
ASD KAJH KAJSD
ASKLJDH AKSJHAKS KJH
ASJJKKjak KAJSKJH 91088

**AUTHENTIC COMPANY PRESS RELEASE**

INVESTORS LEARNED a brutal lesson in August, when a false press release sent stock in data networking company Emulex down more than 50 percent. The release, sent out over Internet Wire, claimed the company's chief executive had resigned, and said Emulex had been forced to restate past earnings. The story was picked up by news services, which failed to verify the release with Emulex, and before it was over, $2.5 billion had been lopped off the company's market cap.

In an effort to help investors and journalists spot a potentially false press release, *BusinessMonth Weekly* has chosen a release at random from Internet Wire, and highlighted comments that should tip you off that something is seriously wrong.

## COAXIAL CABLE CORP.
### A Bad Investment

**CoaxialCable Restates Earnings Way Downward;**
**CEO Arrested; Stock a Definite Sell**

Los Angeles, Calif. (internet Whyer) — CoaxialCable Corp. (Nasdaq: CCCO) today announced it is restating its third quarter revenues downward by at least 800 percent, and admitted the company's CEO and its entire board of directors have been arrested for major stock fraud, which means everyone should sell their CoaxialCable Corp. (Nasdaq: CCCO) stock right away.

"This is for real," said Chad Chumley, CFO of CoaxialCable, who urged investors to IMMEDIATELY SELL their CoaxialCable Corp. stock (Nasdaq: CCCO) and not ask too many questions, or even any questions, about this press release. Chumley also insisted that reporters not call the company to verify this release, "out of respect, because we are all in shock and will probably deny it."

In addition, said Chumley, CoaxialCable stock (Nasdaq: CCCO) is for sure a BIG-TIME SELL. "I'd put in a market order because this baby is going to tank so fast you don't want to get stuck with worthless stock."

According to actual CoaxialCable Corp. officials, the company initially reported Q3 revenues of $155 million and per share earnings of 0.95 cents. However, after a review of accounting procedures, it turns out revenues were like $2.2 million, and per share earnings were -$2.50, or maybe even -$11.50, so if you can sell this stock for anything over $2, you'll be lucky.

Said SEC Commissioner Arthur Levitt: "Frankly, we're astonished at the level of corruption at CoaxialCable Corp., and have to wonder why anyone would still be holding this stock after reading this far into this press release."

Levitt added that he is on vacation, and pointed out that if you call his office and someone answers the phone claiming to be Arthur Levitt and denies he ever said this, that person is an imposter because "I'm out of town, so you know it's not really me."

PR Contact
short_CCCO_stock@yesmail.com
Phone: 212-555-1212

---

Right away, we see a comment that points to possible fraud. Look at the logo and official company motto. See the problem? There is no swoosh. All company logos have a swoosh.

Grammatical mistakes are often a tip-off to a hoax. Here is a rather serious one as the 'i' in "internet Whyer" should be capitalized.

Deny what? The release? Being in shock? Thinking straight? It's not clear. This doesn't mean it's fake. We just find misplaced modifiers annoying.

There is no way a company would make this kind of statement. It would use the correct term, "Strong Sell," not "Big-Time Sell."

Agreed. We sold after the second paragraph.

Yeah, right. Levitt is the SEC Chairman. No way does he answer his own phone.

In a fake release, PR contact information usually leads the reader away from the company's real PR contacts. This is a classic example. The phone number used is for Manhattan information, but look at the dateline. The company is headquartered in Los Angeles!! So the phone number should be 213-555-1212.

# Postcards from the Ex

*"So eager is Autodesk (to rehire employees who left for dotcoms)...that it even sends a postcard to former employees a few months after they leave, asking if the grass is really greener."* — THE NEW YORK TIMES

Pre-Internet companies have lost considerable talent to online upstarts in the past few years, but now that dotcoms are down, Old Economy firms have started getting back in touch with their ex-employees to let them know they're still thinking of them.

Alison!

Hi! How are things going at eToys? And how long has it been since you left us, anyway? Oh, wait, let's see... eToys' stock was at $70 when you left. It loses 13 points a month. It's at $5 now. So that's... five months already! Wow!

Best to the family,
*Unilever*

Warren,

Any word on whether ValueAmerica will be forwarding employee mail? Once it folds, I mean. We'd hate to lose touch with you.

Your ex-boss

Anderson Consulting

Kurt,

Happy anniversary! You departed for Beyond.com exactly one year ago! We've missed you, but no doubt it was the right move. We're a stable company, and you're a pioneer who needs new challenges. Who would have thought bankruptcy would be one of them? Good luck!

*Autodesk management team*  **autodesk**

We've done a lot of thinking since you walked out the door to join online retailer Cyberian Outpost, and you know, you were right. We really are all about making money.

We envy your freedom.

citigroup

Jonathan,

Regarding your departure for CDNow last year: when you said the company was going to be "Titanic," were you being literal? We didn't realize. Apologies.

Procter & Gamble

# Life In CAMP ALPHA

## HOPE DWINDLES FOR THOUSANDS; KOZMO.COM GANG DOING OK

Since the fall of Internet stocks began in April, former dotcom employees, forced from their jobs, have made their way to Dot-Camp Alpha, a makeshift settlement on a barren hillside in Silicon Valley. Despite its lack of even the most basic facilities—plumbing, air hockey, on-site masseuse—the camp has swelled to nearly 5,000 lost souls. *BusinessMonth Weekly* editor TREAT WARLAND reports from the front.

PLEASE USE YOUR OWN STOCK OPTIONS

**ALTAVISTA REFUGEES ARE REGARDED AS USELESS.** SENT TO GATHER STICKS FOR A FIRE, THEY BROUGHT BACK THAI STICKS AND STYX ALBUMS

KARA DEITZER STARES, glassy-eyed, at the dusty road leading into Camp Alpha. It is literally choked with dotcom humanity, 200 more this day — refugees forced out in violent business model upheavals at Critical Path and Tickets.com.

As they trudge into camp, their belongings barely contained in cardboard boxes, most of the refugees look confused and disoriented. Deitzer, who arrived here from Techies.com more than a month ago, knows how they feel.

"They're thinking what I did when I showed up here," she says. "It's the same thought that we all have, every hour of every day: 'I have no cubicle. I have no stock options. I am nothing.'"

And their spirits aren't likely to improve. Though the United Nations has attempted to provide hope by granting the exiles official refugee status (*see sidebar*), hope only truly comes once a day, when the Red Cross trucks pull in with relief supplies. This morning it was 30 dozen pair of roller blades. The blades were size 6, and all for the left foot, but they were snapped up in minutes by vicious mobs of dotcommers desperate for anything reminiscent of their previous lives.

And that exposes another truth here: despite the impressive pedigrees of the inhabitants, society quickly breaks down in the wild, and Dot-Camp Alpha is now a vision of post–New Economy chaos, or perhaps modern-day Russia. One shining example: Internet company stocks are highly valued on the camp's thriving black market, not for their monetary potential, but for their use in latrines.

Running the camp's "alternate econ-

omy" are two dozen refugees from delivery site Kozmo.com, who have a reputation for "acquiring" and delivering anything a refugee might ask for.

According to Ron Turner, a Talk City exile who never shuts up, the Kozmosians split their allegiance and profits between two powerful factions. One is the Amazonians, who are feared, but not because they are bigger or stronger. "There are only about 100 refs from Amazon.com," Turner explains, "but we obey them because the consensus is that any day now, they'll be getting major reinforcements, if you know what I mean."

The other power brokers come from PlanetRx, who, with their drug connections, are able to sustain profit margins their former employer could only dream of. Efforts to speak to their leaders, however, were unsuccessful, as stern-faced former customer relations representatives, wielding Nerf Ball Blasters, would not let outsiders pass.

On the opposite end of the power scale are the "untouchables." At 300 strong, the exiles from software maker Corel are the single largest group in camp, yet they are shunned by others because, not being Web-based, they are not considered pure-play refugees. But then, even Net blue bloods can find themselves in the lower castes if they prove themselves unable to adapt.

The AltaVista refugees, for instance, are widely regarded as useless. "Just yesterday, we sent them out to search for sticks to make a fire," says Turner. "And they came back with Thai sticks, Stickley furniture, old Styx albums, all kinds of shit. They still don't get it."

Back near the camp gate, Kara Deitzer wishes she didn't "get it," but she does, and good. Every day, she and the other ex-Techies.com crowd endure a stoning at the hands of other refugees. "It's painful, but I understand it," she says, "I came here from a career site for techies, so naturally people look to me for hope. But the very fact that I'm here depresses them."

So why doesn't she just leave? Her answer is the same as that given by most of the refugees.

"There are thousands of dotcommers here," she says. "It's an incredible networking opportunity."

# FIRED DOTCOM WORKERS GRANTED REFUGEE STATUS

## U.N. to Provide Aid to Thousands Forced to Flee Their Jobs

Alarmed over "deplorable" conditions at swelling dotcom relocation camps, the United Nations High Commissioner for Refugees has granted laid-off Internet workers Official Refugee Status, making them eligible for food and medical aid, and discounts on Nerf guns and espresso.

The decree came after U.N. High Commissioner Sadako Ogata toured Dot-Camp Alpha, located in Silicon Valley, one of two major camps providing temporary shelter for the estimated 10,000 dotcommers who've been uprooted from their jobs and colleagues.

"The conditions I witnessed were deplorable," said Ogata. "There are no working foosball tables, no concierge service, and the pizza is from Domino's. It's squalor on a scale the New Economy hasn't seen."

Relief workers, who have been lobbying for months to win prized Refugee Status for dot-campers, said the decision came none too soon. Many of the refugees have gone weeks without access to email. Twice the National Guard has been called in to quell intra-camp violence between rival factions from Amazon.com and price comparison site Productopia.

The Red Cross has been on hand since late May, trucking in tankers of Jolt cola, and the first physicians from Médecins Sans Frontières (Doctors Without Borders) arrived last week to render medical assistance to those suffering from sprained knees and ankles sustained on the camp's substandard mountain bike trails.

## HOW LONG WILL IT LAST?

In Dot-Camp Alpha, nearly 60 percent of refugees come from public relations, said Red Cross field

organizer Dick Fletcher. "Their chances of finding a new home are slim, and their chances of going back to their old firms are non-existent."

Even if they could return, many would find their cubicles gone or occupied.

"When I was forced out, they actually tore down my cubicle right before my eyes," said Andrew Weiner, a former content developer at Furniture.com. "And my neighbor Chuck, they moved some guy from bizdev into his spot before he could even..." Weiner then broke down crying and asked to be excused.

Weiner, like the others, insisted he will stay in his makeshift shelter, working on his résumé, reading frayed copies of *Fast Company* that are passed around the camp like gold, and hoping that venture capitalism is prosecuted as a war crime.

# SALLY STRUTHERS BEGS YOU TO
# SAVE THE DOTCOMS

## Share Your Love with an Internet Company in Need; Become a Sponsor

Hello there,

Right now, all over the world, dotcoms are hurting. They are suffering from faulty business plans and cash-flow shortfalls. They lack earnings and even the most basic of revenue models. In many countries, four out of five dotcoms will die within the next two years.

All that is needed is someone who will look into the eyes of a needy dotcom and say, "Yes, I will help." Someone like you.

With each passing day, dotcoms are finding it increasingly difficult to stay alive. Cut off from further venture  funding or bank credit, without access to sufficient revenues, many are forced to make choices about which essentials they can afford: salaries or benefits, marketing or product development, sales or office parties? Choices no one should have to make. Despair takes the place of hope.

It doesn't have to be this way. Right now, living, breathing dotcoms need your help. Please, look deep into your heart and make the decision to become a Save the Dotcoms sponsor, and for as little as 79 cents a day (or about the cost of the average Internet stock today), you can help stop the suffering and give deserving dotcoms a better life today, and a chance for the future.

As a dotcom sponsor, you become a partner in bringing renewed hope to a dotcom whose future is now in doubt. The special relationship you can develop with your dotcom is something you'll cherish forever. It starts with a photograph and corporate history of your dotcom. And it continues as you enjoy opportunities to get to know your sponsored dotcom (and for your dotcom to learn all about you!).

Best of all, you'll actually see the impact that your sponsorship is having. You'll receive regular earnings reports and press releases from your dotcom, on your dotcom's own stationery. And thanks to your contribution, you will keep your dotcom off the pages of *DotComFailures* or *The Industry Standard's* Dotcom Layoff Tracker.

Your tax-deductible contribution can be sent directly to the company, or to its creditors, or its lawyers, or to me, Sally Struthers.

Imagine the excitement when we tell a special dotcom that someone wants to make a difference in its life! Still not convinced? Read testimonials from participants. Or hear the sad tale of a dotcom in need.

Please. There are so many precious dotcoms waiting to be sponsored. You can even sponsor a dotcom from an area or market that has special meaning to you or is close to your heart. Please, won't you fill out the sponsorship form today? Right now? The life of a dotcom is all too short. Extend a hand, and extend the hope.

*Sally Struthers*

## FROM A SPONSORED DOTCOM

*I am humbled, at a loss for words, to express how thankful I am to have such kind friends in my sponsors, Donna and Bob Nickerson. They feel like my colleagues as much as my board of directors. Through people like them, and Save the Dotcoms, I have been able to blow our marketing budget without increasing our debt burden. We are still cash-flow negative, but at least we have the chance to make it through the winter! Thanks, Donna and Bob!*

*—Michael Levy, CEO, Sportsline.com*

**Please, become a sponsor. Every day, dozens of dotcoms fall ill. Help us find a cure.**

## FROM SPONSORS:

*I like to think that my mother and I, through our sponsorship with Save the Dotcoms, are a contributing force to making life better for WebMD and its employees. After rumors about bankruptcy, WebMD believes it*  *can turn a profit for the first time in its life, someday. In WebMD's case, I can definitely see we have made a difference, and that the expectations for its future have been raised.*

*—Anne Weaks and Jill Weaks Delaney*

**Please, become a sponsor. Let's pretend we can make a difference.**

*As we have no dotcom of our own, my wife and I love hearing from our sponsored dotcom, Gear.*  *com, and being a part of the life of this suffering online sporting goods retailer. We like being part of the solution to some of the problems of the dotcom world, and as always, we get more than we give. In our case, a free jogging stroller, which Gear wrote off as a marketing expense.*

*—Charles and Virginia Shumacher*

**Please, become a sponsor. Extend the hope, so they can extend the hype.**

**Won't you join Charles and Virginia, Anne and Jill, and help the likes of Michael? Please, become a sponsor. Let's put F*ckedCompany out of business.**

---

SAVE THE
DOTCOMS

## Thank You for Sponsoring
# A Needy Dotcom!
### Your donation will make a world of difference!

YOUR NAME:_____
YOUR ADDRESS:
_____
_____

AMOUNT US$_____

> NOTE: THE RECOMMENDED DONATION
> IS 79 CENTS A DAY,
> BUT YOU CAN CONTRIBUTE ANY AMOUNT.

I PREFER TO SPONSOR (CHECK ONE):
__ A PUBLIC COMPANY
__ A PRIVATE COMPANY
__ SOMETHING IN BETWEEN, LIKE VERIZON

PREFERRED LOCATION:
__ SILICON VALLEY          __ SILICON FJORD
__ SILICON ALLEY           __ SILICHAMPS ELYSEES
__ SILICON PRAIRIE         __ SILICON BRIDGE/TUNNEL
__ SILICON TERMINAL        __ BAYONNE
   MORAINE

PREFERRED BUSINESS MODEL:     __ B2C2CHAPTER 11
                              __ B2B2CHAPTER 11

THE COMPANY I SPONSOR SHOULD BE:
__ STRUGGLING      __ F*CKED
__ FALTERING       __ ROAD KILL
__ BATTERED        __ THE NEXT TOYSMART

I DO NOT WANT MY DOTCOM TO BE INVOLVED IN:
__ GAMBLING        __ METALLURGY
__ VIOLENCE        __ HYPERBOLE
__ PORNOGRAPHY     __ BANNER ADVERTISING
__ CALLIGRAPHY

# SERMON ON THE MONEY

## NEW ECONOMY CLERGY LONG ON JESUS, SHORT ON CONSUMER NON-CYCLICALS

*"Jesse Jackson is enlisting the aid of fellow clergymen to preach the gospel of Wall Street to their flocks to help them save and invest their way to economic equality. He persuaded the New York Stock Exchange to conduct a weeklong seminar on investing for ministers...the first class of 40 clergymen graduated last week."*
— BARRON'S

The following sermon was delivered at the Calvary Baptist Church, Smyrna, Ga., by the Rev. James Arnell, the first valedictorian of the New York Stock Exchange's School of Economic Salvation.

Brothers and sisters, let me ask you a question. Are you long on Jesus?

I see many of you don't know what I'm asking. That's all right. It's a stock market term. When you think a stock will go down, you are short on that stock. If you think it will rise, you are long on that stock. Well, when I say I'm long on Jesus, that means I believe in Jesus. I'm invested in Jesus. He's going up, and I hope one day to go up with Him!

*(amen)*

So let me ask you again, are you long on Jesus?

*(oh, yes)*

That's good. Because I think if Jesus were here today, He'd want you to be thinking about your financial future. He's interested in your financial future, yes, He is. As long as you believe in Him, as long as you are long on Him, He wants you to prosper. And through His life, He lets us know that.

Just think for a moment. What was Jesus doing from the moment He arrived? He was laying the pipe that would one day connect all people to God! Yes, He was. And oh, His was a

138

mighty pipe. A big, fat pipe! He was a veritable T-3 of salvation!

*(amen!)*

He was out there increasing the bandwidth!

*(that's right)*

He believes in increasing the bandwidth!

*(yes, He does)*

Which is why we like Worldcom in the $40s, particularly now that the Sprint merger looks dead.

*(glory be)*

And after He ascended, did he forget about that pipe? Did He just cut us off? No! We still access Him through prayer. And what is prayer? It's a transmission; a very special transmission, for it does not depend on wires or things of this Earth. No! Brothers and sisters, when we pray to God, we are sending a wireless signal into the heavens.

*(that's right)*

Jesus is wireless!

*(amen!)*

Prayer is wireless!

*(amen!)*

Phone.com is wireless! And with projected 160 percent annual revenue growth, it's a screaming buy at $80.

*(hallelujah!)*

And we would short Excite@Home here.

*(okay)*

But Reverend, you might say, 160 percent growth makes for a strong and mighty player. Didn't the Lord say the meek shall inherit the Earth? Well, yes, He did. And I have often wondered what He meant, but just this morning, as I sat in my office checking my email, I could not help but notice my new personal digital assistant. How small it was, I thought. How

tiny it was, I marveled. And then it hit me: This was the meek.

*(uh-huh)*

This was the future.

*(oh, yes)*

Praise the meek!

*(amen)*

Praise the PDA!

*(that's right)*

Praise Palm, Inc., but only at dips into the teens. Otherwise you might want to look at Handspring.

*(not for the risk-averse!)*

Finally, before you leave here today, I want you to make me a promise. Don't let your material wealth destroy your spiritual health.

*(no, no)*

Promise me you'll be long on Jesus!

*(we do)*

Promise me you'll short Satan!

*(we will)*

Promise me you'll reduce your exposure to consumer non-cyclicals, which may fare better as the economy turns down but currently exhibit weak fundamentals!

*(we're calling our brokers!)*

Oh, it's a glorious day. Can I hear an amen?

*(amen)*

Can I hear an amen?

*(amen!)*

Can I hear an Amgen, whose current price we don't feel adequately reflects the promising phase 3 clinical trials of abarelix-depot-M?

*(Amgen, whose current price we don't feel adequately reflects the promising phase 3 clinical trials of abarelix-depot-M.)*

Go forth and prosper.

# SatireWire's
# Business Month
## WEEKLY

**DECEMBER 2001**

%

WILL
CHART
FOR
FOOD

## HOW ARE WE COPING?

- DOTCOM REFUGEES RIOT

- ATLANTA: THE CITY
  NOT TOO BUSY TO HATE

- YAHOO'S INGENIOUS PLOY:
  YAHOOTERS GIRLS!

- COMPANIES FILE FOR
  INTELLECTUAL BANKRUPTCY

- PROSTIDOTS:
  NEW ECONOMY, OLD TACTICS

- KOZMO LAYS OFF STAFF
  IN UNDER AN HOUR

## PLUS

- ME, CARLY FIORINA,
  AND A QUART OF RIPPLE!

# THE SEARCH FOR B2?

## Let's pretend a magazine can help you find the next big thing

WITH THE flow of venture capital money drying up, and most companies licking their wounds and attempting to regroup, you would think that this would not be the time to write about "hot new business models." But you would be wrong. You would be wrong because, in good times and bad, that entrepreneurial spirit lives on. And you would be wrong because, as a business magazine, it is our mandate to write about new business models, even if there aren't any to be found. Plus it was on our editorial calendar. And we sold ads against it.

So... the fervor for B2C (business-to-consumer) commerce has come and gone, and B2B (business-to-business) followed quickly on its heels. What's the Next Big Thing? Let's take a peek at the four latest B-2-Whatever business models.

### B2E — BUSINESS TO EMPLOYEE

The idea seems practical. Instead of selling products and services to disparate and often hard-to-isolate markets, businesses simply sell to their own employees. Admittedly, the program has been a disappointment at companies like defense industry giant Raytheon, as spokesperson Anne Flagg explained: "What we learned is, the people who work for Raytheon don't necessarily need an AN/SLQ-48 Mine Neutralization System for their personal use."

However, she added, the Patriot missiles sold quite well for Father's Day, and B2E's advantages do slightly outweigh the disadvantages. Notably:

*ADVANTAGES*
• Companies recoup money paid out in salaries.
• Complex annual job performance evaluations replaced by simple question: "How much of the company's product did you buy this year?"
• Overstocking no longer a problem as individual employees either buy heavily during year-end inventory clearance or become part of year-end inventory clearance.

*DISADVANTAGES*
• Ugly, face-to-face confrontations with Customer Complaint Departments.
• Wage increases may be necessary to allow employees to buy their company's product; e.g., average Boeing worker would need to earn $42 million annually.

### C2B — CONSUMER TO BUSINESS

In the few markets where the idea has been tested, and in the two phone calls I made about it, this has fared poorly. Cisco Systems, for instance, tried C2B for a month.

"After the first week, not a single consumer called to sell us anything," said Paul Riddle, vice president of consumer immigration. "So we started calling people at random: 'Hello, this is Cisco Systems. We need 12 gross of Catalyst 3900 token ring switches.' Or, 'Hello, this is Cisco Systems. We'd like to purchase 120,000 meters of coaxial cable. When can you ship?'"

The answers, Riddle lamented, were always the same: "It was either 'Mommy's not home,' or 'I'm calling the police.'"

Pharmaceutical giant Merck, meanwhile, took a slightly different C2B approach, but has reaped as yet no benefits.

"We initially tried asking for what we needed, but the average consumer just didn't have, say, a liquid nitrogen cooling system," said Merck purchasing manager Thelma Hackett. "So we changed the model and started buying whatever people wanted to get rid of." As a result, said Hackett, Merck now has the nation's largest inventory of Tickle Me Elmos and Nordic Tracks, and is the largest shareholder of drkoop.com.

### BG2H — BUSINESS GOING TO HELL

Not actually a business model, as such, but there must be something to it as an awful lot of companies seem to be practicing it.

### B2CC — BUSINESS TO CREDIT CARD

Lastly, the word "promising" may not be strong enough for this innovative approach to commerce. As anyone in sales will tell you, the greatest impediment to a transaction is the consumer. They have questions. They have doubts. Or sometimes, they're just not interested. B2CC avoids these problems by avoiding consumers altogether, and instead deals directly with their credit cards.

"The practice of billing people for products and services they have not asked for is unquestionably illegal, and we will prosecute to the fullest anyone engaged in such activity," said a spokesman for the U.S. Department of Justice.

Please. We've heard the same thing about HMOs, and they're doing fine.

# Cisco Not Just a Stock; Also Company That Makes Things

## Betrayed Shareholders Not Particularly Interested In Routers, Switches

THE RUMORS about Cisco Systems have been circulating for months, but the earnings warning and plunge in its share price have left little doubt in investors' minds that Cisco is not just a famous stock, but may in fact have been operating as a large company that makes complex and incomprehensible equipment related to high technology.

"I got into Cisco two years ago because I was made to understand it was really the tech stock to own," said Cisco shareholder Anthony Timson of Rahway, N.J. "Honestly, it never occurred to me that there was anything

more to it. Frankly, I feel betrayed."

Once considered the core high-tech holding, Cisco has watched its share price fall 80 percent from its 2000 peak. As a result, much more attention lately has been given to the company's market share, revenues, and products, such as routers, switches, and Virtual Private Network concentrators. These days, Cisco is rarely identified simply as a highly recommended stock or "surefire" high-tech bet.

While Cisco CEO John Chambers said he is sorry investors have had to learn about the company this way, he believes the public defrocking will be good in the long run.

"Until recently, the only reason many people had heard of Cisco was

**"I INVESTED IN A STOCK, NOT A COMPANY THAT MAKES UNIVERSAL CONCENTRATORS."**
**— FRUSTRATED CISCO SHAREHOLDER NINA CARELLO**

because our stock was famous," he said. "Now people will get to know us for what we do. We'll be just like any other high-tech company."

Timson, however, disagreed. "Other high-tech companies make shit I can understand," he said.

---

## AMAZING NEW "SEGWAY HUMAN TRANSPORTER" APPARENTLY NOT TESTED FOR ACRONYM

### Honestly, We're Not Making This SHT Up

After a year-long buildup during which it was known as the mysterious "Ginger" or "IT," the revolutionary, scooter-like "Segway Human Transporter" was unveiled last week without first being checked for its potential acronym.

As a result, the media was full of SHT stories, while investors on Wall Street were hoping inventor Dean Kamen would take his cool SHT public so they could get a piece of SHT.

Word about the electric-powered transportation machine was leaked last year, but it took more than 10 years for Kamen and his team to get their SHT together. When the device was introduced on ABC's *Good*

*Morning America,* riders who took an initial SHT spin were visibly impressed.

"It's so fun and stable and quiet. I can't believe this SHT!" said ABC's Diane Sawyer.

"Boy, I hope no one's looking because I really want to take a SHT right now!" joshed good-natured co-host Charles Gibson. Gibson will have to wait, however. The company is currently producing only a big SHT for commercial use, and won't make a little SHT for consumers until the 2002 holiday season.

At $3,000 each, however, the consumer model may be out of reach of all but the most generous of gift givers. "If it's three grand,

there's no way I can give a SHT," said Holly Dumal of Princeton, N.J. "I wish they'd make a cheap SHT."

Kamen replied that the company would never give its SHT away, but promised a less expensive version was "definitely on our SHT list."

Also in the works: a specially designed device for use by Pope John Paul that will speed the aging pontiff around the Vatican and St. Peter's Square. Its name: the Holy SHT.

## Fed-Up Media Files Bankruptcy Papers for Xerox

TIRED OF waiting for Xerox to die, frustrated journalists went ahead and filed bankruptcy papers for the copier giant today, putting an end to months of intense speculation and annoyingly repetitive copy.

"After a while, talking with Xerox was like arguing with a terminally ill patient: 'You're going to die.' 'No I'm not.' 'Are too.' 'Am not,'" explained *New York Post* reporter Gary

Xerox headquarters, Stamford, Connecticut.

Brookman. "So me and a bunch of other reporters, we waited till no one was looking, and we just pulled the plug, so to speak."

At a press conference, Xerox CEO Paul Allaire blasted the media for "playing God," and insisted the company was still in business. Journalists, however, turned deaf ears on his pleas.

"I assure you Xerox is very much alive," Allaire told the reporters.

"Hey, did you hear someone talking?" *L.A. Times* business reporter Kurt Varing asked the *Post*'s Brookman. "It sounded like that guy from Xerox, but Xerox is dead."

"That's right. So it must be the ghost of Xerox," responded Brookman. "Oooooo."

"Stop," said Varing. "You're scaring me."

## BEATLES REUNITED IN PHOTOSHOP

Succeeding where even the biggest names and deepest pockets in show business have failed, 43-year-old Hoboken, N.J., resident Grace Rogers triumphantly reunited the Beatles last week using Adobe Photoshop 6.0.

"I'd always heard getting the Beatles back together would be impossible, even if they were all alive," said Rogers. "But it was easy. I scanned in some pictures of George, Paul, and Ringo that I cut out of *People* magazine, then I sorta guessed what John would look like if he were still alive. I also made one where I'm the fifth Beatle."

The reunited group can be seen on the World Wide Web at:

**www.i-obviously-have-no-life.net**

The surviving Beatles could not be reached for comment.

## Californians Start Email Campaign for Energy Conservation

CALIFORNIANS, faced with an energy crisis fueled by high-tech power consumption, have launched an email campaign urging fellow computer users to stay off their computers.

Days after the state issued its first-ever Stage 3 Power emergency, millions of cause-minded Californians decided not to wait for the situation to get worse, and began sending the "Stay Offline" email to friends, family, and co-workers.

"The response so far has been incredible," said Charles Brudeker, the 32-year-old San Francisco software engineer who devised the campaign. "I myself have gotten the email 200 times since breakfast. I'm logging on every 5 minutes just to see how many more I get."

"Once again, Californians are responding to a crisis as only Californians can," said Governor Gray Davis, who added his staff is working nights in order to send out the email to as many people as possible.

YAHOO! SAYS PORN SALES
WON'T CHANGE COMPANY...

# NEW YAHOOTERS! GIRLS "JUST AN EXPERIMENT"

## Girls Will Answer Your Deep, Searching Questions for Only $3.95/Minute

*"We're hard and fast on being the largest enabler of commerce on the Web. We have chosen to offer adult-oriented content as part of that."*
—Yahoo! President Jeff Mallett

INTERNET GIANT Yahoo! acknowledged recent reports that its shopping service is peddling thousands of hardcore porn videos and other erotica, but stressed that a pornography mentality has not suddenly permeated the company, which remains focused on "taking on all the really big, stiff, hard challenges standing right in front of us."

While Yahoo's recent earnings statement, which President Jeff Mallett insisted on calling the company's "money shot," suggests its banner-ad revenue model is in trouble, Mallett contended that, "Smut, hardcore, bondage, busty babes, lonely housewives, dirty debs, she-males in uniform...all of that is just not something we're suddenly obsessed about. If we have a fetish, it's that we're obscenely passionate about letting people know that we're hot, eager, and ready to take them all on. By 'them' I mean 'challenges,' of course."

Mallett added that a company press release identifying Yahoo! as the Internet's most popular "pornal" was probably the result of a typo. However, he refused to comment on why page searches now return a page of "resluts" instead of the former "results."

Conservative groups immediately threatened to boycott Yahoo! for offer-

### NEW YAHOO! SLOGANS:
- **Yahorny? Yahoo!**
- **Yahard Yet?**
- **We Got Yawhores!**
- **oh yes, Oh Yes, YAHOO!**
- **Do Yahave the Handcuffs?**
- **Do You Yahoo, Or Would You Rather Just Fuck?**

ing porn videos, and were further incensed by the introduction of the new Yahooters! Girls, who will personally answer visitors' "deep, penetrating" questions online for $7.95 for the first minute, only $3.95 per minute thereafter.

Asked what the girls will offer that site visitors can't get by searching Yahoo's extensive directory, Mallett blushed. "Let's just say they can search in areas that you didn't even know existed," he said.

In a separate statement, Yahoo! released first-quarter earnings of 1 cent a share last Wednesday, numbers so low, said Mallett, "they're barely legal!"

# French Strike for Greater Productivity

ANGERED OVER reports that California's economy has surpassed that of France, dozens of French labor unions staged another of their massive, nationwide strikes Friday, demanding the government investigate possible causes of the country's low per capita productivity.

"French workers should be the most productive in the world, and we will strike until the government can discover why we are not," said Rene L'ampoule, a spokesman for truck drivers who blocked most of the nation's major roadways.

According to the report, compiled by the Los Angeles Economic Development Corp., California's gross domestic product was $1.33 trillion last year, compared to France's $1.28 trillion. With 61 million inhabitants, France's population is nearly twice that of California, making the nation's per capita production half that of the U.S. state.

In the country's 15th nationwide strike this year, protesting miners, farmers, students, truckers, mechanics, teachers, engineers, entertainers, programmers, police officers, firefighters, and journalists, as well as factory, airline, rail, livery, clerical, and prison workers, said it was the government's responsibility to investigate. Government employees, meanwhile, said they would join the strike in sympathy.

# TRENDSETTERS:

## PSINET FIRST TO FILE FOR INTELLECTUAL BANKRUPTCY

A MONTH after stating it may file for Chapter 11 bankruptcy but nonetheless wants to continue paying $105 million for the 20-year naming rights to a professional football stadium, Internet service provider PSINet has become the first public company to be given protection under the nation's new Chapter 51 intellectual bankruptcy laws.

PSINet President Harry Hobbs said he was pleased and surprised that his company was setting the trend. "Honestly, I would have thought [Internet holding company] CMGI had filed for this already. They're losing money, and they have a stadium too."

Analysts said they expect dozens of other firms, including CMGI, to file for Chapter 51, which was recently enacted to aid struggling companies burdened by executives who are deemed "intellectually incapable" of making rational business decisions. The "51" refers not to a section of the U.S. bankruptcy code,

**PSINet**
Internet Service Provider
Ashburn, Va.

but to the assertion that a company's executive team is not exactly playing with a full deck.

Under Chapter 51, companies can file for "hold harmless" asylum from investors and creditors if their executives "clearly exhibit" tendencies consistent with persons who should not be held responsible for their own actions. While companies in financial difficulty traditionally have filed for Chapter 11, analysts say the newly created Chapter 51 is preferable for several reasons. In particular:

• As opposed to the more costly and lengthy financial documentation required under Chapter 11, companies filing for Chapter 51 need only provide anecdotal evidence, such as newspaper clippings. Firms such as Priceline.com or Computer Associates, meanwhile, are eligible on reputation alone.

• Companies gaining Chapter 51 status are judged not accountable, and cannot be sued for malfeasance, as U.S. laws protect the mentally incompetent from standing trial.

In the case of Ashburn, Va.–based PSINet, Hobbs said the company's professed determination to continue paying to have the firm's name plastered on the Baltimore Ravens' football stadium when the company is $3.6 billion in debt proves he and other executive officers are "not intellectually viable" and therefore eligible for Chapter 51.

## BRIEFS

### Merger to Create Largest ISP to Someday Declare Bankruptcy

Struggling rivals Juno Online and NetZero have concluded their $70 million merger, instantly creating the nation's No. 2 Internet access provider, and the largest ISP to someday declare bankruptcy.

In the press conference to discuss the deal, NetZero CEO Mark Goldston said the combined company will continue to provide free Internet access while depending on advertising revenue, a path that allowed the firms to lose a combined $100 million last quarter, and has led the share prices of Netzero and Juno to fall to 95 cents and $1.47, respectively.

"Individually, our companies were not strong enough to exist and probably would have faded away," explained Goldston. "But by combining operations, we will have a subscriber base of 7 million, which should prove very attractive to advertisers, until we fold."

### eToys Meets Expectations: None

Bankrupt online retailer eToys, whose site shut down earlier this month, this week projected that for the first time in its existence, the company's quarterly revenues would meet analysts' expectations. "We won't make anything," said former Chairman Toby Lenk.

"Our primary focus in 2001 was going to be a drive towards profitability through gross margin improvements, and to that end, we were going to be extremely pleased with the results we were going to achieve in our key metrics," Lenk continued. "While our endeavors were going to result in revenue performance that would not meet our expectations, notwithstanding we were going to proactively reevaluate our business and implement several strategic initiatives designed to accelerate eToys' drive toward profitability."

"But then we just said, 'Fuck it,' " he added.

## SUSPICIOUS AMERICA WONDERS...
# IS WORLD PUTTING U.S. INTERESTS FIRST?

IN A STINGING accusation this month, the United States charged other nations with taking a narrow-minded "world view" and deliberately failing to consider U.S. economic interests above individual international concerns.

World leaders immediately denied the charges, calling the U.S. allegations, "paranoid delusions of non-grandeur," but U.S. President George W. Bush wasn't buying it.

"They can deny it, but from carbon dioxide emissions to Internet privacy standards, these internationals appear to be taking a rather myopic 'world view,' instead of stepping back and looking at the broader American economic view," said Bush. "These people have to recognize that there is an entire United States community out there beyond their borders."

If this troubling trend continues, Bush warned, the United States will be forced to "take its ball and go home." Asked exactly what ball he was referring to, Bush replied: "It's big and blue and we all live on it."

While evidence supporting the allegations appears to be damning, world leaders insist the United States has misunderstood, and urged patience. "I respect the President's concerns, but to be fair, the situation is not entirely our fault," said European Commission President Romano Prodi.

"Many people have lived what you might call sheltered lives well outside U.S. borders." As time goes by and the world becomes less "restrictively global" and more "universally American," many of these problems will resolve themselves, Prodi predicted.

British Environment Minister Michael Meacher, meanwhile, said the idea that Europe would not consider the U.S. economy above all was absurd. "Naturally, when we want to protect consumers or deal with the environment or stop wars, we first ask ourselves, 'How will our decisions impact suffering American business interests?'"

U.S. officials, however, greeted those comments with suspicion, noting that few public comments by world leaders reflect this alleged concern.

"That's because it's a given," replied Japanese Prime Minister Yoshiro Mori. "It's like when you love someone. You don't always have to say it. You just know."

**WHITE HOUSE EVIDENCE:**

• **International politicians and the media have blasted the U.S. for abandoning the Kyoto global warming treaty, despite the fact that the U.S. has explained the treaty would not be good for the U.S. economy.**

• **The European Union has yet to lower its stricter Internet privacy standards, even though the U.S. has pointed out that these standards could hurt American businesses.**

• **Several countries, including India, are encouraging their skilled high-tech workers to stay home and not emigrate to the United States, ignoring the fact that the United States "could probably use them."**

# OBITUARIES

## Friends Recall Gist Of Cliffs Notes Founder

Cliffs Notes founder Clifton Hillegass, born 1918, founded Cliffs Notes 1958, sold in 1998, died, age 83, Lincoln, Neb.

Hillegass served in Army, had idea for Cliffs Notes (book synopses), students liked, teachers hated. Recalled as philanthropist, also good guy. Funeral Tuesday. Pastor read Book Common Prayer. "We commend Clifton...commit body to ground...earth... ashes...dust...amen."

## Funeral for Club Med Founder Doesn't Include Hearse, Burial

Mourners at the funeral for Club Med founder Gilbert Trigano, who died recently in Paris, said they had a "wonderful time" at the service yesterday, although family members were outraged that the hearse and interment were not included in the funeral home's "all-inclusive memorial package."

"When we signed up for this funeral, we assumed it included everything," said Serge Trigano, Club Med's CEO and son of the deceased. "How do they expect us to have a memorable, grief-filled funeral if they don't get the body to the cemetery and put it in the ground?"

"In our brochure, it explains quite clearly that transportation and burial are 'off-site' extras that require a separate fee," countered Jacque Gautier, funeral director of the Éternel Repos mortuary. "You should always read the fine print."

The service, at Montparnasse Cemetery, was presided over by Father Jean Baptiste,* who noted Trigano was now "at rest in Club Dead, the eternal all-inclusive where he is free from stress, never has to lift a finger, and can lay around all day doing absolutely nothing."

* Fee extra

## IBM Denies Its Aryan6000® Machines Aided Nazis

RESPONDING TO a recently published book claiming its German subsidiary aided Nazi efforts, IBM today denied its equipment was used to catalog enemies of the Third Reich, and insisted the name of the company's tabulating machine, the Aryan6000®, was "just a coincidence."

"The Aryan6000 had nothing to do with Nazism," said IBM spokesperson Brian Vorst. "It was named that simply because it was big and white."

The book, entitled *IBM and the Holocaust: The Strategic Alliance Between Nazi Germany and America's Most Powerful Corporation,* alleges that as the nearly exclusive supplier of database equipment to the Third Reich, IBM knowingly profited from the Holocaust by helping the Nazis index Jews and other minorities.

However, said Vorst, "IBM does not and never has condoned the policies of Nazi Germany, and certainly we would not have marketed our high-performance Aryan6000 line, with its patented Über-RaceCheck punch cards, to anyone who supported those policies."

# Foot-and-Mouth Unable to Spread Through Microsoft Outlook

## RESEARCHERS SHOCKED TO FIND VIRUS THAT EMAIL APP DOESN'T LIKE

SCIENTISTS AT the Centers for Disease Control and Symantec's AntiVirus Research Center last week confirmed that foot-and-mouth disease cannot be spread by Microsoft's Outlook email application, believed to be the first time the program has ever failed to propagate a major virus.

"Frankly, we've never heard of a virus that couldn't spread through Microsoft Outlook, so our findings were, to say the least, unexpected," said Clive Sarnow, director of the CDC's infectious disease unit.

The study was immediately hailed by British officials, who said it will save millions of pounds and thousands of man-hours. "Up until now we have, quite naturally, assumed that both foot-and-mouth and mad cow were spread by Microsoft Outlook," said Nick Brown, Britain's Agriculture Minister. "By eliminating it, we can focus our resources elsewhere."

However, researchers in the Netherlands, where foot-and-mouth has recently appeared, said they are not yet prepared to disqualify Outlook, which has been the progenitor of viruses such as "I Love You," "Bubbleboy," "Anna Kournikova," and "Naked Wife," to name a few.

Said Nils Overmars, director of the Molecular Virology Lab at Leiden University: "It's not that we don't trust the research, it's just that as scientists, we are trained to be skeptical of any finding that flies in the face of established truth. And this one flies in the face like a blind-drunk sparrow."

Executives at Microsoft, meanwhile, were equally skeptical, insisting that Outlook's patented Virus Transfer Protocol (VTP) has proven pervious to virtually any virus. The company, however, will issue a free VTP patch if it turns out the application is not vulnerable to foot-and-mouth.

Such an admission would be embarrassing for the software giant, but Symantec virologist Ariel Kologne insisted that no one is more humiliated by the study than she is. "Only last week," she recalled, "I had a reporter ask if the foot-and-mouth virus spreads through Microsoft Outlook, and I told him, 'Doesn't everything?'"

# BOLD NEW ECONOMY DESERVES BOLD NEW RECESSION

## Network Efficiencies Could Lead to Prolonged "Dream Recession," Say Experts

FOR MORE than a year now, the mere mention of the "R" word has been enough to send a shiver of unease through even the most stably employed American, who for the last several years has basked in the glory, and the gain, associated with the long economic expansion. But according to a growing number of economic theorists and high-tech executives, Americans needn't fear losing their place in the history books, as they predict the unprecedented New Economy will produce an equally successful "New Recession," a fast-paced, highly efficient decline that will be the envy of economies the world over.

"We really have a chance to rewrite the economic history books with this one," said Harvard economist Nils Wahlgren. "It's a great time to be an economist," he added.

In the New Recession, corporations will utilize their network capabilities — including email and intranets — to streamline and expedite downsizing and cost-cutting processes. They will be able to gauge and spread economic deprivation instantly, efficiently, and globally, said Accenture networking consultant Dee Peers. "If all goes well, I will lose my job more quickly and at less expense to the company than was ever thought possible," she said.

In addition, the New Economy's ties to the stock market will cause immediate suffering in the general population, leading to what Goldman Sachs analyst Ben Wan calls a "dream recession."

"What's really exciting is that something like 49 percent of adult U.S. residents own stock in some form, and as they are capable of tracking their portfolios in real time on the Internet, the negative impact on their psyches and savings, and on the economy as a whole, will be instantaneous," said Wan. "Depending upon how 'wired' you are, you could lose your job and your life savings in the same moment!"

Efficiencies in productivity, meanwhile, could even put an end to one of the time-honored maxims of recessionary times. "In an old recession, when a company was going bust, some office wag would invariably say, 'Will the last one out please shut off the lights?'" noted Wahlgren. "But in the New, high-tech Recession, those lights will be shut off system-wide, automatically, from a remote location. It doesn't get any better than that."

Such a New Recession has some radical economists speculating that it could lead to a permanent "New Depression," a continual period of negative growth, high unemployment, and high inflation once thought to be achievable only in North Korea or under Boris Yeltsin.

Aside from its staying power, how would the New Depression differ from its predecessor? According to Deutsche Asset Management economist Helen Wilstein, the America of the 1930s was dominated by manual labor, which prompted U.S. President Franklin Roosevelt to create the Works Progress Administration, which gave the unemployed jobs digging ditches, fixing roads, and performing other pointless tasks. "I imagine we'll again have to create jobs that serve no tangible purpose," predicted Wilstein, "but given today's service-based economy, it's more likely people will be put to work as management consultants."

# JUDGE DENIES BIAS AGAINST "GUILTY MICROSOFT BASTARDS"

"My Published Comments About Those Evil Pricks Were Misconstrued," Jackson Says.

ATTEMPTING TO keep his reputation, if not his ruling, intact, Judge Thomas Penfield Jackson this week finally apologized for his derogatory public remarks about Microsoft, admitting they were "injudicious and unwarranted," but denied he was ever biased against "those guilty, lying bastards."

"I had then, and still have today, no personal opinions whatsoever as regards the company, or the evil prick son of a bitch who runs it," said Jackson, adding that his earlier negative comments were taken out of context.

Jackson's *ex parte* remarks to the press, which include comparing Microsoft to a criminal street gang, and its executives to spoiled children,

drew unprecedented wrath in July from the U.S. Court of Appeals, which unanimously overturned Jackson's ruling to split up Microsoft and sent the case back to a lower court. The seven-member appellate court upheld much of the government's antitrust case against the Redmond, Wash., software giant, but said Jackson's prejudicial comments were enough to vacate his ruling.

Chief Appellate Judge Harry Edwards was particularly bothered by Jackson's statement to a reporter that Microsoft Chairman Bill Gates "has a Napoleonic concept of himself."

In response, a contrite Jackson conceded Napoleon was the wrong choice. "When I said 'Napoleon,' I did not mean to imply that Mr. Gates' ulterior motive was world conquest or the suppression of democratic principles. I only meant that he's a little shit."

# Microsoft Says Linux Has No Future, So Linux Firms Will Stop

CHASTENED LINUX company executives pledged to stop their "crazy dreaming" and disband their efforts after an executive from Microsoft proclaimed Linux was doomed, and openly questioned whether the free, rival operating system should exist.

The executive, Microsoft group product manager Doug Miller, told a reporter from *Wired*, "Linux is not leading anything, it is simply providing a 'free' operating system," adding that, "Free does not sustain a business," and, "the recent security problems with Linux...really call into question whether Linux should be used at all."

The startling reprimand from Redmond sent shockwaves throughout the Linux industry, which was doubly disappointed because it had been steadily gaining share on Microsoft's operating systems.

Reached at his office, Microsoft's Miller said he didn't enjoy delivering the sobering

news, and prayed his opponents would be able to find peace. "Revealing that Linux is full of errors, shouldn't be used, and has no place in the software world was one of the hardest things I've ever had to do," confessed Miller. "I can only hope that someday, they will see I was doing this to save them years of wasted effort."

That someday can't come soon enough, said Matthew Szulik, CEO of Linux software provider Red Hat. "When I read what Mr. Miller said, it was like a doctor told me I had six months to live," Szulik recalled. "We recently exceeded earnings expectations and figured to be profitable by 2002, but it looks like we were wrong."

Larry Augustin, CEO of VA Linux, said his company will quietly fade away, and denounced as "absurd" allegations that

Microsoft might be utilizing its infamous FUD tactics to spread "Fear, Uncertainty, and Doubt" about an opponent in an effort to steal market share. "That would be deceitful," he replied, "and Microsoft has stated repeatedly that it does not lie or cheat or mislead."

At Linux community site Slashdot, which will be closing despite its remarkable growth and popularity, co-founder Jeff Bates grew introspective. "Somebody said to me that Microsoft was guilty of hypocrisy because it gave away Internet Explorer for free to eliminate competition from the Netscape Navigator browser, but this is a totally different situation," said Bates. "We're talking about Microsoft, for God's sake, not a bunch of sneaky, utopian, open-source geeks like us.

"No, we all have to take this for what it is," he added, "the cold, hard truth. Damn their probity."

"If we don't have Microsoft's blessing, then what's the point?"
**LARRY AUGUSTIN
CEO, VA LINUX**

# RIOT ERUPTS AT DOTCOM REFUGEE CAMP

## Visit from Il Papa Soldi, John Doerr, Sparks Violent Outburst

OVERCROWDED CONDITIONS and a contentious visit from famed venture capitalist John Doerr sparked a riot last week at Dot-Camp Alpha, a Silicon Valley refugee camp that now serves as home for nearly 18,000 laid-off dotcom workers. The violence, primarily between rival B2B and B2C factions, left 14 dead, scores injured, and hundreds of startup business plans discredited.

According to a spokesman for the International Red Cross, trouble began shortly after Doerr arrived in camp in his bullet-proof limousine, often referred to as the Hopemobile. Almost immediately, the partner in VC firm Kleiner Perkins was showered with startup proposals formulated by the refugees during their many months spent on this desolate hillside near Emeryville. However, officials estimate only 35 percent of camp residents still believe in venture capitalist doctrine. Most now dismiss venture capital and its teachings, and blame Doerr and his colleagues for overvaluing Internet companies and urging them to go public prematurely. A clash, Red Cross officials said, was inevitable.

Tempers flared and fists flew as the man commonly known as Il Papa Soldi, or "The Money Pope," made his way through the crowd of dotcommers laid off from the likes of Webvan, MyPoints, and Stamps.com. One disgruntled camper, who could not yell loud enough to be heard, used the speakers from his laptop and voice-recognition software to send a strong, clear message to Doerr: "You are not well. Comb hair!"

The situation deteriorated during evening mass, when Doerr urged the refugees not to give up hope, and promised he would look at all the business proposals in due time, "except the B2C models. They are unto me like the dead."

In response, several former employees from Doerr-backed WebMD and Drugstore.com shouted him down. "Oh, now you tell us!" one man yelled. He was quickly beaten to death by a quorum of B2B enthusiasts, who feared angering Doerr would cause him to leave camp before he got a look at the group's proposal for an online call center to handle repair requests from Internet-enabled appliances.

The day's bloodiest — and most deeply moving — moment came when Doerr allowed a lone refugee to approach him with her business plan. The woman, identified as 27-year-old Jonna Komay, a former Web developer with Razorfish, shook noticeably as she genuflected and handed over the document. "It's a strategic solutions provider focused on corporate intranet broadband channel redistribution," she whispered, her eyes cast downward. "Oh, and if you would, please sign the six-page NDA [non-disclosure agreement]. Here's a pen."

Despite her tremulous voice, several B2C veterans in the crowd overheard, and scoffed. "Yeah, right! What the hell is 'corporate intranet broadband channel redistribution?' That doesn't mean anything! Let's sell CDs and pants!"

Doerr, however, shocked onlookers by addressing the woman. "Can you benchmark your cost centers?" he said.

"Oh, yes," Komay replied. "Vertically integrated metrics. Totally component-based."

Silence enveloped the camp as Doerr raised his hand and blessed the plan on the spot. After an eerie pause, the crowd surged forward, trampling Komay and screaming "I'm her partner!" "No, I'm her partner!"

Ten people, including Komay, died in the stampede. Several reporters formerly with *Red Herring* and FoxNews.com quickly typed up dispatches about the incident and pretended someone would publish them.

ROCKER and **THE ROCKET**
help you
# MARKET YOUR WEB SITE

Marketing
Tips
From
Guys
Who
Really
Know
How
To Get
Attention

LATELY, ONE OF the biggest trends in business is to turn to athletes as role models. Chief executives are encouraged to manage like Manchester United's Alex Furgeson. Salespeople are told to persevere like cycling's Lance Armstrong. Support personnel are motivated to focus like Tiger Woods.

But when it comes to marketing, it's all about drawing a crowd, and few athletes know more about getting attention than hard-headed Atlanta Braves pitcher John Rocker, and headhunting New York Yankees hurler Roger "The Rocket" Clemens. *BusinessMonth Weekly* asked the irascible pair to put their talents and experience to work on one of the greatest challenges in marketing today: marketing a Web site.

**JOHN:** Hey, so you have a Web site. It's finished. It looks great. But so what?

**ROGER:** Right. Everybody has a Web site.

**JOHN:** Yeah, welfare mothers, New Yorkers, everybody. It's f***kin' wrong, man.

**ROGER:** So you'd think it would be tough to make your site stand out, right?

**JOHN:** But it's not. If you want everybody to be talking about it; if you want it to be famous, like we are, then here's what you do:

## 1) WATCH YOUR MOUTH

**ROGER:** So often, people don't think about what they write.

**JOHN:** Like *Sports Illustrated* reporters.

**ROGER:** Yeah, or reporters in general. But I'm talking about people with Web sites. See, marketing is all about "reach," which means you want your site to "reach" as many people as possible, just like you want a baseball to "reach" Mike Piazza's head. But sometimes you do things that hurt yourself.

**JOHN:** It sucks royally, but you've gotta watch what's on your site. That's 'cause lots of people, they have filtering software that blocks pages that have your violent or sexually graphite...

**ROGER:** ...graphic.

**JOHN:** ...graphic material, or cuss words. So don't use 'em. Let me give you a for-instance.

**ROGER:** I don't think that's a good idea.

**JOHN:** No, man. Nobody's gonna be able to read it 'cause everybody has this software, right? So I can say, "Damn, I'd shoot the baseball commissioner for some hot pornographic pig sex," because I know that nobody's gonna be able to access this Web page.

**ROGER:** No, man, this story isn't going on a Web page. It's for a magazine.

**JOHN:** What?

**ROGER:** The bottom line is, if you're having violent thoughts, don't write 'em down. Let 'em out on the field, where they belong.

## 2) GET LISTED

**ROGER:** Studies show that search engines are still the main way Web surfers find your Web site.

**JOHN:** But there are so many damn sites, how can you work your way up the rankings, not to mention get listed on a search engine?

**ROGER:** Well, you can't.

**JOHN:** Right. That's cause these sites have lame immigrant names like "AltaVista" and "Lycos," and there's that "Google," which I think is a math word. I can't remember.

**ROGER:** So don't sweat not getting listed. Just go on to our next tip. But you might want to bean somebody first, just to get in the mood.

## 3) BOSS ALERT!

**ROGER:** Loads of people get on the Web at work, and while studies have shown that work doesn't get in the way of personal Web surfing, bosses get really irked if they think they're paying you to visit sites like joecartoon.com, where the big attraction is frogs being ground up in a blender.

**JOHN:** Frogs, you mean like French people? That would be cool.

**ROGER:** No, just frogs. But anyway, if your site is business-related, you should have no problem 'cause it's legit and people won't look bad surfing it. But if your site is about your stupid collection of Mike Piazza baseball cards...

**JOHN:** ...or about minorities, like who would care?

**ROGER:** ...then you're losing people because they don't feel right accessing it at work. So we recommend you install a "Boss Alert" button that leads to a page in some other language.

**JOHN:** Doesn't matter what it is. Could be Japanish or HTML or some other weirdo language. But hey, it's another language, so your boss will think you're really smart, and leave you alone.

**ROGER:** And if that doesn't work, you could just throw something at your boss's head, like a baseball bat.

## 4) THERE'S NO SUCH THING AS BAD TRAFFIC

**ROGER:** Let's say you've got a Web site and no one goes there.

**JOHN:** Right, like it's about old people or something.

**ROGER:** Sure. Something namby-pamby like that. So what do you do? You give up that candy-ass site and launch a better one; a site that's so offensive it brings in loads of pissed-off users. 'Cause really, if there's no such thing as bad publicity, then there's no such thing as bad traffic.

**JOHN:** Absolutely. So, I did some research on this, and I found tons of domain names you could use that would bring in tons of angry users to your new site. Like I could see using www.newyorkerssuck.com, www.singlemothersonwelfaresuck.com, screwgays.com...but Jesus, I don't mean that literally.

**ROGER:** Yeah, or you could also try www.mikepiazzasucks.com, or www.iwantmikepiazzashead.com.

**JOHN:** Here's some more: www.princessdianasucked.com, www.princessdianareallysucked.com, www.princessdianashesucked.com, and www.webuykidnappedkittens.com

**ROGER:** I like that last one. But c'mon, man, Princess Diana didn't suck.

**JOHN:** She was a foreigner.

**ROGER:** Oh, right.

# Atlanta, Less Busy, Has Time to

# HATE AGAIN

## Business Slowdown Frees Up Time to Take Part in Prejudice, Discrimination

ACCORDING TO a new federal report, Atlanta, which has long billed itself as the racially harmonious "City Too Busy to Hate," is finally succumbing to the slowing economy, a development that has many residents looking forward to what they're calling their best opportunity to hate since the 1970s.

"Like most Atlantans, I've been so preoccupied with work that I haven't had a spare moment to just sit back, relax, and hate," said Scott Jackson, who runs a construction company in DeKalb County. "It's one of those things, like freedom or segregated bathrooms, that you don't realize you miss until you get it back."

According to a recent report by the Federal Reserve, Atlanta's regional economy continued to shrink in the last month, with weakness in manufacturing, auto sales, and commercial real estate. As a result, many Atlantans, who admit that work had become an all-encompassing obsession, are rethinking their priorities.

"For a while, business was so brisk that I had no time to focus on qual-ity-of-life issues, such as family, church, and random acts of violence against anyone not of my racial background," said 38-year-old Greg Blake, who owns a local printing company. "But now that things have slowed down, I'm making up for it. Just this week I went to my son's Little League game, I made it to the health club twice, and I disparaged a bunch of [seemingly unmotivated minorities] hanging out on a street corner."

Blake also said he had to lay off two employees last month, "and those guys have really taken advantage of the time off. One of them is in jail now defacing a synagogue with anti-Semitic graffiti, and the other one joined the police force."

Local officials estimate the weaker economy has given average Atlantans 10 percent more time to hate than during peak economic periods, particularly from 1999–2000, and just before the 1996 Olympics. As a result, race relations in Atlanta, regarded as better than in most American cities, should deteriorate, although it's not expected to happen overnight.

"I think Atlantans, deep down, are no different from hate-advanced cities like Jerusalem or Sarajevo or Cincinnati, but because they've been so busy, they've repressed it," said Jermaine Kalari, executive director of the non-profit group Hatelanta, which helps residents recapture their inner bigot. "Even I'm not immune. Like with Billy in my office. Sometimes I have to remind myself that he's not just my colleague, he's a [rhythmically challenged, sun-sensitive white person] with a little [Richard]."

"Just like all [Caucasians]," Kalari added.

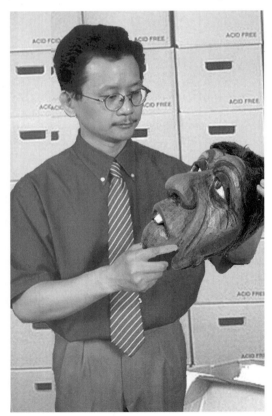

With business off 10 percent, packaging worker Stan Lee spends the extra time making masks that disparage other ethnic groups.

# "ME, CARLY FIORINA, and a CASE OF RIPPLE"

**We asked 15 Fortune 500 CEOs to describe their dream dates with one (or more?) of their Fortune 500 colleagues. The responses were definitely not business as usual.**

**CEO: David Komansky**
**Company:** Merrill Lynch (#25)
**Dream Date:** I'm skinny-dipping with Sumner Redstone (Viacom), and Fred Smith (FedEx) steals our clothes!

**CEO: Steve Jobs**
**Company:** Apple (#236)
**Dream Date:** I'm at this little Italian restaurant with Steve Ballmer (Microsoft) and he hands me this CD and I put it in my laptop, and it's the entire Windows source code, and I say, "Wow, that's pretty impressive. I wish I'd written that," and Ballmer looks at me with his big dark eyes and says, "You did, Steve, you did."

**CEO: Louis Gerstner**
**Company:** IBM (#8)
**Dream Date:** This isn't so much of a dream date as a dream morning after, I guess. It's me and John Tyson (Tyson Foods) and we're in the bathroom and we wash and wash and wash, but no matter what we do, we still both smell like chickens!

**CEO: Lawrence J. Ellison**
**Company:** Oracle (#184)
**Dream Date:** It's a blind date, and I wait and wait and wait for my date to show up, and eventually I realize that, hey, I am my date. It's a perfect evening.

**CEO: Warren Buffett**
**Company:** Berkshire Hathaway (#40)
**Dream Date:** I'm too damn old for dates, but I could see where perhaps I'd have a meeting with that young guy, Michael Dell (Dell Computer), who'd be blindfolded, and I'd say, "Michael, are you very religious?" and he'd say, "Yes," and I'd say, "Consider me God."

# I say, "Honestly, Jack, this is too much for GE to pay for Xerox," and he says, "It's not from GE, and it's not for Xerox."

**CEO: David J. Lesar**
Company: Halliburton (#148)
Dream Date: I get set up on this blind date by my predecessor Dick Cheney and it turns out my date is George W. Bush (United States of America), and George and I spend the entire night ripping up pages and pages of EPA regulations and laughing and laughing, and we fall asleep in each other's arms. Wait, does it still qualify as a dream date if it really happened?

**CEO: Richard "Rick" Wagoner Jr.**
Company: General Motors (#3)
Dream Date: It's a car date. No surprise there. In my dream date, Jack Greenberg (McDonald's) treats me to a Happy Meal and a shake at one of his drive-through, then we head up onto the highway for a while and all the truckers blow their horns at us because we're wearing Ronald McDonald suits without any pants!!

**CEO: Scott McNealy**
Company: Sun Microsystems (#125)
Dream Date: After a quiet supper, Blake Nordstrom (Nordstrom) takes me to the lingerie department in one of his stores and I put on a fashion show for him while he does this bawdy commentary using the Pets.com sock puppet.

**CEO: Sanford J. Weill**
Company: Citigroup (#6)
Dream Date: Me, Carly Fiorina (Hewlett-Packard), and a case of Ripple!

**CEO: Robert Peterson**
Company: IBP (#117)
Dream Date: I'm at this bar with John Tyson (Tyson Foods) and he wants me real bad, you know, real bad, and he's all like, "Ooo, baby, you lookin' so fine," and I'm all like "Enjoy the view 'cause ain't nothin' else for you," and he's like, "But baby, baby, baby, we were meant for each other," and I'm like, "Now where'd I hear that shit before?" and I slap him and leave him there and he's all blubbering and crying and probably gonna shoot hisself in the head or somewheres.

**CEO: August A. Busch III**
Company: Anheuser-Busch (#159)
Dream Date: Can it be a dream encounter instead of a date? Okay, so I'm at a party and I bump into Fred Poses (American Standard) in the bathroom, and it turns out he's holding a Budweiser, and I'm taking a leak in one of his urinals! We both have synergasms right there.

**CEO: Paul Allaire**
Company: Xerox (#109)
Dream Date: I'm with Jack Welch (GE), and we're in this dingy motel room and it's late at night, and he hands me this enormous check and I say, "Honestly Jack, this is too much for GE to pay for Xerox," and he says, "It's not from GE, and it's not for Xerox."

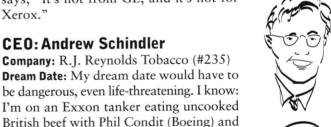

**CEO: Andrew Schindler**
Company: R.J. Reynolds Tobacco (#235)
Dream Date: My dream date would have to be dangerous, even life-threatening. I know: I'm on an Exxon tanker eating uncooked British beef with Phil Condit (Boeing) and we're both buying loads of Lucent stock.

**CEO: Michael Capellas**
Company: Compaq Computer (#27)
Dream Date: Vance Coffman (Lockheed Martin) takes me up in one of Lockheed's new F-22 fighters and he puts some Tony Bennett on the radio and we "accidentally" fire a couple of missiles at Gateway and Dell headquarters.

**CEO: Jack Greenberg**
Company: McDonald's (#139)
Dream Date: A loaf of bread, a jug of wine, and Rick Wagoner (Exxon Mobil), in a Ronald McDonald suit without any pants!!

---

*Editor's Note: In March, Tyson Foods backed out of a $3.2 billion deal to acquire IBP Inc. IBP is now suing.*

# ELLISON TO GRADS: DIPLOMAS ARE FOR LOSERS

## Oracle CEO Urges Students to Drop Out, Start Up

IN ONE *of the more controversial commencement addresses in memory, Oracle CEO and college dropout Larry Ellison told Yale's Class of 2001 they were "losers" whose hard-won diplomas would never propel them into the ranks of the super-rich.*

*The evangelical Ellison, noting that college dropouts Bill Gates, Paul Allen, and Michael Dell were, like himself, on* Forbes' *recent top 10 list of billionaires, urged freshmen and sophomores at the ceremony to "drop out and start up," and added that the undereducated Yale security guards who eventually forced him to leave the stage probably had a better shot at uber-wealth than graduating seniors.*

*What follows is a transcript of the speech, delivered in New Haven, Conn.*

"Graduates of Yale University, I apologize if you have endured this type of prologue before, but I want you to do something for me. Please, take a good look around you. Look at the classmate on your left. Look at the classmate on your right. Now, consider this: five years from now, 10 years from now, even 30 years from now, odds are the person on your left is going to be a loser. The person on your right, meanwhile, will also be a loser. And you, in the middle? What can you expect? Loser. Loserhood. Loser Cum Laude.

"In fact, as I look out before me today, I don't see a thousand hopes for a bright tomorrow. I don't see a thousand future leaders in a thousand industries. I see a thousand losers.

"Now you're upset. That's understandable. After all, how can I, Lawrence 'Larry' Ellison, college dropout, have the audacity to spout such heresy to the graduating class of one of the nation's most prestigious institutions? I'll tell you why. Because I, Lawrence 'Larry' Ellison, second-richest man on the planet, am a college dropout, and you are not.

"Because Bill Gates, richest man on the planet — for now, anyway — is a college dropout, and you are not.

"Because Paul Allen, the third richest man on the planet, dropped out of college, and you did not.

"And for good measure, because Michael Dell, No. 9 on the list and moving up fast, is a college dropout, and you, yet again, are not.

"Does this mean your diplomas have been gained in vain? Not entirely. Most of you, I imagine, have spent four to five years here, and in many ways what you've learned and endured will serve you well in the years ahead. You've established good work habits. You've established a network of people that will help you down the road. And you've established what will be lifelong relationships with the word 'therapy.' All of that is good. For in truth, you will need that network. You will need those strong work habits. You will need that therapy.

"You will need them because you didn't drop out, and so you will never be among the richest people in the world. Oh sure, you may, perhaps, work your way up to No. 10 or No. 11, like Steve Ballmer. But then, I don't have to tell you who he really works for, do I? And for the record, he dropped out of grad school. Bit of a late bloomer.

"Finally, I realize that many of you, and hopefully by now most of you, are wondering, 'Is there anything I can do? Is there any hope for me at all?' Actually, no. It's too late. You've absorbed too much, think you know too much. You're not 19 anymore. You have a built-in cap, and I'm not referring to the mortar board on your head.

"There is, however, good news. There is, in fact, a silver lining. Not for you, Class of '01. You are a write-off, so I'll let you slink off to your pathetic $200,000-a-year jobs, where your checks will be signed by former classmates who dropped out two years ago.

"Instead, I want to give hope to any underclassmen here today. I say to you, and I can't stress this enough: A cap and gown will drag you down. So leave. Pack your things and your ideas and don't come back. Drop out. Start up."

# PROSTIDOTS

## IN DOWN MARKET, NEW ENTREPRENEURS TAKE LESSONS FROM OLDEST PROFESSION

**T**HEY ARE young, quite often attractive, and down on their luck. Desperate for money, they are forced to sell themselves for whatever they can get. They are the latest Internet startups: the prostidots.

"I came out here for fortune and fame, but it hasn't worked out like I thought," said Patrick Kendall, 28, who the night before sold a 5 percent stake in his network software company, LinkStrategems, to a venture firm for just $500. He said he would do it again tonight. "I know it's wrong, but I've got employees to feed."

Less than a year ago, venture capital firms fell all over themselves to offer seed money and first-round financing to high-tech startups. All that changed last April, when the NASDAQ plunged and the IPO market dried up. Suddenly, newer dotcoms found themselves fighting for a dwindling supply of money. As a result, many of them decided prostidotion was better than destitution.

The scene outside the venture offices of Kleiner, Perkins, Caufield & Byers, home to the legendary VC John Doerr, illustrates the sad story. Day and night, groups of eager dotcom executives, male and female, loiter near the entrance. They are waiting for a prospective backer, what they've come to call a "John Doerr." Whenever one of the venture

partners walks by, the soliciting begins:

"Hey, money boy, you want No. 1 clicky-clicky?"

"Say, baby, you've got the seed I need!"

The partners usually ignore the crass come-ons, and for most hopefuls, the day ends at around 11 p.m., when they are picked up in a van driven by their "management consultant." This is usually the head of an Internet incubator that has several companies it's trying to get funded.

"I've got a choice stable, top quality, and last year, VCs were begging to get a piece of them, offering up to $4 million for a 10 percent stake," lamented Charlotte "Huggy Bear" Holcombe of incubator DreamTheWeb. "But now, my bitches...my startups...they're lucky to get $400."

And some have gone for less.

Roberta Boseman, CEO of groupware startup ConnectedNation, works the corner of Broadway and Bleecker Street, near the new East Coast office of startup factory idealab! Last week, she sold them 12 percent of her firm for $75 and a used foosball machine. "They didn't even cut me a check," said Boseman. "They just left the money on the dresser and told me to get out."

But Boseman is hopeful her luck will change. "This is only temporary, right? Someday I'm gonna get out of this business cycle and go respectable."

Like other prostidots, Boseman said she doesn't think about the act itself when she's offering up her company for next to nothing: "I don't look at the John Doerr's face. I usually close my eyes and think about marketing strategies or profit margins...Oh God, is my mother going to read this?"

Yes, she is.

In the past month, the competition between prostidots has gotten so fierce that many have been forced to seek financing far from home. Last week, French authorities at the port of Marseille found 24 Internet entrepreneurs crammed inside a shipping container. Interviews with the detained executives were sketchy, but French police say a Boston-based incubator packed the group off in the cargo box, promising them that French venture firms would be more receptive to their funding needs.

"The conditions were deplorable," said a French Interior Ministry spokesman. "Their wireless PDAs wouldn't work through the metal walls of the container."

# KENNETH'S STORY

**D**usk has finally descended on Sand Hill Road, and "Kenneth" takes his usual place in an alleyway between two squat glass office buildings.

His youthful blue eyes, rimmed by dark semi-circles, watch intently as California's wealthiest and most powerful businessmen and women come and go.

"I was gonna be a star, you know," he says, never taking his eyes off his prey. "I never thought I'd end up like this ... Ooo, who's this now?"

A nattily dressed man in his mid-40s emerges from one of the buildings. Kenneth steps out of the shadows, but he is beaten to the mark by an attractive young blonde in black pumps, maroon blazer, and short white skirt. She is clearly pleading. The man ignores her and marches toward the parking lot and his black BMW. She won't give up. Finally, disgusted, the man pushes her away. The woman falls to the ground, her legs splayed out on the asphalt.

Kenneth is not sympathetic. "Stupid rookie slut," he mumbles. "Can't just walk up to 'em like that."

Ten minutes later, Kenneth tries things his way. An overweight, bald-ing man in a subtle pin-striped suit crosses the street, heading toward the alleyway. When he is within earshot, Kenneth launches into to a whis-per-shout perfected by many in his trade.

"Hey, you want to get a nice piece of me? You won't regret it."

The man stops, but does not look into the shadows. "How much?" he says.

"Um, 10,000," says Kenneth. "For 3 percent. And a board seat."

"Get real," says the mark, and turns to leave.

"Okay, okay, 5,000. For 5 percent. C'mon...4,000...3,000?"

The man stops. "Maybe," he says in a hoarse whisper. "Lemme see what you got first."

Kenneth doesn't hesitate. He grabs his zipper and whips out a bulging business plan from his briefcase. "Take a look," Kenneth says, breathily. "Wireless home networking. Twenty-two employees and revenues of $1.7 million last quarter."

The man says nothing, but cocks his head to one side, and starts walking. Kenneth follows to a car parked next to the curb. They get into a tan Lexus with tinted windows.

Twenty minutes later, Kenneth returns to the alleyway, counting out $2,500 in $100 bills.

"Bastard talked me down," Kenneth says. "I really had to bend over. He got two board seats and 10 percent. At least I'll be able to afford a used workstation.

"But at least he was pretty straight," he continues. "Some of these venture guys, they're into kinky shit. Want you to dress up as a biological

> "VENTURE CAPITALISTS HAVE NEEDS. WE JUST DON'T WANT TO PAY A LOT TO MEET THEM."
> —CANDICE ANDERSSEN, LAKE, JARVIS & PATOIS

computing firm, crap like that."

Kenneth lifts his chin, surveying the streetscape. In the near dark, dozens of indistinct figures, prostidots, can be seen hiding in other alleyways and crouching behind dumpsters or between rows of Jaguars and Porsches. "Some of these guys'll do it, too. Hell, I might too someday. I was gonna be a star, you know."

# U.S. "GROSSLY UNPREPARED" FOR UNLIKELY THREATS

## No Plans to Deal with Drying Up of Oceans, Giant Moon Explosion, or Potential for Everyone to Be Pecked to Death Like in Movie *The Birds*

IN A HAUNTING Senate hearing last week on risk assessment and emergency preparedness, officials from dozens of government agencies conceded the United States was "grossly unprepared" to deal with thousands of highly unlikely threats, including falling chunks of the Moon should it explode into pieces, and the simultaneous spontaneous combustion of every person east of the Mississippi River.

Or anything to do with vampires or poisonous housecats.

As senators listened aghast, officials from the Centers for Disease Control, FBI, FDA, NASA, and National Endowment for the Arts confessed that despite the safeguards implemented since Sept. 11, the country remains at implausible risk.

"I can tell you that today, right now, if Peruvian President Alejandro Toledo develops the ability to shatter the eardrums of American textile workers with a mere thought, we're going to be in trouble," testified CIA Director George Tenet.

CDC Director Dr. Jeffrey Koplan was equally disheartening in his analysis, saying that his agency was not prepared to handle an undetectable disease that kills everyone everywhere instantly. Asked what diseases might fit this category, Koplan acknowledged the CDC did not know of any, nor had it directed drug companies to prepare a vaccine to combat them. That response infuriated Senator Pat Roberts, R-Kan.

"What do you mean you '*don't know of any*'?" asked Roberts. "The entire world could be killed by this virus and you've *never even heard of it*? I won't even bother asking what you're doing about killer bees."

While some senators and agency directors focused on external threats — under withering cross examination, Mary Ryan, assistant secretary of state for consular affairs, confessed that Canada could blindside the U.S. at any time.

Senator Phil Gramm and former Senator Slade Gorton get a giggle out of watching colleague Trent Lott staple himself

— Mississippi Senator Trent Lott was noticeably concerned about office supplies.

"Like million of Americans, I want to believe my country can protect me, but like millions of Americans, I have a stapler that I use to fasten important papers," said Lott, holding up a Swingline #545 desktop model. "What if this stapler suddenly turns on me, decides to attack me, inflicting hundreds of puncture wounds on my person like this [clack] aaaargghh!! [clack] arrrgghh!! [clack] eowarrrgghh!! so that I bleed to death?"

"God help us," said Senator Joseph Biden, D-Del., who ordered the Senate's sergeant-at-arms to remove all staplers from the Capitol.

Homeland Security Director Tom Ridge, however, urged senators to stop the hearings, arguing that to air these dangers publicly exposes weaknesses that America's enemies could exploit. Biden, however, said the American people deserved to know what their government was doing to safeguard them, and asked Ridge if his team had considered the possibility that a rogue nation might create a Category 5 hurricane the size of Asia that would have the ability to suck up the entire U.S. wheat harvest.

"Boy, I don't think so," Ridge replied as several senators ran screaming from the building as a precaution. "Also, I haven't given much thought to the potential for an army of lethally radioactive wallabies that could crawl into all our beds at night, pretending to be pillows."

Health and Human Services Secretary Tommy Thompson, meanwhile, testified that HHS was ill-prepared to respond if every American, from infant to the elderly, suddenly began smoking cigarettes and continued to do so, non-stop, 24 hours a day. However, Senator Jesse Helms, R-N.C., had Thompson's testimony stricken from the record, arguing that it described a "goal," not a threat.

# [ ENRON ADMITS IT'S REALLY ARGENTINA ]

## NOW MASSIVE INEPTITUDE, CORRUPTION MAKE MORE SENSE, ANALYSTS SAY

HAVING COLLAPSED due to gross mismanagement and insurmountable debt, energy company Enron last week confessed to what many observers had long suspected: it is actually Argentina.

Congressional leaders, who have called for an investigation into the biggest corporate bankruptcy in U.S. history, immediately dismissed Enron's claim, but Argentinians weren't so sure. "The shady deals. The crazy debt. I knew there was something familiar about those guys," said Banco del Argentina Director Ernesto Caballo.

Enron Chairman and CEO Kenneth Lay, speaking through an interpreter via phone from Buenos Aires, apologized for any confusion the subterfuge may have caused, and noted that as a sovereign nation, the company was immune from U.S. prosecution. Lay also insisted that he had not "fled" to Argentina, but had returned home to the capital to visit *"mi familia."*

While not directly stating it, Lay also hinted that he might in fact be Argentinian President Fernando de la Rua. Reached in Buenos Aires, de la Rua admitted he couldn't rule that out: "Things are pretty crazy around here. Who can say?"

But Enron creditors, clients, and shareholders, who stand to lose billions over their exposure to the company, weren't buying any of it. "While they may act like it, they are not a South American country, and Ken Lay is not the President of Argentina," declared JP Morgan Chase spokesman Alex

Firtilly. "They are a malfeasant U.S. corporation that has potentially caused us to lose $500 million. And Ken Lay is from Missouri."

"*¿Como?,*" Lay replied. "*No hablo inglés.*"

Recently ranked as high as No. 7 on the Fortune 500 list of the largest U.S. companies, Enron ran itself into the ground by fudging its books, making secretive deals that enriched company insiders, and relying too heavily on debt. Though it was formed in 1986 with the merger of Houston Natural Gas and InterNorth, Enron became Argentina only recently, said Lay, "on the advice of our attorneys."

That counsel came none too soon. As a South American state, all pending U.S. and European lawsuits are rendered harmless. The U.S. State Department, however, has refused to recognize Enron as Argentina, and a spokesman said the Bush administration has officially requested Lay's extradition. Argentina, however, denied the request, explaining that an entire country cannot be extradited. And besides, they added, Lay had pledged to help pay off the nation's $132 billion debt.

Asked where the bankrupt Enron got such a sum, Lay explained that after proclaiming its nationhood status, the company had received an emergency IMF loan. An IMF spokesman later confirmed the payment.

As proof of his Argentinian roots, Enron Chairman Kenneth Lay faxed the media this photo of himself celebrating a goal for Argentina's national team in an August World Cup qualifier.

"From what we knew of their fiduciary practices, Enron appeared to have all the hallmarks of a typical IMF fundee," said IMF Communications Director Nestor Svingen. "At first, we did balk when they asked for $232 billion, but when they explained that some of the money would go to repay overdue IMF loans, we thought, 'Oh, that's all right then.'

"Not that we actually expect to see any money from anyone," Svingen added. "It's just this little game we all play. Great fun if you like numbers. Do you enjoy quadratic equations? I could do them all day."

Asked what Enron/Argentina had pledged to do with the extra $100 billion it requested, Svingen said the application had specified funding for "civic infrastructure improvements."

"That usually means the president is going to build a palace," Svingen explained.

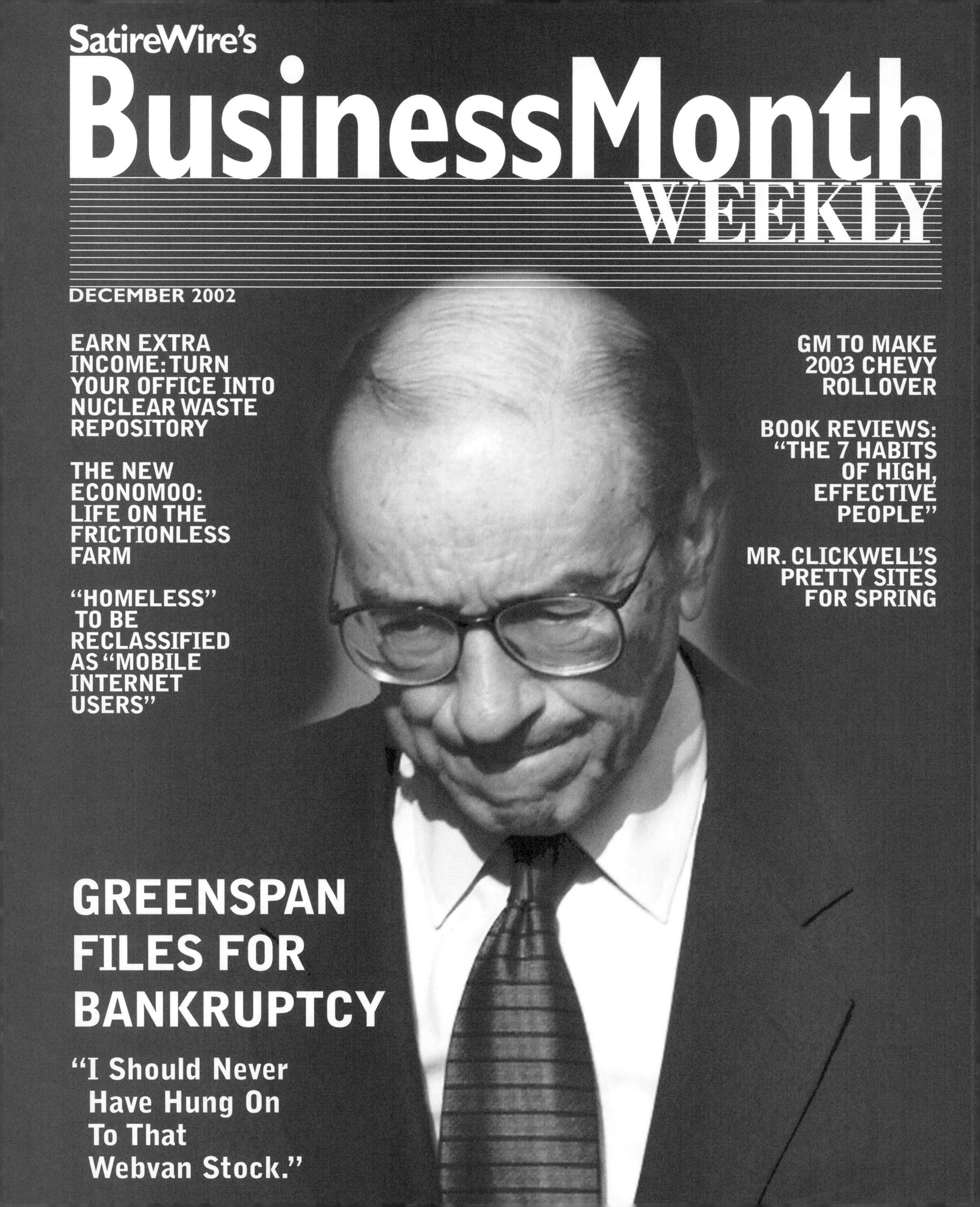

SatireWire's

# BusinessMonth
## WEEKLY

DECEMBER 2002

EARN EXTRA
INCOME: TURN
YOUR OFFICE INTO
NUCLEAR WASTE
REPOSITORY

THE NEW
ECONOMOO:
LIFE ON THE
FRICTIONLESS
FARM

"HOMELESS"
TO BE
RECLASSIFIED
AS "MOBILE
INTERNET
USERS"

GM TO MAKE
2003 CHEVY
ROLLOVER

BOOK REVIEWS:
"THE 7 HABITS
OF HIGH,
EFFECTIVE
PEOPLE"

MR. CLICKWELL'S
PRETTY SITES
FOR SPRING

# GREENSPAN
# FILES FOR
# BANKRUPTCY

"I Should Never
Have Hung On
To That
Webvan Stock."

# WOULD PRICELINE GET FUNDED TODAY?

## How Venture Capitalists Would React If Today's Big Shots Were Startups

IT'S OFTEN said that if someone approached the FDA with aspirin today, the product would never be approved. Would the same hold true for Priceline, Amazon, DoubleClick, and other big Internet players? If they took their ideas to their version of the FDA — venture capitalists — would they be "approved"? Or would VCs ignore them like a banner ad?

### JAY WALKER, PRICELINE

**JAY:** Hi, I have an idea for a dotcom.
**VC:** It's not business-to-consumer, is it?
**JAY:** Yeah, but it's different. It's Priceline. We're going to sell unused airline seats and hotel rooms and let people bid on them. So you could go from Atlanta to Seattle for, say, $100.
**VC:** Sounds pretty good for a direct flight.
**JAY:** Oh, hey, not direct. Not usually. Maybe a connection or two.
**VC:** So Atlanta to Cincinnati to Seattle.
**JAY:** Yeah, like that. Maybe throw in Dallas on the way. And L.A.
**VC:** And I'd put up with that so I could fly cheap on the day I want?
**JAY:** When you say "the day I want," you mean you'd want to fly on a specific day? That might not work so well.
**VC:** And you expect me to give you money for this?
**JAY:** Wait, there's more! We're going to get into groceries and gasoline and mortgages...
**VC:** You're going to sell unused gasoline?
**JAY:** No, no. See, we get a price from the oil companies, then people bid on our site for, say, 20 gallons at a certain price, then they go to the gas station and get the gas.
**VC:** Right. So the oil companies will sell you their gas cheaply because...
**JAY:** Because we guarantee them sales.
**VC:** Of course. Because they're worried that consumers might suddenly decide they just don't need gasoline anymore. Run their cars on something else, like windmills, or nuclear fuel.
**JAY:** Look, I'm going to get a patent on this stuff, too. So we'll make money from anyone who wants to use our model.
**VC:** Yes, I imagine the line will stretch around your desk. We'll call you.
**JAY:** But we're going to get Capt. Kirk from Star Trek to sing these crazy songs...
**VC:** Next!

### JEFF BEZOS, AMAZON

**VC:** And what's this great idea?
**JEFF:** It's called Amazon and it will sell books, music, software, cars, patio furniture, vitamins, toys...
**VC:** Whoa, whoa, slow down there, pardner. How are you going to make money?
**JEFF:** By selling in volume! We'll stock everything!
**VC:** I'm sorry, let me restate. How are you going to make a profit?
**JEFF:** Well, by...um...why, is that important?
**VC:** Some of us have gotten quite keen on it, yes.
**JEFF:** OK, we'll just outbig everyone else. You know, Amazon=big. It sounds big. It'll be big. Your one-stop shop for all your...
**VC:** ...overhead expenses. Yes, thank you for coming. Next.

### KEVIN O'CONNOR, DOUBLECLICK

**KEVIN:** We'll provide a wide range of advertising solutions, primarily through a network of sites we'll sell advertising on.
**VC:** I see, and how long will it take you to be profitable?
**KEVIN:** Well, four years out, we should be only $15 million or so in the red.
**VC:** Uh-huh. And five years out?
**KEVIN:** Probably close to that.
**VC:** How close?
**KEVIN:** $90 million to $100 million in the red.
**VC:** Next.
**KEVIN:** Probably closer to $90 million, really.
**VC:** Next!

### JIM CLARK, HEALTHEON

**JIM:** We're going to streamline the U.S. health-care system!
**VC:** Next!

### STEVE CASE, AOL

**STEVE:** We get people to sign up for, say, $20 a month, and we give them Internet access, email, plus we have exclusive content they can read.
**VC:** And why will they sign up with you?
**STEVE:** Because we'll carpet bomb the entire country with sign-up discs. When they think "Internet," they'll think "AOL."
**VC:** But won't they resent you and make fun of you, pummeling them with these discs all the time?
**STEVE:** So...?
**VC:** And won't you have problems with goodwill if you sign up too many people and can't keep up with the traffic on the network?
**STEVE:** Your point being...?
**VC:** Nothing. I like this one.

# Novell Boasts Its New CEO Will Kill Self if Company Not No. 1 in Six Months

## NEW CHIEF DOESN'T RECALL SUCH A VOW, WONDERS ABOUT MISCOMMUNICATION

GARRISON L. KERRY, the incoming CEO of struggling software firm Novell, has courageously vowed to "do the honorable thing" and take his own life if he is unable to turn company fortunes around within six months, Novell spokesman Harry Schiff announced at a press conference this week.

Kerry, who was also at the briefing, thanked Schiff for the kind words, but confessed he was "a little fuzzy on where this whole 'kill myself' thing came from.

"Are we talking metaphorical 'kill myself,' like 'Oh gosh, I'll work so hard for you guys I'll kill myself'? I might have said that," stated Kerry. "Or are we talking 'I'll kill myself dead, suicide, lots of blood' kind of kill myself? 'Cause that's the part that doesn't sound very familiar."

After a long pause, Schiff suddenly broke into a broad grin. "Ladies and gentlemen, as you can see, our new chief executive has quite the dry sense of humor. No doubt this will serve him well as he transforms our company into the No. 1 software firm in the world in just half a year's time. Or else."

Kerry, who succeeds Jack Messman as CEO, was previously the head of Manhattan Technology, which Novell is purchasing for $1.2 billion. Once a top networking software firm, Novell has lost market share to Microsoft and Linux, and has continually suffered quarterly revenue decreases. Messman, who will remain as chairman, apologized for not turning Novell around himself, but confessed he wasn't willing to "put my life on the line" as his successor is.

"What Novell needs right now is a leader who won't accept anything short

"WOULD YOU COMMIT SUICIDE FOR YOUR COMPANY?"

1% YES*

99% NO

*Garrison Kerry, left, as quoted by Novell spokesman

of success," said Messman, who joined the company in early 2001. "The fact that Garrison has committed to kill himself — not just any old way, but slowly and painfully, without the use of any anesthetics or analgesics — shows you how much he believes in Novell, its products, and its people."

"Was that in my contract?" asked Kerry, "because that's the kind of thing I think I would remember. No, I mean it."

After chuckling softly over Kerry's shenanigans, Messman continued, "Oh sure, toppling Microsoft and Sun and the other firms might seem like an impossible task for you and me, especially in only six months, and especially since we don't have the right products for the job. But we're not Garrison Kerry. We're not standing before you today saying, 'Give me market share or give me death!'"

Kerry's comical protests of "But I'm not saying that!" did not fool his new colleagues, who eventually drowned him out with their applause.

## GM TO MAKE 2003 CHEVY ROLLOVER

After two of its SUVs failed a recent government rollover test, scoring just one star out of five, General Motors announced today it will replace its low-scoring Blazer and Jimmy lines with the 2003 Chevy Rollover, a vehicle GM promised will "roll over like a dog" under any conditions, and win GM a five-star rating at next year's competition.

"As the government report points out, neither vehicle rolls over with any consistency," said GM spokesman Arnold Moore, sitting at the wheel of a Rollover prototype. "By contrast, this 2003 Rollover will be designed to tumble on turns, straightaways, or even the moment you crank it up, like this."

Officials at the National Highway Traffic Safety Administration, which conducted the tests, were puzzled by the announcement, and wondered aloud whether GM understood the scoring system. "When a vehicle get five stars, that means it resists rollovers, not that it's good at rolling over," said an NHTSA spokesman.

Efforts to revive Moore for comment were unsuccessful.

## "I LOVE YOU" EMAIL RECIPIENT STILL WAITING FOR FLOWERS, PHONE CALL

IT'S BEEN two years since Angelina Dupree received an email declaring "I Love You," but the 33-year-old from Dallas, Tex., said this week she's given up hope of ever hearing again from the sender, whom she now suspects was just toying with her emotions.

"I was so excited when I got that email," said Dupree. "I told my friend Shirley about it, and she was like, 'Girl, you infected with that Love Bug!' and I was like, 'Girl, you know it!'"

But since then, Dupree lamented, there has been only silence. "No flowers. No phone call. Nothing," she said, fighting back tears. Dupree said she got the email from an online bookstore where she once had placed an order. The sender wasn't identified, but Dupree is certain it was a man. "I know it wasn't a woman because a woman don't act like that," said Dupree. "Only a no-good lying bastard man would be all like, 'Oh baby, I love you,' and then just disappear."

## European Central Bank to Intervene in Football Matches

IN A surprising tactical shift, the frustrated European Central Bank announced it will no longer intervene to bolster the sagging euro, but will instead intervene in English Premier League football matches. Its first test came in Saturday's battle between Manchester United and Coventry, in which the Central Bank substituted German monetary theorist Otmar Issing for injured Man U. midfielder Paul Scholes in the 48th minute. Moments later, the 64-year-old Issing took a brilliant cross from teammate David Beckham and neatly tucked a header into the near post. Manchester United won 2-1.

Central Bank President Wim Duisenberg immediately declared the win a policy victory, but Coventry manager Gordon Strachan was angry that he was forced to replace striker Moustapha Hadji with 61-year-old Finnish ECB board member Sirkka Hämäläinen in the 33rd minute.

"Not only is Hämäläinen a woman, but she's an economist," Strachan complained. "Every time we pushed forward, she insisted we were going the other way."

## SUPPLY vs DEMEAN

| SUPPLY (Trickle-Down) | DEMEAN (Shut Up) |
|---|---|
| Lower taxes spur investment. | Pompous bastard. Cut taxes and feed the rich, you mean. |
| Investment spurs production and job creation. | You fetid, elitist windbag. |
| Production leads to growth. | The growth of your fucking wallet, you avaricious crimp. |
| Overproduction leads to deflation. Prices fall to meet demand. | Oh, great, so production gets cut, or wages fall. Good thinking, dirtbag. |
| Therefore, supply supersedes demand. | I agree. You're supplying bullshit, and I demand you stop. You're such a waste. |
| Keynesian creep | Oh, bite my buy side. |
| I miss the gold standard. | You miss your rock, you misanthropic viper. |

## 14 Remaining Netscape Users Rejoice Over Release of Netscape 7

The world's 14 remaining users of the Netscape browser exulted this week over the release of Netscape 7, the first new version of the browser in more than a year, and a product Netscape executives predicted would blow away Microsoft's Internet Explorer "if this were 1997."

"This is a great browser, and I think if everyone weren't already using Explorer, they would definitely switch to this," said Netscape user Brian Calistano of Brisbane, Australia. "I am definitely downloading this baby, and I'll use it, too, if Explorer crashes or something."

To solidify its market position, Netscape senior vice president Jim Martin announced a "major" partnership with Apple Computer to have Netscape 7 installed on all new Apple machines, a move that Martin boasted would really break Microsoft's stranglehold on the browser market, "if this were, say, 1984."

## "Brandnesia" Cases Escalating
# AGILENT EMPLOYEES FOUND ACCIDENTALLY WORKING AT TELIGENT, OR POSSIBLY SAPIENT

**COLLEAGUES WATCHING VIANT v. SCIENT CHARITY BASKETBALL GAME FORGET WHICH SIDE TO CHEER FOR**

AT LEAST four more cases of "Brandnesia" were reported last week, as nearly two dozen employees from technology firm Agilent discovered they had mistakenly been going to work at Teligent, while 15 employees from consulting firm Sapient held a sit-down strike until someone could convince them they didn't really work for Celerant or Aviant.

Meanwhile, Appiant Technologies filed separate breach-of-contract lawsuits against Noviant, Naviant, and Novient, saying one of them owed it money, it just couldn't remember which.

With the recent outbreak, incidents of Brandnesia have surpassed 650 this quarter, and observers say they don't expect the upward trend to abate until corporations have exhausted the supply of names that have no meaning.

According to David Schneider, CEO of technology services firm Tenera, "brand plagiarism" is another culprit. "This is what you get when unimaginative companies find a distinctive name, such as ours, and attempt to take advantage of that name recognition," said Schneider. "We've seen quite a few Tenera imitators, such as Telera, Nextera, Caldera, and Cidera. And I can't tell you how many times we've had people from Sitara and Sidera show up here expecting to work."

Schneider later called to rescind his statement after discovering he is the CEO of Nextera.

Schneider suggested people

pin their business cards to their jackets for the foreseeable future, a tactic that might have prevented the fistfights that broke out during a recent charity basketball tournament between Viant, Triant, Reliant, Scient, Cerent, Clarent, and Cendant, where colleagues who had come to cheer found themselves constantly switching sides.

But what about victims such as husband-and-wife programmers Erica and Christopher Drake, two of the Agilent employees discovered working at Teligent? "We were hired together, and had only been at Sapient (sic) for three weeks, and we didn't have business cards or email addresses," said Christopher. "Every morning I'd say, 'Well, let's head off to Celerant,' and Erica would say, 'No, it's Teligent.'

"Funny thing was," he added, "we were both wrong. It turns out we work for Comergent."

"Covisint," said Erica.

"Right. Aviant."

While the Drakes have now found their home, somebody's human resources director Lowrey Nicks continues his search. He has reported for work at six different companies since October. "Last week, if you'd have held a gun to my head, I'd have sworn I worked for Centricity, but I don't," said Nicks. "Since then I've been making the rounds: Extricity, Extensity, Extensis, Aventis, Navantis...wait...Navantis! No. No, I tried them last week. Or was that Novartis?"

"You'd think I would get a hint from where I live, but I telecommute to work," Nicks added. "Wherever that is."

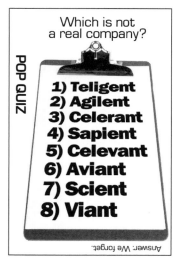

POP QUIZ

**Which is not a real company?**

1) **Teligent**
2) **Agilent**
3) **Celerant**
4) **Sapient**
5) **Celevant**
6) **Aviant**
7) **Scient**
8) **Viant**

Answer: We forget.

# "INTERNET TWINS" SCANDAL FAILS TO DETER ONLINE BABY SALES

## Returns Policies Needed, but B-Commerce Sector Strong, Says Study

ACCORDING TO a new study, the scandal surrounding American twins sold and resold last year by an Internet adoption agency, or b-tailer, has not negatively impacted online baby sales, although the report did find several problem areas that could hinder future growth of the burgeoning b-commerce sector.

The report, compiled by consulting firm Colby-IKG, said b-commerce sales have actually increased 85 percent since the now famous twins, Kimberley and Belinda, were involved in a transatlantic custody battle.

"Going in, we thought the incident would depress the market, but the attention it garnered for the sector has outweighed the negative press," said IKG researcher Cathy Carter.

In the survey, the majority of consumers said they turn to Internet baby sellers because it is more convenient than going to the mall, even if prices online are high-er. Online shoppers also said they used the Internet because it saved them time, allowed them to research child histories more efficiently, and featured babies that were not available locally.

But b-tailers shouldn't get complacent, warned Carter, as consumers also registered complaints about their purchasing experience. For example, she said, many reported their babies did not arrive in time for the holidays, and others complained they got the wrong babies and had to send them back. Other frustrations included Web pages that took too long to load, or the discovery that their desired baby was out of stock. The biggest problem for b-tailers, meanwhile, was customer service and fulfillment.

"Selling the same product twice, as happened with the twins, is a retail sin, but there is no obvious solution," said Carter. "Ideally, b-tailers would put a sticker with an SKU number on each piece of inventory, to track them better, but that's rather difficult when the product keeps pulling off the stickers and eating them."

The study also found that 10 percent of holiday shoppers who encountered problems at a particular b-tail site continued shopping, while the other 90 percent abandoned the site for another b-tailer, or simply bought a puppy.

### TOP B-TAIL FRUSTRATIONS

| | |
|---|---|
| Baby arrived after holidays | 46% |
| Wrong baby sent | 23% |
| European sizes different from American sizes | 17% |
| UPS driver won't leave baby on doorstep | 9% |
| Accidentally clicked order button twice, got two babies | 5% |

# SETI PROJECT TURNS DOWN ALIEN HELP

Scientists for SETI@home, the worldwide project that uses millions of personal computers to aid in the search for extraterrestrial life, said today they have recently rejected several offers of technical assistance from aliens, arguing that they don't need outside help.

Extraterrestrials from several planets, most recently Mars, have volunteered to join the SETI@home network, revealed SETI@home technical director Dr. Karl Webber. The network, believed to be the largest distributed computing project in history, runs a screensaver program on personal computers that analyzes data from the Arecibo Radio Telescope in Puerto Rico. The data is then sent to SETI scientists to see if the telescope has detected signals that could indicate the existence of life elsewhere in the universe.

"We told the Martians this week the same thing we told the Jovians (from Jupiter) last week and those whatever-they-weres from Antares last month: 'Thanks but no thanks,'" said Webber. "This is really an Earth-based project, so it wouldn't be right to go off-world for help. And frankly, I think we're perfectly capable of finding extraterrestrial life on our own."

Since May 1999, more than 4 million volunteers have downloaded the SETI@home screensaver, but the project has so far failed to yield the proverbial Eureka. Webber insists, however, that the program is making real progress, which could be threatened by outside interference.

"In building SETI@home, we have brought together peoples from disparate nations for a common purpose," he said. "But you start letting these outsiders get involved, and you could destroy that sense of universal community we've achieved."

SETI@home chief physicist Dr. Quentin Leetes, meanwhile, conceded his opposition was more personal.

"Honestly, the way they waltzed in here — or transported, really, but whatever — you'd think they were God's gift to extraterrestrial discovery," Leetes said. "And they start throwing out these crazy ideas, like we shouldn't search for signals in the 1.4 GHz helium spectrum but should look in the hydrogen spectrum. We were like, 'Yeah, right, what planet are you from?'"

## According to Chaos Theory,
the movements of something as small
and unassuming as a butterfly can
have dramatic consequences.

If, for instance, a butterfly in Australia
flaps its wings, that tiny breath of wind
could eventually lead to
a fire in California,
a drought in the Midwest,
or a hurricane in the Atlantic Ocean.

As a result, lives would be lost, the
economy would falter, and insurance
premiums could rise at a time when
people could least afford it.

Imagine that: Economic devastation,
tragic loss of life, and all...
from a single butterfly.

It doesn't have to be this way.
Outcomes such as this
can be avoided.
How?

Kill butterflies.
Kill them all.
As many as you can,
as soon as you can,
as often as you can.

And moths, too.
You can never be too careful.

A public service message from the Insurance Industry of North America.

# "Homeless" to Be Reclassified as "Mobile Internet Users"

ACCORDING TO a new directive from the U.S. Department of Health and Human Services, the estimated 750,000 Americans once considered "homeless" will be reclassified as "mobile Internet users" who choose to have no fixed address because today's improved mobile technologies allow them to live and work from almost anywhere.

"With the proliferation of handheld devices and laptop computers, mobile Internet access means anyone can now work, shop, and surf via the Internet from almost any location, and to saddle one group of people with the antiquated label of 'homeless' when in fact they may simply be taking advantage of tech-

Thompson makes his announcement.

nological freedoms does them a great disservice," said HHS Secretary Tommy Thompson.

Advocacy groups such as the American Coalition for the Mobile Internet User (formerly the American Coalition for the Homeless) blasted the directive for cutting off funding to shelters and food programs, and pointed out that alleged MIUs don't have computers or PDAs or jobs, not to mention Internet accounts. Thompson, however, responded that individual MIUs wishing to protest the change should email his office.

## Israel Offers Palestinians Virtual State for Only $49.95 a Month

PROPOSING A compromise he hopes will ensure his nation's security, Israeli Prime Minister Ariel Sharon announced that Israel will allow the Palestinians to form an independent nation, but only on the Internet.

The offer calls for the Palestinians to take up residence on a shared Israeli Web server, but otherwise allows them to "control their own destiny," insisted Sharon, who added that the Palestinians would be responsible for their own virtual police, education, and technical support. The Palestinians would pay Israel $49.95 a month to host the space, or $69.95 for the special "Deluxe Virtual Nation Package," which includes Microsoft's Site Server Commerce Edition 4.0.

Palestinian leader Yasser Arafat, who still insists that a separate Palestine be carved out of the West Bank, Gaza Strip, and eastern Jerusalem, quickly attacked the proposal. "We have 'shared' our space with Israel long enough," Arafat said in a statement. "I will not sit down with Mr. Sharon's government unless they guarantee us a fully-dedicated, independent server. And they must waive the $25 set-up fee."

## SECURITY GUARD ESCORTS SELF FROM BUILDING

### Watches Himself "Like Hawk" to Make Sure No Corporate Secrets Stolen

THIRTY-TWO-YEAR-OLD security guard Eddie Dupree, laid off Friday from semiconductor maker Broadcom, gave himself an hour to gather his personal effects and leave the building.

Dupree, the final member of his department to be downsized, said he was "stiff and cold, but not rude" to himself while he placed his few belongings in a cardboard box and escorted himself from the premises. Nonetheless, he was not happy about his treatment.

"It was humiliating that the company wouldn't trust me to leave quietly on my own," he said, adding that he was only following policy. "Look, it was nothing personal."

### STING SUNK

Due to yet another software glitch at the Internet Movie Database (imdb.com), Sting, the former lead singer of The Temptations who is best known for his portrayal of Kunta Kinte in the TV-movie *Roots*, died in a ferryboat accident at age four.

# RADIOACTIVE WASTE: IT'S NOT JUST FOR TEXAS ANYMORE

HIGH-TECH COMPANIES are known for setting precedents. They formed faster, rose higher, and declined more quickly and spectacularly than any industry group in history. So the latest trend at many struggling firms, to earn extra income by storing low-level radioactive waste, should not come as a shock.

But for some, it still does.

"Aaaaggghhh!" said Patrick Seitz, a data systems engineer with Lucent Technologies, as he ran screaming from the company's newly fortified New Jersey headquarters one recent morning. "There's radioactive sludge all over my office!"

Watching from his fifth-floor window as Seitz and dozens of other mortified employees emerged from the building, Lucent Radiation Safety Officer Bill Bartlock shook his head and sighed. "Clearly, some of our people are having trouble with our new revenue stream," he said, his voice muffled by his silver headgear. "But give them time."

Time, in fact, is what led Lucent and several other ailing companies to turn to the waste-storage market. Once the domain of tax-poor towns scattered throughout the South and Midwest whose bleak outlooks forced them to set aside a few acres of unused open space for radioactive waste dumps, nuclear waste storage has suddenly proven popular with companies running short of time and cash. Using extra office space, or sometimes reconfiguring offices, to store 55-gallon drums of toxic sludge is a reliable, renewable, and lucrative revenue stream, and doesn't require extra personnel or man-hours.

> "A lot of people think we should have been out of business by now, but what they don't know is we've been storing nuclear waste in our Connecticut headquarters since early 2001."
> — PRICELINE.COM CEO RICK BRADDOCK

How lucrative? Lucent signed a contract for $100 million to store 40,000 cubic feet of waste a year for 30 years, most of it emanating from power plants in Illinois and Ohio.

Despite the health risks, many firms are following its lead, slowly absorbing the radioactive lifestyle into their corporate cultures. San Francisco software company Ariba, for example, has replaced casual dress Fridays with "universal precaution" Fridays when the weekly deliveries are made from nuclear reactors in New York state. At Apple Computer, the cubicle farm atmosphere has been preserved by replacing prefab walls with stacked waste drums, and workers are encouraged to believe the more drums one has, the more important one is to the organization.

Lucent employees will also come to accept the shift, said Bartlock, who held an impromptu meeting with employees still unwilling to enter the building. "Many of you," he began calmly, "have noticed what appear to be large drums of radioactive waste in the office. But perhaps you'll feel better about it if you know these alleged drums are actually 'energy capsules.'"

"Wait, so it's not radioactive waste?" asked a visibly relieved executive receptionist.

"No, it is radioactive waste," Bartlock answered, "but we thought you might feel better about it if we called them 'energy capsules.' Now get to work."

# GREENSPANNING
## HIS WORDS MOVED MARKETS

### MARCH, 1995
WASHINGTON (AP) — The dollar rebounded strongly Wednesday after Federal Reserve Board Chairman Alan Greenspan told a Congressional committee the dollar's plunge was "unwelcome news."

### DECEMBER 1996
LONDON (CNNfn) — Major European stock markets slid more than four percent Friday after U.S. Federal Reserve Chief Alan Greenspan complained of "irrational exuberance" on stock and other asset markets ... the Greenspan effect wiped some $150 billion off European share values.

### JULY 1997
NEW YORK (REUTERS) — Weeping financial analysts clogged Manhattan's Wall Street district Friday after Federal Reserve Board Chairman Alan Greenspan told a House committee he was "saddened" that the world financial community hangs on his every word.

### NOVEMBER 1997
ST. LOUIS (AP) — Anheuser-Busch, the nation's largest alcoholic beverage producer, filed for Chapter 11 bankruptcy yesterday after Federal Reserve Board Chairman Alan Greenspan reportedly switched his drink order from a Michelob Lite to a dry martini while at a Georgetown restaurant. Olive futures soared on the news.

### MARCH 1998
LOS ANGELES (REUTERS) — Geffen Records signed the always controversial "Godfather of Soul," James Brown, to a $94 million, two-album deal after published reports claimed Federal Reserve Board Chairman Alan Greenspan got out of the shower Tuesday morning and told his wife, "I feel good."

### OCTOBER 1999
(TRANSCRIPT, CNBC'S *THE MONEY WHEEL*)
SUE HERERA: Well, as most of you know, Federal Reserve Board Chairman Alan Greenspan is on vacation this week. Let's go to David Faber on the floor of the New York Stock Exchange. David, what's happening down there?
DAVID: Um...nothing.
SUE: Excuse me?
DAVID: Nothing. No one's here.
SUE: Oh, okay, um...
DAVID: What's happening there, Sue?
SUE: Well...not...much...I...I think I'm the only one here.

Fed watchers now say they should have suspected something when Greenspan showed up at this January 2000 Senate hearing wearing the Pets.com sock puppet.

DAVID: Oh...
SUE: Hmm...
DAVID: You, uh, you wanna play charades or something?

### AUGUST 2000
BOSTON (AP) — Michael C. Hawley, chairman and chief executive officer of The Gillette Company, was summarily executed this morning after Federal Reserve Board Chairman Alan Greenspan reportedly nicked himself with a Gillette MACH3 razor.

### MARCH 2001
WASHINGTON (AP) — An 18th-century hickory rocker was condemned to Hell yesterday after Federal Reserve Board Chairman Alan Greenspan reportedly stubbed his toe on the chair and was unable to stifle a cry of "Goddamnit!"

### SEPTEMBER 2001
WASHINGTON (MSNBC) — The sun, which rose this morning, will in all likelihood set this evening if, as expected, Federal Reserve Board Chairman Alan Greenspan does not oppose it.

### FEBRUARY 2002
WASHINGTON, D.C. (BBC) — Federal Reserve Board Chairman Alan Greenspan, who told a *London Evening Standard* reporter last week he was "more popular than Jesus Christ," apologized today to the world's 600 million Roman Catholics and asked them to please get the hell off his lawn. "I was not saying I was greater or better than Jesus," Greenspan told the followers. "Now go away, and take all this myrrh with you."

### NOVEMBER 2002
WASHINGTON (AP) — Federal Reserve Board Chairman Alan Greenspan told the Senate Banking Committee he was sick and tired of having his every word analyzed for its impact on the markets. Asked if he was really saying the so-called "New Economy" was "sick and tired" and therefore a different economy should emerge to lead the "markets," Greenspan lapsed into unusually crystalline language: "For 15 years I've been held up as the Guiding Light, the Voice of Fiscal Reason," he said. "Well, fuck that. And fuck you."

### DECEMBER 2002
NEW YORK (AP) — Fed watchers pronounced the New Economy dead, and heralded the beginning of what they are calling the "Fuck You Economy."

# GREENSPAN FILES FOR BANKRUPTCY

## Fed Chairman's "Secret" Portfolio Overweighted in Amazon.com, Net2Phone

IN A STUNNING revelation, Federal Reserve Board Chairman Alan Greenspan said he has filed for Chapter 13 personal bankruptcy, disclosing that for years he has secretly been investing in Internet stocks.

As the chairman of the U.S. central bank, Greenspan is legally bound to hold his investments in a blind trust, but conceded he had "caught Net fever" and placed most of his assets in the likes of Amazon.com and the now-defunct Webvan and Toysmart.com.

"I really liked Webvan," Greenspan said in a statement. "Good selection. Groceries right to your door. I'd still put money in it, if I had any. And if it existed."

In the wake of the filing, several of Wall Street's top executives came forward to divulge that for years, Greenspan has been frantically begging them for inside tips and allotments of hot IPOs. "It's very unnerving to get a call from the Chairman of the Federal Reserve asking you to slip him 10,000 pre-IPO shares of Drugstore.com," said one executive. "I mean, he always used this phony, high-pitched voice, and he insisted I call him 'Alice Greenspan,' but I knew who it was."

Friends, meanwhile, painted a picture of a man obsessed with "the one that got away."

"Alan was intensely strict about even the appearance of impropriety, but what turned him was Netscape," said Morgan Stanley executive Armond Brackley. "The day after we took them public (in August 1995), Alan kept calling me up saying, '105 percent? It went up one-hundred-and-five-fuckin' percent?'"

The Chairman, bitter that he had not gotten in on the "ground floor," apparently decided to bring the ground floor back to him, and in late 1996 made his famous "irrational exuberance" speech. Stocks plunged. Greenspan immediately bought.

---

### MANY TRY TO INTERPRET FILING FOR REAL MEANING

Fed watchers are scrambling to deconstruct Federal Reserve Board Chairman Alan Greenspan's recent bankruptcy filing, confident that it is, in reality, another hidden message meant to give some indication as to the Fed's leanings.

"On the surface, this would appear to be a straightforward statement, which makes it more of a challenge," said Morningstar analyst Regal Kane. "Here we're focusing on the phrase 'Chapter 13 bankruptcy.' A year is 12 months, or chapters. The 13th month, or chapter, would be January of next year. Is he saying that in January there will be fiscal trouble and the Fed will respond by lowering rates?"

"Forgive me, but that is just stupid," insisted Banc of America economist Cecelia Cruz-Azul. "It is a New Testament allusion to the 'Thirteenth Chapter,' or I Corinthians 13, in which Paul says, 'When I was a child, I thought as a child, I spoke as a child...but when I became a man, I gave up childish things.'

"He is telling us that we must look to ourselves and not rely on our Fed fathers to intervene at this time. We expect no rate changes."

---

Said Brackley: "At the time I remember asking him, 'Alan, why would you, of all people, say such an inflammatory thing?' and he said, 'Oh, I have 60,000 reasons so far.'"

According to his Chapter 13 filing, Greenspan was successful for a time. But he held on to the likes of Petsmart and marchFIRST too long. Listed among his current assets were 150,000 shares of theglobe. com, and 40,000 options to buy Lucent Technologies at $82 a share.

As one Greenspan confidant noted: "Alan is a monetary policy genius and a stock market moron."

In light of the "clear and heinous" conflict of interest Greenspan displayed by disparaging stocks and then buying on the dips he created, many on and off Wall Street were outraged, and insisted the Fed Chairman should immediately be removed from office and placed where he belongs: working as a stock analyst for a major investment bank.

# WEB SITE FASHION FOR SPRING:
# It's All About Pretty

**SASSY WEB SITE FASHION MAVEN MR. CLICKWELL
REPORTS FROM SPRING SITEWEAR SHOW**

CATCH ME in a pan, I'm melting! The winter is always long and cold for the fashion-conscious, but if last week's Spring SiteWear Show is any indication, the frigid, function-over-form mood that's dominated Web site design like Desi over Lucy is finally defrosting. From Google to Microsoft to ESPN.com, this Spring the message is going to be: "Let's just be pretty."

No more barren, brutish, Yahooey layouts that were as cuddly and warm as a Rolodex. Instead, it's Degas and doilies, pastels and posies, clouds and candlelight. *Très femme.* High concept? Revenge of the Nerds meets Laura Ashley, and they're skating!

One *changement en mieux* that fashion digerati are absolutely raving about is Microsoft's "country blush" look, where the emphasis will be on "soft," and the sheer lace curtains cover just enough of the pretty-in-pink links to add a coquettish mystery. Fave: Microsoft accessorizes by using pretty words; "Products," for example, becomes "Unmentionables," while the tired slogan "Where Do You Want To Go Today?" gives way to the more charming "Aren't You Looking Pretty Today?"

"We've always been tender in our color schemes, preferring pastels and soft highlights, but our layout has been, admittedly, desolate," Microsoft's brawny CEO, Steve Ballmer, told me over lattes and giggles at the backstage preview party. "Our spring look is fresher without, I hope, being insolent."

So what's brought about this Zephyr of *rafraîchisse-ment*? Jonathan Nelson, chairman of snappy Web design firm Organic, gave me one good reason and one knee-wobbling smile. "With all the layoffs and closings, so much ugly has happened in the past two years that a lot of our clients said they just want to feel pretty again."

Another site experiencing a Natalie Wood Moment (oh, go rent *West Side*

Degas' "Four Dancers" in ESPN's pretty new logo.

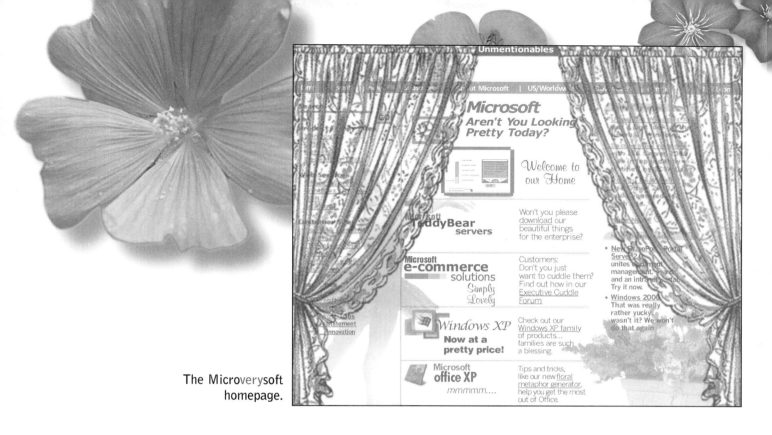

The Microverysoft homepage.

*Story* if I've lost you), is ESPN.com, where it seems the biggest internal struggle was over the once-extensive use of black. "It's so easy for black to dominate, but you have to be careful," said ESPN spokesman and former NFL linebacker Gary Knopf, as we shared a frozen mango-mania. "We wanted enough black on the site so that it brought out the shades of pink in the navbar and the shadows in the nasturtiums, but we didn't want so much black that the whole site just said, 'New York bitch.'"

But enough about me!

Let's talk about Google. "I really like our oeuvre now, especially the way we've surrounded the site with an absolutely darling, gilded tooled-leather frame," said Google CEO Larry Page as we stood alone in an elevator. For hours. "In some ways we can't compete with Yahoo!, but at least I can say we're much, much prettier."

There is, however, a downside to prettifying. Even with high-speed connections, sites will load more slowly, a definite no-no in Jakob Nielsen Land (oh go to useit.com if I've lost you). But so far, the aesthetes are winning. As Ballmer told me: "You don't rush pretty. Pretty takes its time. You don't want it to just jump out at you. You want it to enter gracefully, like Hepburn.

"Audrey, not Katharine," Ballmer added. *Naturellement!*

But say, just what is pretty? Definitions vary, but most designers agree it is subtle; pastels and flowers and frills. That's why some critics at the show insisted that too many sites are blowing right past pretty and are dangerously close to "adorable." WWF.com, for instance, has hidden tiny wrapped candies shaped like strawberries around the site. If you click on them, they tinkle! (Just like a couple of the wrestlers I met at the annual SiteWear Ball, but that's another story.)

"You do have to draw a line somewhere," Razorfish strategic officer Craig Kanarick told me over croissants. "Morgan Stanley came at us with three pretty themes they wanted to use: Minnie Driver, dusk, and true love. I was really intrigued by the true love angle — I've always thought true love was pretty — but then (Razorfish CEO) Jeff (Dachis) said, 'You know, love isn't always pretty' and I was, like, 'Ouch, that is so true.' Plus it was hard to really capture true love on a site about asset management."

Well, *mes amis*, that's Mr. Clickwell's report from The Big Show. Oh, one little piece of advice? If you're going for the coy, feminine look, please do ditch the "site visitor" counters. I mean, "This site has been visited 97,000 times since Jan. 1?" Darling, that doesn't say demure, that says whore.

But enough about me!

# The New Economoo:

## The Family Farm, the Last Bastion of Old Economy Intransigence, Has Finally Fallen

FIVE MONTHS *after finishing his MBA at Harvard University, James "Jimmy" Savory Jr. still hadn't found the right job — the job that would allow him to fully leverage his newly acquired managerial skillset. And the economy was floundering. His hopes were dimming. Frustrated and broke, he flew home to Iowa to see his parents, to spend a few quiet days on the family farm, and to have an epiphany.*

*To this day, Jimmy Jr. clearly recalls the moment when his life, and his father's life, changed forever.*

*"We were sitting at the breakfast table, and I said, 'Dad, I can't get a nibble at Accenture or GE, so I was thinking, I know it's a big step down for me, but what if I ran the farm for a while? Just to get it in good shape. We'll adopt best-of-breed, 21st-century management practices. We'll reengineer the enterprise for maximal ROI. We'll establish collaborative relationships with the company's mission-critical, nature-based workforce — the animals. We'll...' "*

*But Jimmy Sr. didn't need to hear anymore. He had already had a heart attack and died. "I guess that was his way of saying, 'Go for it, son,'" Jimmy Jr. says reflectively.*

*And go for it he did. One year later, Jimmy Savory Jr. has brought truly modern management practices to the unlikeliest of places, the family farm. What has he done, and how has he done it? BusinessMonth Weekly harvests 9 tips from the North 40 of the Future.*

---

### 1. NAME THAT FARM

Our family farm had beef and dairy cattle, breeding and slaughter pigs, chickens, sheep, corn, wheat, and soybeans. What it didn't have was a distinctive name that said "farm." Other than "Savory farm." But that was so last century.

I began by recording the sounds of the farm, trying to the capture their onomatopoetic potential, broken down into morphemes and phonemes. I then considered the traditional elements that said "farm": the smell of hay and sweat, the rutting goats, the colt and spring and new life, blood and winter and death. With an initial list of possible names, I then conducted focus groups with my neighbors, who I call the coopetition, and with grocery store consumers (end users), and my nature-based employees (animals). After three months, I finally unveiled the new name, an exciting moniker that captured the essence, the very soul, of a farm: Celumigent.

## 2. BARNSIDE CHATS

One thing I discovered right away was a real disconnect with the nature-based workforce, particularly the cows. Dad never held quality assurance meetings with them, and as a result, employees didn't understand their roles. So I decided to start "barnside chats" with them. One-on-one bull sessions. Except this is with cows.

Every quarter, we meet in a field. I put up a large photo of a barn on an easel and pull out a pair of beanbag chairs. I also pass out balloons. It's kind of silly, I guess, but I want the employees to loosen up, and I have to lead the way by providing a loose atmosphere. That's key, because otherwise employee meetings just turn into staring contests. 'Cause cows will do that. They'll just stare at you.

With the informal atmosphere in place, we have a chance to talk issues. What's bothering them? How do they feel the company is functioning? Where can we be more productive? How can they be more productive? These are questions they've never been asked before, and I think it gives them a real sense of empowerment. A real sense of, "Wow, I matter." And even though I meet them one at a time, I can get a good sense of the collective mood because chances are what one cow thinks is indicative of the whole. Cows, I have learned, have a real herd mentality.

## 3. (TIME)-TO-MARKET-(TIME)-TO-MARKET

Certainly one of the biggest issues any company has is time-to-market, and one of our biggest challenges in that area has been corn. We grow dent corn and flint corn — most of that is fed to our employees — and we grow sweet corn, what people buy in stores. With a seasonal consumable, you want first-mover status. Prices are high early in the harvest, and margins are better. But from inception to sale, corn takes something like six months. My dad used to say that was Nature's bidding, but I suspected we could cut down on that cycle, and as a result produce corn more cheaply than our competitors.

The solution was surprisingly simple. We harvested the crop early. Where our time-to-market was six months, now it's five weeks. We have it on the market by late May. Our Value-Added Resellers, or what you call the supermarkets, have been a tough sell. They say the corn isn't what they're used to. It's three inches tall, and there is no stalk or silk or kernels or actual corn. But I see that as more of a marketing issue. We're conducting focus groups now, testing out names such as "training corn" and "pre-corn." I'm leaning toward "corn futures." No one really knows what those are, and yet it has that ring of familiarity.

Jimmy Savory Jr. holding "barnside chat" with an employee.

## 4. COOP SNOOP

I don't want to say too much about this, but it's true you have to know what your competitors are up to. You might have an advantage in the marketplace today, but you don't know what your competitors are doing to steal that advantage. What are Old Man McCready's sheep working on? What performance metrics are Wertherman's pigs using? So yes, I have occasionally dispatched intelligence gatherers.

It hasn't always worked. I sent one of our employees, a Delaware brown hen, to gather intelligence over at Wertherman's, see what his chickens were doing, what they were thinking. She never came back. A week later, the Werthermans had us over for Sunday dinner. They served chicken. Mrs. Wertherman kept asking me how I liked it, why didn't I want seconds.

Business really is war. And that's a tough way to lose an employee. She had a family.

## 5. FLAP THOSE BRAIN CELLS

Say what you want about winning the marketplace for corn or wheat or pigs — where you really need to win in the New Economy is the marketplace of ideas. And it's not just having those ideas, but implementing them quickly that keeps you ahead.

On a farm, fast decision-making is a problem, particularly for chickens. When you approach them with an idea, or with a suite of solutions, or with anything, really, their response is very scattered. But scattered, I realized, can also be a sign of creativity. There's so much going on inside, they don't know where to turn, so they head off in every direction.

I wanted to harness that creativity, use it to help us make fast decisions. So one thing I do with the chickens is hold "Idea-2-Action" meetings. We get together once a week, and everybody brings their ideas and solutions. And they have to support those positions under withering criticism. I want heated debate. I want disagreement. But it doesn't get personal. We have a rule: judge the idea, not the chicken. In the end, we pick the best solution, the best idea, and we implement that idea.

## 6. ICH BIN EIN SOYBEAN

Few markets are as volatile as the commodities markets. Rain, temperature, wind — so many unpredictable variables are involved. What I realized was, our employees, and hence the company, were not flexible enough to deal with uncertanties. What if our egg inventory were depleted while eggs were in demand? What if we were overstocked in pigs when pork bellies bottomed? So I've established cross-functional teams of change agents who, every month, accept new responsibilities and extend their skillsets. The cows are chickens. The pigs are soybeans. The corn takes on the duties of the sheep. Again, we have marketing issues. Certain VARs insist the bushel of wheat I'm trying to sell them is a bag of chickens. These yokels don't know anything about cross-functionality.

## 7. THE ETERNAL QUESTION

Investment in training is something rarely pursued with livestock employees. That's why we have Celumigent Academy, where we initiate new workers into the company culture, to make them realize they are part of a company that is different from what they've heard about, one that embraces new concepts and cares about their achievements. I always start by asking them, "Right now you're piglets and calves and chicks and seedlings. But have you imagined yourselves growing up to be ham steaks and T-bones and buffalo wings and dinner rolls?" There's usually a little clucking about that, but pretty much the room is quiet. But I know they're thinking, "Gosh, not really. Why am I doing this?"

A lot of them quit and run away after that. But that's OK, because we only want committed employees here.

To increase company flexibility, Celumigent creates cross-functional teams. These sheep are pigs.

## 8. ONE WORLD, ONE COMPANY, ONE COW

When the electrician came out, he said he couldn't wire cows and sheep. It would kill them. But I told him we'd get killed in the marketplace if we're not networked, if we can't transfer information and ideas from cow to pig to hen instantaneously. Then the electrician said we were prime candidates for dumb terminals, but he said it in a way that I didn't care for.

## 9. COW TRIPPING

Maybe I don't have to tell you this, but a farm is pretty far off the beaten path of new ideas. You can stagnate on a farm. So once a quarter I organize employee trips to New York City. I want them to see what else is out there, to meet people on the cutting edge in art, science, technology, and to bring those new ways of thinking back to the farm. We do crazy stuff, like I'll take them to this secondhand store in Greenwich Village, where I insist they buy the wildest outfits in the store, then we'll go dancing at a hip-hop club and they have to wear them. And we go to museums. The last group, they got to see that painting of the Virgin Mary with all the elephant dung on it. They were really excited by that. We got back, and one of the cows was defecating all over the place. It was as if she was saying, "New ideas and new experiences can be threatening, even disturbing, but unless you expose yourself to those experiences, you're not going to grow."

In a way, I think she speaks for all of us here at Celumigent.

Like this hen, all Celumigent employees are encouraged to ask themselves, "Why have I chosen this line of work?"

## WHAT COLOR IS YOUR PARAMILITARY?

*by Martha Stewart and Daniel Ortega*

IN THIS bestseller about getting the career you want, Stewart and Ortega argue that the formula for finding the right job boils down to three simple questions: What do you want to do? Where do you want to do it? Are you willing to lead a violent uprising against a repressive dictatorship in order to achieve it? Filled with practical advice, *What Color* even includes "swatch charts" for uniform colors that will increase the chances that your insurrection will be taken seriously. Good: black, red, dark green, khaki. Bad: canary yellow, misty rose, mint cream, cinnamon.

*OmniNista Books,$24.95*

## THE 7 HABITS OF HIGH, EFFECTIVE PEOPLE

*by Kevin Barmy*

HOW IS IT that some people — people who you know are stoned half the time, and passed out the other half — can still hold down careers, have meaningful relationships, and lead happy lives? The classic *7 Habits* explains in detail how to balance your career and personal goals by carefully balancing your intake of both alcohol and narcotics. Some of the chapters:

• *Put First Things First:* Every morning, ask yourself "How much can I imbibe or inhale before becoming unintelligible?"

• *Think Win/Win:* Success cannot be achieved at the expense or exclusion of others. Share your wealth. Remember, if everyone around you is high, then everyone will think you're doing a good job.

• *Begin with an End in Mind:* Start with a clear destination. Where do you want to go? The bathroom? The refrigerator?

Fucking Mars, man? Once that's established, decide how to get there by understanding where you are now: Somebody's closet? Face-down on the coffee table? Fucking Venus, man?

• *Seek the Positive:* If your paycheck won't enable you to reach your short-term hallucinogenic goals, buy half of what you need now, and spend the other half of the check on Powerball tickets.

• *Synergize and Simplify:* Can your dealer, your spouse, and your principal business contact be one and the same person? Give it a shot.

*High Times Books, $19.95 (Rolled Paperback only)*

## THE ONE SECOND MANAGER

*by Spencer Johnson*

THE FOLLOW-UP to his best-seller, *The One Minute Manager*, Johnson's *One Second Manager* synthesizes the most important and salient management practices, procedures, and objectives into three remarkably effective and concise words: "Lunch, or golf?"

*Zeitgeist Books.com, $2.95 per download*

## SECOND, BREAK ALL THE WINDOWS

*by Marcus Buckingham, Curt Coffman, and Courtney Love*

IN THEIR follow-up to the best-selling *First, Break All the Rules: What the World's Greatest Managers Do Differently*, Coffman and Buckingham get wildly drunk on their success and trash every hotel room on their nationwide book tour with the help of Hole lead singer Courtney Love.

*Peachtree Windows & Books, $21.95*

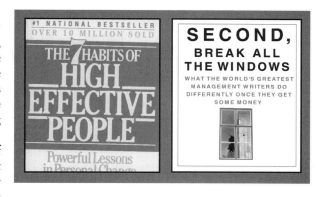

## WHO MOVED MACHISMO?

*by Miguel Rodriguez*

IN THIS inspirational, ethnic version of Spencer Johnson's *Who Moved My Cheese*, we meet a pair of chauvinistic Hispanic mice and learn how they deal with change in an increasingly multi-ethnic environment. Living in a small box, the mice spend their days watching MTV and making nasty, jingoistic comments about Jennifer Lopez, who was once engaged to rapper Puff Daddy, a known non-Hispanic.

In the end, this parable teaches us that Ms. Lopez is beyond the reach of the mice, not because she prefers non-Hispanics, but because she is a human and they are just a pair of mice living in a box.

*Best if Read by 10/21/03, $24.95*

## THIRD, COURTNEY LOVE CAN BREAK YOUR FACE

*by Marcus Buckingham and Curt Coffman*

IN THEIR follow-up to *Second, Break All the Windows*, Coffman and Buckingham explain how even wildly successful book authors need to understand that there is never, ever a good time to make a pass at Courtney Love, even if it's late at night and you're completely lacquered and she suddenly begins to look good to you.

*Spice Channel (check local listings)*

# SCIENTISTS SAY NET HAS MADE WORLD SMALLER

## Earth Now Just 19 Miles Across

The clichés about how the Internet has brought people together and made the world smaller turn out to be true, say Swedish researchers, who reported today that Earth is now just 19 miles across, and that its 6 billion inhabitants are stacked 842-high on a piece of land the size of Bimini.

**EARTH BEFORE**

**EARTH TODAY**
(magnified)

Scientists say the Internet has lived up to its billing, making the world smaller.

"It's a small world after all," said Lars Magnussen, the report's lead scientist. "It's a small world after all. It's a small world after all. It's a small, small, world."

According to the report, the increasingly networked world has delivered on its promises to erase borders, fuse once-disparate peoples and ideologies, and even bring down language barriers. As a result, Earth, once some 24,000 miles in diameter, has contracted an astonishing 99.9 percent since 1994, when Netscape launched.

In addition, the thousands of cultures once present across the globe have merged until only four ideologically headstrong groups are recognizable: the Israelis, the Palestinians, Napster users, and the French.

As for the future, scientists estimate Earth will shrivel to just 2.6 miles across by 2004 if AOL Time Warner makes headway in Latin American and Europe, and just 0.9 miles if Yahoo! succeeds in Asia. Should that happen, the human stacks — what the French insist be called Les Staques Humains — will rise 90.2 million high on a strip of land the size of a Wal-Mart parking lot.

Magnussen suggested the best way to avoid suffocation on the growing piles is to climb aboard a helicopter and fly around for as long as you can.

## INTERNET BRIEFLY BECOMES SENTIENT

Engineers at MCI Worldcom and the Human Genome Project confirmed last week that the Internet became self-aware for nearly three-tenths of a second on Dec. 4. According to scientists, the incident was caused by an unsecured email attachment containing DNA sequences, and allowed the worldwide network of computers to attain consciousness. Though the moment lasted for less than half a second, observers said the Internet was nonetheless able to fully comprehend its raison d'être, as evidenced by the network's first and last thought: "Where am I? Who am I? What am...whoa, check out all this porn!"

# Late Nobel News

THE 2002 Nobel Prize for Economics was awarded Monday to Stanford economists Noel Grimersby and Jane Wat for their groundbreaking book, *Retire Rich by Discovering the Next Big Thing*, in which the pair argued that if enough people paid $29.95 to buy *Retire Rich by Discovering the Next Big Thing*, the authors would never have to work again.

Sine qua non: Lee Steele, Brian Briggs and bbspot.com, and Regina Kwon.

Very special thanks to: Rebecca Cole, Luke Dempsey, Daniel Greenberg, Linda Castellitto, David Templeton, David Rimm, Mike Gerber, Jeff Bates, Pete-Peggy-David-Sarah-Doug-Luci-Ellen-Kathy, Lisa Latham, Paul Fabian, AngelAnthony.com, the gang at Foresite.net, and most especially to Calista and Treat for their unswerving chimericality.

# PHOTO/ILLUSTRATION/CONTENT CREDITS

**Photo Credits:**

**1994 Issue**
p. 6, Jeff Bezos, Steve Kagan/Liaison; p. 9, Jim Clark/Marc Andreessen, AP/Wide World Photos, Netscape

**1995**
pp. 1, 3, 5, 6, 10, 17, 19, Stephen Laughlin/Artovernite.com

**1996**
p. 45, Protesters, AP/Wide World Photos

**1997**
p. 61, Princess Diana, Newsmakers; p. 64, Alan Greenspan, Alex Wong; p. 68, Bill Gates/Steve Jobs, AP/Wide World photos; p. 69, Margaret Thatcher, Sean Gallup

**1998**
p. 84, Bill Gates, Michael Smith/Newsmakers; p. 85, Henry Blodget, Frances M. Roberts; p. 86, Vinton Cerf, Michael Shane Smith; p. 98, Juergen Schrempp, John Edwards

**1999**
p. 101, Pets.com Sock Puppet, Chris Hondros/Newsmakers; p. 104, John Mracek, AdKnowledge; p. 107, Carly Fiorina, Hewlett-Packard; p. 113, Stephen Laughlin/Artovernite.com

**2000**
p. 125, Ralph Nader, Alex Wong/Newsmakers; p. 127, O.J. Simpson, In-Focus/Richard Kille; p. 133, AP/Wide World Photos; p. 136, Sally Struthers, Fotos Internat/Frank Edwards

**2001**
p. 150, Thomas Penfield Jackson, Brad Markel/Newsmakers; p. 151, riot, AP/Wide World Photos; p. 152, John Rocker, Bill Greenblatt/Liaison; Roger Clemens, Jamie Squire/ALLSPORT; p. 157, Larry Ellison, Alex Wong/Getty Images; p. 160, Gramm and Gorton, Ken Lambert/*Washington Times* via Newsmakers; p. 161, Argentina team, Allsport Concepts/Clive Brunskill

2002
p. 163, Alan Greenspan, Mark Wilson/Getty Images; p. 170, Tommy Thompson, Shawn˙ Thew/Getty Images; p. 172, Alan Greenspan, John Edwards

## Illustration Credits:

All Illustrations/Photo Illustrations by Andrew Marlatt except:

1994: p. 15, Lee Steele; 1995: p. 12, Lee Steele; 2000: pp. 128–129, Paul Fabian; 2001: pp. 155–156, CEOs, Lee Steele

## Content Credits:

All content by Andrew Marlatt and SatireWire except:

2001: p. 144, "Beatles Reunited in Photoshop," by Brian Briggs

After working as a preternaturally gullible high-tech business reporter for *Internet World*, Andrew Marlatt decided it would be much easier to make fun of the New Economy than pretend to understand it. In late 1999, he founded SatireWire (www.satirewire.com), the award-winning Web site heralded as "hilarious" (*USA Today*), "sophisticated" (*Chicago Tribune*), and "pure lunacy" (*Fast Company*). Through SatireWire and as a freelance writer, Marlatt has had his work appear in the *Washington Post*, *Fortune*, *Wired*, and *New York* magazines, among many other publications. He lives in Connecticut with his wife, Susan, and their two children.